CONCENTRATE
COMPANY LAW

CONCENTRATE COMPANY LAW

LAW REVISION AND STUDY GUIDE

Lee Roach

Senior Lecturer in Law, School of Law, University of Portsmouth

SEVENTH EDITION

OXFORD
UNIVERSITY PRESS

Great Clarendon Street, Oxford, OX2 6DP,
United Kingdom

Oxford University Press is a department of the University of Oxford.
It furthers the University's objective of excellence in research, scholarship,
and education by publishing worldwide. Oxford is a registered trade mark of
Oxford University Press in the UK and in certain other countries

© Oxford University Press 2023

The moral rights of the author have been asserted

Sixth Edition 2020
Fifth Edition 2018
Fourth Edition 2016

Public sector information reproduced under Open Government Licence v3.0
(http://www.nationalarchives.gov.uk/doc/open-government-licence/open-government-licence.htm)

Published in the United States of America by Oxford University Press
198 Madison Avenue, New York, NY 10016, United States of America

British Library Cataloguing in Publication Data
Data available

Library of Congress Control Number: 2023937469

ISBN 978–0–19–888140–7

Printed in the UK by
Bell & Bain Ltd., Glasgow

Dedication

To Tom and Sandra Roach

New to this edition

- Coverage of relevant reforms proposed by the Economic Crime and Corporate Transparency Bill 2023.
- Coverage of proposed revisions to the UK Corporate Governance Code.
- Coverage of the Law Commission's review of corporate criminal liability.
- Updated coverage of the proposed ban on corporate directors.
- Updated coverage of boardroom diversity developments, including the passing of the EU's boardroom diversity directive.
- Coverage of relevant reforms proposed by the government's white paper on restoring trust in audit and corporate governance.
- Coverage of the reforms introduced by the Corporate Insolvency and Governance Act 2020.
- Coverage of new case law including:
  (a) *Broadcasting Investment Group v Smith* [2020] (reflective loss principle)
  (b) *BTI 2014 LLC v Sequana SA* [2022] (s 172 duty and creditors)
  (c) *Burnford v Automobile Association Developments Ltd* [2022] (reflective loss principle)
  (d) *Chu v Lau* [2020] (winding up due to deadlock)
  (e) *Hurstwood Properties (A) Ltd v Rossendale Borough Council* [2021] (disregarding corporate personality)
  (f) *Nectrus Ltd v UCP plc* [2021] (reflective loss principle)
  (g) *Okpabi v Royal Dutch Shell plc* [2021] (duty of care)
  (h) *Primeo Fund v Bank of Bermuda (Cayman) Ltd* [2021] (reflective loss principle)
  (i) *Re Amicus Finance plc* [2021] (restructuring plan)
  (j) *Re Avanti Communications Ltd* [2023] (fixed and floating charges)
  (k) *Re DeepOcean 1 UK Ltd* [2021] (restructuring plan)
  (l) *Re Glam and Tan Ltd* [2022] (summary remedy and breach of duty)
  (m) *Re Klimvest plc* [2022] (winding up due to loss of substratum)
  (n) *Re Virgin Atlantic Airways Ltd* [2020] (restructuring plan)
  (o) *Sevilleja v Marex Financial Ltd* [2020] (reflective loss principle)
  (p) *Shah v L3 Commercial Training Solutions Ltd* [2021] (duty of care)
  (q) *Tradition Financial Services Ltd v Bilta (UK) Ltd* [2023] (fraudulent trading)
  (r) *WM Morrison Supermarkets plc v Various Claimants* [2020] (vicarious liability)

Preface

Company Law Concentrate has two clear aims. First, it aims to provide a clear and succinct guide to help you better understand a number of prominent and regularly assessed company law topics. Second, it offers a number of useful hints and tips to aid you in revising for, and undertaking, a company law exam or other written assessment. *Company Law Concentrate* does not aim to provide an overview of an entire company law syllabus, nor could it do so without being appreciably lengthier. Nor does it aim to provide the level of detail and analysis that a good textbook should provide. In other words, *Company Law Concentrate* cannot and does not seek to replace the knowledge you will gain from a high-quality textbook and accompanying research. Instead, *Company Law Concentrate* aims to complement your existing textbook. Company law texts can be complex, technical, and difficult to understand. Further, company law texts are required to cover a broad syllabus without necessarily indicating which topics are assessed most regularly. *Company Law Concentrate* aims to address both of these issues by covering those topics that tend to arise in exams in a simple and easy to understand manner, and to provide you with clear guidance on how best to discuss these topics whilst avoiding common mistakes and pitfalls. Having said that, students should not assume that the topics discussed within are guaranteed to arise in an exam, and the content of company law courses does vary substantially—for example, some company law courses might not discuss the various rescue and insolvency procedures discussed in Chapter 9.

It is hoped that *Company Law Concentrate*, alongside existing textbooks and further research, will provide you with the foundation you need to effectively revise for, and obtain a high mark in, your company law assessments. Bear in mind, however, that in essay-style assessment, high marks come from the sort of critical analysis that is usually not found in textbooks, but is found in journal articles and other specialist academic works. Accordingly, reference will be made to useful articles that you might wish to consider reading.

The law continues to develop and this edition has been updated fully to reflect these developments. The author's Twitter account (@ UKCompanyLaw) will provide you with updates on these issues and on all company law and corporate governance developments.

I offer my thanks to the publishing team at OUP for their hard work. In particular, I would like to thank Liana Green, Katherine Jones, Anjandevi Karthikeyan, Seemadevi Sekar, and Henry MacKeith whose encouragement and aid were of enormous help. I would also like to thank the anonymous reviewers whose insightful comments were of great benefit.

I have attempted to state the law as at June 2023.

LRR
Portsmouth, June 2023

Latest News

Several legal developments occurred too late to be incorporated into the main text. Accordingly, they have been noted here.

The Economic Crime and Corporate Transparency Bill 2023

At the time of writing, the **Economic Crime and Corporate Transparency Bill** is making its way through Parliament and will likely be passed by the time this book is published. Mention has been made of relevant reforms at various stages in the book, but it is worth noting here the principal reforms that will be made based on the current version of the Bill:

- the registrar of Companies House will be subject to a legal obligation to uphold several objectives relating to promoting the integrity of the register (e.g. ensuring that documents are filed on time and accurately);
- the application for registration will require additional material to be included (e.g. that the subscribers wish to form the company for a lawful purpose);
- additional restrictions regarding company names will be introduced (e.g. a name cannot be used to suggest a connection with a foreign government);
- the obligation placed upon companies to keep certain registers (e.g. register of directors, PSC register) will be abolished;
- a system of identity verification will be introduced for specified 'registrable persons' (e.g. directors);
- the registrar of Companies House will be given additional powers to help promote the integrity of the register (e.g. the power to reject documents for discrepancies), and;
- several new offences will be introduced relating to the provision of false information (e.g. delivering to Companies House a document that contains misleading, false or deceptive material).

Proposed revisions to the UK Corporate Governance Code

At the time of writing, the 2018 version of the UK Corporate Governance Code is currently in force. In late-May 2023, the FRC published a consultation document setting out proposed changes to the Code. Most of the changes are relatively minor, but more noteworthy proposed revisions include:

- a new Principle in Section 1 that states that companies should focus on outcomes and impact when reporting on their governance practices;
- expanding the role of the audit committee to cover sustainability and ESG reporting;
- increased reporting obligations on the company's internal control system, and;
- increased reporting obligations relating to malus and clawback provisions.

The consultation ended in September 2023. No indication has yet been given as to when the proposed revised Code will come into force.

Fixed and floating charges

At 7.3.1.3, the distinction between fixed and floating charges was discussed. In *Re Avanti Communications Ltd* [2023], the High Court provided further guidance on the distinction, notably to what extent can a chargor deal with the assets covered by a purported fixed charge before that charge is more likely to be characterised as floating. Traditionally, commentators have interpreted the law in this area as being a charge that allows the chargor to deal with the charged assets without the chargeholder's consent is likely to be a floating charge and not fixed. However, in *Avanti*, at para 118, Edwin Johnson J stated:

> I can see that it is helpful, in considering the question of whether a charge is fixed or floating, to look at the range of possibilities as a spectrum, with total freedom of management at one end of the spectrum, and a total prohibition on dealings of any kind at the other end of the spectrum…. What I cannot see is that a charge will only be fixed if it is located at the total prohibition end of the spectrum. The case law seems to me to support a more nuanced approach, which depends upon a combination of factors.

In *Avanti*, the court held that the charge was indeed a fixed charge, even though the chargor had the right to deal with the charged assets (albeit a limited and restricted right that would not arise in the ordinary course of business). As noted, this approach appears to be somewhat at odds with how commentators have interpreted the courts' approach prior to this, so it will be interesting to see how future cases treat the more nuanced approach of Edwin Johnson J.

Contents

List of abbreviations

The following is a list of abbreviations used in this text.

AGM	annual general meeting
ARGA	Audit, Reporting and Governance Authority
CA 1985	Companies Act 1985
CA 2006	Companies Act 2006
CDDA 1986	Company Directors Disqualification Act 1986
CIGA 2020	Corporate Insolvency and Governance Act 2020
CVA	company voluntary arrangement
EEA	European Economic Area
EU	European Union
FCA	Financial Conduct Authority
FRC	Financial Reporting Council
FSA	Financial Services Authority
HMRC	HM Revenue & Customs
IA 1986	Insolvency Act 1986
IR 2016	Insolvency (England and Wales) Rules 2016
LLP	limited liability partnership
LLPA 2000	Limited Liability Partnerships Act 2000
NED	non-executive director
PA 1890	Partnership Act 1890
SBEEA 2015	Small Business, Enterprise and Employment Act 2015
TFEU	Treaty on the Functioning of the European Union

Table of cases

Table of legislation

Table of codes and rules

Business structures

1

KEY FACTS

- The four principal business structures are the sole proprietorship, the partnership, the limited liability partnership, and the company. The company is the most popular business structure.

- Sole proprietorships involve little formality, but the liability of the sole proprietor is personal and unlimited.

- Two or more persons who wish to conduct business can form an ordinary partnership. Such partnerships are subject to greater regulation than sole proprietorships, but less regulation than limited liability partnerships and companies. The liability of the partners is personal and unlimited.

- Limited liability partnerships were created primarily to be a suitable business vehicle for large professional firms. In many respects, limited liability partnerships closely resemble companies.

- Public companies are so called because they can offer to sell their shares to the public at large. Private companies cannot offer to sell their shares to the public at large. There are other notable differences between public and private companies.

- The vast majority of companies are limited companies, and so their members will usually have limited liability.

CHAPTER OVERVIEW

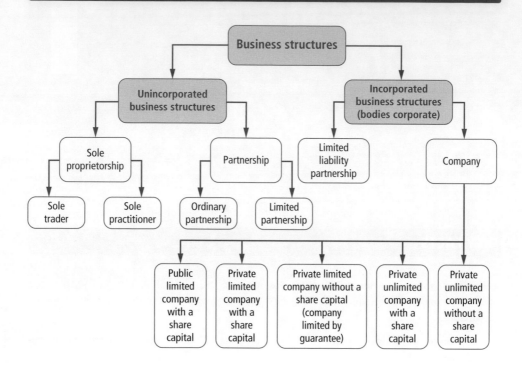

Introduction

A person who wishes to engage in some form of business activity will need to do so via some form of business structure, with differing business structures providing different advantages and disadvantages. In the UK, four principal business structures can be identified, namely:

1. the sole proprietorship,
2. the ordinary partnership,
3. the limited liability partnership (LLP), and
4. the company.

The LLP and the company are created via a process called **incorporation** and are therefore known as incorporated business structures or, as they are referred to in their respective statutes, as 'bodies corporate'. The sole proprietorship and the ordinary partnership are not created via incorporation and so are known as unincorporated business structures.

REVISION TIP

Although company law focuses on the regulation of companies, it is important to understand the advantages and disadvantages that companies have when compared to other business structures. Indeed, an essay question may require you to discuss such advantages and disadvantages. Alternatively, a problem question may provide you with a set of facts involving the setting up of a new business, and you might have to advise which business structure would be most suitable for the new business.

1.1 Sole proprietorships

The simplest business structure is the **sole proprietorship**. A sole proprietor is simply an individual carrying on some form of business activity on their own account (i.e. is self-employed). Whilst a sole proprietorship will be operated for that individual's benefit, sole proprietors can take on employees, although the vast majority do not. The key point is that the sole proprietorship is not incorporated, nor does the sole proprietor carry on business in partnership with anyone else.

Unlike incorporated structures, there is no separation between a sole proprietor and their business, and sole proprietorships do not have corporate personality (discussed at 2.3). Accordingly, the sole proprietor owns all of the assets of the business and is entitled to all the profit that the business generates, but they are also liable for all the business's debts and liabilities.

1.1.1 Formation and regulation

Commencing business as a sole proprietor is extremely straightforward and involves much less formality than creating an LLP or company. All that the prospective sole proprietor need do is register themselves with HM Revenue & Customs (HMRC) as self-employed. Sole proprietorships are not generally subject to the **Companies Act 2006 (CA 2006)**, so do not need to file accounts at **Companies House** and are subject to much less regulation than companies. However, being self-employed, sole proprietors are required to complete their own tax returns (or appoint an accountant to complete them), so sole proprietors should maintain clear and accurate records of all transactions entered into.

1.1.2 Finance

In terms of raising finance, sole proprietorships are can be at a disadvantage when compared to other business structures. Partnerships can raise finance by admitting new partners. Companies, especially public companies, can raise finance by selling shares. Neither of these options is available to a sole proprietor who wishes to remain a sole proprietor. A sole proprietor will either need to invest their own money into the business (and risk losing it should the business fail) or obtain a loan. Given that many sole proprietorships are small affairs, banks are cautious when lending to sole proprietors and obtaining large amounts of **debt capital** is usually impossible.

1.1.3 Liability

The principal disadvantage of carrying on business as a sole proprietorship is that the liability of the sole proprietor is personal and unlimited. Whereas partnerships and companies can be limited, sole proprietorships cannot. Accordingly, the sole proprietor's assets (including personal assets such as his house, car, and bank accounts) can be seized and sold in order to satisfy the debts and liabilities of the sole proprietorship. If the sole proprietorship's debts/liabilities exceed the assets of the sole proprietor, they will likely be declared bankrupt.

1.2 Partnerships

Two or more persons who wish to carry on business together cannot do so as a sole proprietorship for obvious reasons. For such persons, a **partnership** may be a more appropriate business structure, of which there are three different forms:

1. the ordinary partnership (also referred to simply as a 'partnership' or as a 'general partnership'), on which this section will focus;

2. the limited partnership, which is a form of partnership that can be formed under the **Limited Partnerships Act 1907** (limited partnerships are rare and need not be discussed further here);

3. the limited liability partnership which, being an incorporated business structure, is discussed later in this chapter at 1.3.

Section 1(1) of the Partnership Act 1890 (PA 1890) defines an ordinary partnership as 'the relation which subsists between persons carrying on a business in common with a view to profit'.

LOOKING FOR EXTRA MARKS?

This seemingly simple definition contains a number of notable words and phrases that have proven difficult to define clearly in practice. For a more detailed discussion of the definition found in **s 1(1)**, see Geoffrey Morse and Thomas Braithwaite, *Partnership and LLP Law* (9th edn, OUP 2020) ch 1.

1.2.1 The relationship between the partners

The **PA 1890** establishes rules regarding the relationship between the partners. Many partnerships will have in place a written partnership agreement that sets out the rights and obligations of the partners. Where a partnership agreement does not exist, **ss 24 and 25 of the PA 1890** imply a number of default terms that will apply to the partnership. In fact, these implied terms will apply even where a written partnership agreement does exist, unless the implied terms are inconsistent with, or are excluded by, the terms of the written agreement. Examples of these implied terms include the following:

- All of the partners are entitled to share equally in the profits of the firm and must also contribute equally towards the firm's losses.

- Every partner may take part in the management of the firm.

- No new partners may be admitted to the firm without the consent of all the other partners.

- The agreement between the partners can only be altered with the express consent of all the partners.

- The majority of the partners cannot expel a partner unless an express power to do so has been agreed upon by all the partners.

1.2.2 The relationship between partners and third parties

Sections 5–18 of the PA 1890 regulate the relationship between the partners and third parties. This includes the extent to which the partners can contractually bind the firm and the other partners to a third party, and the extent to which the firm and the other partners can be liable for the acts or omissions of a single partner that cause a third party to sustain loss.

1.2.2.1 Agency

Regarding a partner's ability to bind his partnership and co-partners to a third party, the key provision is **s 5 of the PA 1890**, which provides that each partner is an **agent** of the firm and of his co-partners. Accordingly, providing a partner acts within his authority, he is able to contractually bind his firm and his co-partners to a third party. In fact, in certain cases, a binding contract may exist where the partner has exceeded his authority, or even where he has no authority. As each partner has the power to contractually bind his co-partners, it follows that every partner is jointly liable for the debts and obligations of the firm incurred while he is a partner. As with a sole proprietorship, the liability of the partners is personal and unlimited.

1.2.2.2 Liability for tortious and other wrongful acts

Partners may be held liable in tort or found guilty for the criminal acts of other partners. **Section 10 of the PA 1890** provides that the partnership and each partner is vicariously liable for the wrongful acts or omissions of another partner, providing that the partner was acting within their authority, or that the act or omission was done whilst in the ordinary course of the firm's business.

EXAMPLE (FICTIONAL)

Coffey & Sons is a UK-based firm of accountants consisting of fifty partners. One of the firm's partners, Kirsty, is conducting an audit of BioTech plc, but she conducts the audit negligently. Under s 10, Coffey & Sons and the other forty-nine partners face liability for Kirsty's act of negligence.

Liability under s 10 is **joint and several**, meaning that the claimant can sue a single partner, each partner in turn, or all the partners at the same time, until they have recovered the full amount of their loss. Liability is both personal and unlimited.

1.3 Limited liability partnerships

With the passing of the **Limited Liability Partnerships Act 2000 (LLPA 2000)**, two or more persons can now form a **limited liability partnership (LLP)**.

REVISION TIP

Students often confuse limited liability partnerships with limited partnerships, but the two business structures are very different. An LLP is a body corporate created under the **LLPA 2000**, whereas a limited partnership is merely a specialized (and rather rare) type of partnership that can be created under the **Limited Partnerships Act 1907**. Although both offer limited liability, the limitations placed upon the limited partners of a limited partnership (notably the inability to take part in management) make LLPs a more attractive option generally.

In order to understand the purpose and functions of LLPs, it is vital to understand why the **LLPA 2000** was enacted. For large professional firms (e.g. accountants and solicitors) who may have thousands of partners worldwide, the joint and several liability of the partners meant that, for example, one partner in London could be personally liable for the unlawful acts of a New York-based partner that he had never met. The largest accountancy firms therefore lobbied the UK government to create a new form of partnership that provided its partners with limited liability similar to that enjoyed by the members of limited companies. The result was the **LLPA 2000**.

REVISION TIP

An essay question in this area might require you to discuss the LLP and the extent of its usefulness. The story of the passing of the **LLPA 2000** is significant as it is largely professional firms that have expressed a significant interest in adopting LLP status. It is not therefore a business structure of widespread use and it is certainly not a structure designed to cater to the needs of small businesses. This is demonstrated in that, as of March 2023, there were only 52,626 LLPs incorporated in the UK (compared to nearly 5.1 million companies).

Some argue that LLPs are hybrid organizations that combine the characteristics of a partnership and a company. Whilst this is true, there is little doubt that LLPs have more in common with registered companies than with partnerships:

- Like a registered company, an LLP is created by registering documents with the **Registrar of Companies** at Companies House.
- Like a registered company, an LLP is a body corporate (**LLPA 2000, s 1(2)**) and therefore has corporate personality (discussed at 2.3).
- The **LLPA 2000** refers to the partners of an LLP as 'members'.
- The members of an LLP, like the members of most registered companies, will have limited liability.
- Generally, LLPs are regulated by company law, although there are notable areas in which they are regulated by partnership law. Many provisions of the **CA 2006** and virtually all the provisions of the **Insolvency Act 1986** will therefore apply to LLPs as well as companies.

LLPs also differ notably from ordinary partnerships, as Table 1.1 demonstrates.

Table 1.1 The differences between an ordinary partnership and an LLP

	ORDINARY PARTNERSHIP	LLP
Formation	Can be formed informally by two or more persons agreeing to carry on business in partnership	Formally incorporated by registration with the registrar of companies
Corporate personality	Ordinary partnerships do not have corporate personality	LLPs do have corporate personality
Regulation	Regulated by partnership law, notably the **PA 1890**	Regulated by company law, unless the **LLPA 2000** states otherwise
Designation of partners	The partners of an ordinary partnership are known as 'partners'	The partners of an LLP are known as 'members'
Liability of partners	The partners of an ordinary partnership are jointly liable for the debts of the partnership and are jointly and severally liable for its liabilities	The members of an LLP are not generally liable for the debts and liabilities of an LLP—the LLP itself is liable
Disqualification	The partners of an ordinary partnership cannot be disqualified from acting as a partner of an ordinary partnership	The members of an LLP can be disqualified from acting as a member of an LLP (or as a company director)

1.3.1 Liability

In the event of a partnership being dissolved, the partners are liable for the debts of the firm, with such liability being personal and unlimited. Conversely, the members of an LLP need contribute nothing when it is wound up, although there are several exceptions to this (e.g. the members of an LLP can be found liable for wrongful trading). Accordingly, the LLP remedies the principal weakness of the partnership, namely the personal and unlimited liability of its partners. As the LLP has corporate personality, it follows that the LLP itself will be liable for its debts and can be vicariously liable for the acts of its members, agents, and employees.

1.4 Companies

The processes by which a company can be created and the advantages and disadvantages of conducting business through a company are fundamental issues and are therefore discussed more fully in Chapter 2. Here, the discussion will focus on the different forms of company that can be created. The **CA 2006** provides for a number of different forms of company that are classifiable by reference to three principal characteristics, namely:

1. Is the company to be public or private?
2. Is the liability of the company's members to be limited or unlimited? If liability is to be unlimited, then the company must be private—the law does not allow for the creation of unlimited public companies.
3. Does the company have a share capital or not? Public companies must have a share capital, but private companies need not, although the vast majority do.

These three characteristics will now be discussed in more detail, along with the distinction between quoted and listed companies.

1.4.1 Public and private companies

When creating a company, the **promoters** are required to state whether the company is to be registered as a private company or as a public company. A public company is a company limited by shares, or limited by guarantee and having a share capital, whose certificate of incorporation states that it is a public company (**CA 2006, s 4(2)**). A private company is simply defined as any company that is not a public company (**CA 2006, s 4(1)**). These definitions do not, however, help us understand why a promoter would choose one company over another. To understand that, the differences between public and private companies need to be discussed, with the key differences being the following:

1. A public company may offer to sell its shares to the public at large and, to facilitate this, it may offer to sell its shares on a stock market, with the principal market in the UK being the London Stock Exchange. This allows public companies to raise massive amounts of capital very quickly (e.g. Facebook's **initial public offering** on Nasdaq allowed it to raise over $16 billion in one day through the selling of shares). Private limited companies are not permitted to

offer their shares to the public at large (**CA 2006, s 755(1)**), nor can their securities be admitted to the official list (**Financial Services and Markets Act 2000, s 75(3)** and **Financial Services and Markets Act 2000 (Official Listing of Securities) Regulations 2001, reg 3**). As a result, private companies can find it difficult to obtain sufficient levels of share capital.

2. Whilst private companies can be created with a trivial amount of capital (e.g. a single 1-penny share), public companies are required to have an allotted share capital of at least £50,000 (discussed in more detail at 7.1.4).

3. Both private and public companies can be created with only one member. However, whereas a private company can be formed with only one director, a public company must have at least two directors (**CA 2006, s 154**).

4. Public companies are required by law to appoint a **company secretary (CA 2006, s 271)**, whereas private companies are not, unless their articles state otherwise.

5. Private limited companies are required to add the suffix 'Ltd' to their name (**CA 2006, s 59(1)**). Public companies must add the suffix 'plc' (**CA 2006, s 58(1)**).

Table 1.2 summarizes the differences between public and private companies.

Table 1.2 The differences between a public company and a private company

	PUBLIC COMPANY	PRIVATE COMPANY
Number of companies	As of March 2023, there were 5,617 public companies registered in the UK (0.1 per cent of the total number of companies)	As of March 2023, there were nearly 5.1 million private companies registered in the UK (99.9 per cent of the total number of companies)
Share capital requirement	Must have a share capital	No share capital required, but the vast majority do have a share capital
Liability of members	Must be limited. It is impossible to create an unlimited public company	Can be limited or unlimited, although the vast majority are limited
Public offering of shares	Can offer to sell its shares to the public at large	Cannot offer to sell its shares to the public at large
Official listing	Can list its securities on the official list (although most do not)	Cannot list its securities on the official list
Minimum capital requirement	Must have an allotted share capital of at least £50,000	No minimum capital requirement
Minimum number of directors	Two	One
Suffix required	plc	Ltd
Company secretary	Must appoint a company secretary	Need not appoint a company secretary, unless its articles so require
Level of regulation	The **CA 2006** regulates public companies more stringently than private companies. Listed companies are regulated even more stringently by having to comply with **Pt VI of the Financial Services and Markets Act 2000** and the **FCA Handbook**. The **UK Corporate Governance Code** applies to companies with a premium listing	

REVISION TIP

It is vital that you are aware of the differences between public and private companies as the **CA 2006** regulates public companies more heavily than private companies. In problem questions, distinguishing between public and private companies will usually be straightforward due to the requirement to state Ltd or plc after the company's name. Listed companies are regulated even more strictly by additional rules contained in the **FCA Handbook**.

1.4.2 Limited and unlimited companies

The terms 'limited' and 'unlimited' do not actually refer to the company itself, but to the liability of its members. As noted, the liability of the members of a public company must be limited **(CA 2006, s 4(2))**. Where the promoters decide to form a private company, they will need to decide whether the liability of the company's members will be limited or unlimited.

1.4.2.1 Limited companies

The vast majority of companies are limited companies. As of June 2022, there were around 4.9 million companies registered in the UK, of which only 4,500 were unlimited companies. Where the liability of a company's members is limited, the form and extent of the limitation will depend upon whether their liability is limited by guarantee or by shares:

- A limited company without a share capital is said to be 'limited by guarantee'. This is because, when such companies are incorporated, the promoter is required to submit to Companies House a statement of guarantee, which states how much the members will be required to contribute in the event of the company being liquidated **(CA 2006, s 3(3); Insolvency Act 1986, s 74(3))**.

- Where a company is limited by shares, the liability of the company's members will usually be limited to the amount that is unpaid on their shares **(Insolvency Act 1986, s 74(2) (d))**. Members who have fully paid for their shares are generally not liable to contribute any more to the company. The vast majority of limited companies are limited by shares, and so the following example will demonstrate the operation of limited liability in a company limited by shares.

EXAMPLE (FICTIONAL)

A newly incorporated company, FakeCo plc, issues 100,000 shares, and provides that subscribers can pay fully for their shares immediately, or can pay half now and the remainder at a later date. The shares have a **nominal value** of £1. Tom decides to buy 1,000 shares and takes advantage of the ability to pay half the amount. He therefore pays £500. A few months later, before Tom has paid the remaining amount, FakeCo is liquidated. The liquidator will be able to recover from Tom the remaining £500 (i.e. Tom's liability is limited to £500). Had Tom paid the full £1,000 prior to liquidation, then the liquidator would not have been able to recover any more money from Tom.

As this example demonstrates, limited liability remedies the principal weakness of sole proprietorships and ordinary partnerships, namely personal and unlimited liability.

1.4.2.2 Unlimited companies

Less than 0.1 per cent of all companies are unlimited. The reason why there are so few unlimited companies is simple: in an unlimited company, upon winding up, the liability of the members is personal and unlimited, so their personal assets (e.g. house, car, bank accounts, etc.) can be seized and sold to satisfy the company's debts.

 LOOKING FOR EXTRA MARKS?

The obvious question is why would a company choose unlimited liability. The principal answer is that unlimited companies are subject to less regulation than limited companies. For example, unlimited companies do not generally need to file their accounts with Companies House (**CA 2006, s 448(1)**), so their affairs can be conducted with more privacy and with less formality. However, such concessions are, for most businesses, not a worthwhile trade-off for the loss of limited liability.

1.4.3 Companies with and without a share capital

As noted, only public companies are required to have a share capital, although most private companies have a share capital too. The reason why the vast majority of companies have a share capital is because doing so serves several useful purposes, including:

- it allows the company to raise capital by selling shares;
- the allocation of shares can be used to establish who has control of the company, and;
- shares are transferable, thereby allowing the company's shareholders to exit the company simply by transferring their shares to someone else.

1.4.4 Quoted and listed companies

Certain laws or governance principles only apply to companies that are quoted or listed and so it is important to understand what these terms mean:

- A listed company is one that has a class of securities listed on the UK's official list (FCA Handbook, Glossary).
- A quoted company is a company (i) whose share capital has been included on the official list (so some listed companies will also be quoted, but see the example that follows), or (ii) whose share capital is officially listed in an EEA State, or (iii) whose share capital is admitted to dealing on the New York Stock Exchange or Nasdaq (**CA 2006, s 385(2)**). A company that is not quoted is unquoted.

EXAMPLE

- The shares of Vodafone Group plc are on the official list, so Vodafone is a listed company and a quoted company.
- The shares of Meta Platforms Inc (formerly Facebook) are not listed on the UK's official list, but they are listed on Nasdaq. Accordingly, Meta is a quoted company, but it is not a listed company.
- A2D Funding plc only has debt securities listed on the official list. Accordingly, it is a listed company, but as it has no share capital listed, it is an unquoted company.
- The shares of Boohoo Group plc are traded on AIM, a market of the London Stock Exchange. However, its securities are not on the official list and so it not a listed company and it is unquoted.

It is important to know whether a company is listed or quoted for several reasons:

1. Listed companies are required to comply with a range of additional laws, notably the provisions of **Pt VI of the Financial Services and Markets Act 2000** and those rules created by the FCA under the 2000 Act (notably the FCA Handbook).

2. The **UK Corporate Governance Code** (discussed at 6.2.1) applies to companies with a premium listing.

3. Quoted companies are subject to numerous additional statutory requirements (e.g. the directors of quoted companies must prepare a directors' remuneration report).

REVISION TIP

Be aware of the full range of rules and principles that a company is subject to. Larger companies especially can be subject to a range of laws, quasi-legal rules, codes, principles, and best practice recommendations. Company law is no longer just about the law; complying with other forms of rules and principles can be just as important as complying with legal obligations.

KEY DEBATES

Topic	Partnership law reform
Author/Academic	Law Commission and the Scottish Law Commission
Viewpoint	Recommends a number of extremely far-reaching reforms to modernize partnerships and partnership law (sadly, most of which have not been implemented).
Source	*Partnership Law* (Law Com No 283, 2003)

Topic	The limited liability partnership
Author/Academic	Stuart R Cross
Viewpoint	Discusses the operation and background of the **LLPA 2000** and highlights a number of problem areas that are likely to impede the usefulness of LLPs.
Source	'Limited Liability Partnerships Act 2000: Problems Ahead' [2003] JBL 268

Topic	Forms of company
Author/Academic	Andrew Hicks, Robert Drury, and Jeff Smallcombe
Viewpoint	Argues that the private limited company is not a suitable business structure for many small businesses. Argues that the regulation that small businesses wish to avoid is a consequence of limited liability, and so a new company form should be made available which does not offer its members limited liability, and is regulated by partnership law.
Source	*Alternative Company Structures for the Small Business* (Association of Certified Chartered Accountants, 1995)

 EXAM QUESTIONS

Essay question

'The limited liability partnership is an ideal business structure for small businesses as it combines the best features of a partnership and a company.'

Do you agree with the above statement? Provide reasons for your answer.

See the 'Outline answers' section in the endmatter for help with this question.

Problem question

Dean is a successful sole practitioner offering business consultancy services to a number of local companies. His chief competitor is Caroline, who offers similar services. Caroline and Dean decide that they wish to work together, but are unsure as to which business structure would be most appropriate. They seek your advice regarding which business structure would be most suitable, bearing in mind:

- they wish to avoid significant levels of formality and regulation
- they want to have flexibility in establishing the procedures by which the business is to be run
- they want to be able to run their affairs in private
- they want to avoid personal liability for the debts and liabilities of the business

- the process of creating the business should be relatively cheap and quick
- they do not want to invest significant amounts of their own capital in setting up the business and will probably wish to raise capital from outside sources
- they wish to take on employees

Discuss to what extent the various business structures fulfil all, or some, of these aims and advise Dean and Caroline which business structure would be most suitable for their business.

Online resources

For an outline answer to this problem question, as well as multiple-choice questions and further reading, please visit: www.oup.com/he/roach-concentrate7e.

Incorporation

2

- Companies (and LLPs) are formed via a formal process known as 'incorporation'.

- The vast majority of companies are incorporated by registration, which involves registering specified documentation with Companies House.

- A company can do many things that a natural person can, including entering into contracts, owning property, and commencing legal proceedings.

- In the vast majority of companies, the liability of the members will be limited.

- A company has corporate personality, which means that, at law, it is a person.

- The courts can set aside a company's corporate personality where statute so provides, or where a company is interposed in order to evade, or frustrate the enforcement of, a legal obligation.

- Companies can be found liable for committing a civil wrong or guilty of committing a crime.

CHAPTER OVERVIEW

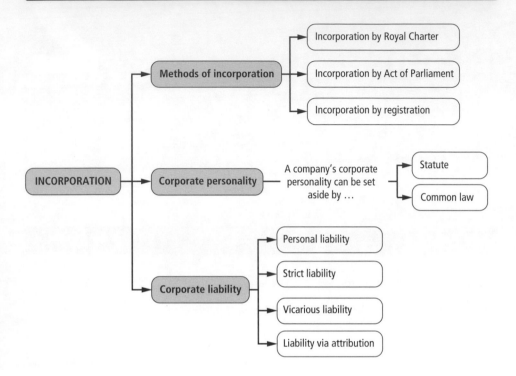

Introduction

Sole proprietorships and ordinary partnerships can be brought into existence very easily and with minimal state involvement. Conversely, companies (and LLPs) are brought into existence at the discretion of the state via a formal process known as 'incorporation'. The word 'incorporation' is used because successful incorporation brings into existence a 'corporation' (or as **s 16(2) of the CA 2006** terms it, a 'body corporate'). In this chapter, the process of incorporation and the advantages and disadvantages of conducting business through a company will be discussed.

2.1 Methods of incorporation

There are three principal methods by which a company can be incorporated:

1. incorporation by Act of Parliament;
2. incorporation by Royal Charter;
3. incorporation by registration.

The vast majority of companies are incorporated by registration, but it is still worth understanding all three methods of incorporation.

2.1.1 Incorporation by Act of Parliament

Parliament can create a company by passing an Act of Parliament. For example, organizing the London 2012 Olympic and Paralympic Games was the responsibility of a company called the Olympic Delivery Authority, which was created by the **London Olympic Games and Paralympic Games Act 2006**.

2.1.2 Incorporation by Royal Charter

A company can be created by Royal Charter. Historically, such so-called chartered companies were created personally by the monarch through the exercise of the Royal Prerogative, but today they are created by the monarch upon advice from the Privy Council. Prominent examples of companies incorporated by Royal Charter include the Bank of England, the Law Society, and the BBC. Today, very few companies are created in this way (in 2022, no chartered companies were created and only around 900 chartered companies still exist), with modern charters being granted almost exclusively to bodies engaged in regulatory, educational, or charitable work.

2.1.3 Incorporation by registration

Petitioning Parliament or the monarch is not the most accessible or efficient way of creating a company. Accordingly, a simpler and quicker method of incorporation was created by the **Joint Stock Companies Act 1844**, namely incorporation by registration. Today, the overwhelming majority of new companies are incorporated by registration under the provisions found in **Pt 2 of the CA 2006** (in 2021/22, over 750,000 companies were incorporated by registration).

2.1.3.1 The registration process

Incorporation by registration is so called because it involves submitting 'registration documents' to Companies House. These documents, once registered by Companies House, bring a registered company into existence. **Section 9 of the CA 2006** provides that the required documents are the memorandum of association (discussed at 3.1.1), an application for registration, and a statement of compliance. The most important document is the application for registration (known as Form IN01), which will provide specified information on the proposed company, including:

- the company's proposed name;
- the address of the company's registered office;
- whether the company is to be public or private;
- whether the members' liability is to be limited or unlimited and, if limited, whether it is to be limited by shares or by guarantee;
- if the members' liability is to be limited by guarantee, then a statement of guarantee must be included;
- if the company is to have a share capital, a statement of capital and initial shareholdings must be included;
- a statement identifying the company's proposed officers (i.e. the first director(s) and, if applicable, the first company secretary);
- a statement identifying persons who have significant control over the company, and
- if the company is private, and the promoters have elected to have Companies House keep its statutory registers, then a notice indicating this must be delivered to Companies House upon registration.

The **Economic Crime and Corporate Transparency Bill** (which, at the time of writing, is making its way through Parliament) will require additional information to be included in the application for registration, including:

- a statement confirming that the identities of directors and persons with significant control have been verified,
- a statement confirming that the subscribers wish to form the company for a lawful purpose, and
- a statement confirming that no one named as a director is disqualified or ineligible to act as director.

A statement of compliance must be registered which states that the statutory requirements regarding registration have been met.

If the registrar of companies is satisfied that the documents are complete and accurate, he will, upon payment of the registration fee, issue a certificate of incorporation, which provides conclusive proof that the company is validly registered under the **CA 2006 (s 15(4))**. From this date, the company has all the powers and obligations of a registered company, and the proposed directors will formally become directors, subject to a range of statutory duties (discussed at 4.4).

LOOKING FOR EXTRA MARKS?

Be aware of the practicalities of incorporating a company (e.g. methods of incorporation by registration, costs of incorporation, etc.) and how practice in this area is changing. For example, Companies House has stated that it eventually intends for all incorporations to be completed electronically and strongly encourages paperless incorporation via the registration fee, which is notably less for electronic registration than for paper registration.

A wealth of practical and up-to-date information relating to the process of incorporation and the number of incorporations can be found at the Companies House website (www.gov.uk/government/organisations/companies-house), and the Companies House blog (https://companieshouse.blog.gov.uk) also provides useful updates.

2.1.3.2 'Off-the-shelf' companies

Preparing the registration documents is not unduly burdensome, but it does require knowledge of the procedures by which a company is created. Persons who lack such knowledge, or who wish to avoid the time and effort associated with preparing the registration documents, may instead prefer to take advantage of the services of an incorporation agent (also known as a company formation agent). Incorporation agents register the relevant documents and then leave the newly registered company 'on the shelf' until such time as it is purchased from them. When purchased, the agent will notify the registrar of companies of the new owner's identity and relevant changes (e.g. change of registered office, change of directors, etc.).

REVISION TIP

The Company Law Review Steering Group estimated that around 60 per cent of all new companies are initially created as off-the-shelf companies. Be aware of the importance of this method of obtaining a company, and also the advantages (e.g. speed and lack of expense) and disadvantages (e.g. the company may not be tailored to the purchaser's needs) of purchasing an off-the-shelf company.

2.2 Consequences of incorporation

To understand the true importance of the company, it is vital that you appreciate the consequences of incorporation, especially the advantages and disadvantages that arise when conducting business through a company.

REVISION TIP

Students are often aware of the advantages of incorporation, but frequently are unaware that incorporation carries some notable disadvantages. Despite the numerous substantial benefits that incorporation brings, it is not suitable for all businesses, as evidenced by the notable number of sole proprietorships and partnerships.

2.2.1 Advantages

Carrying on business though a company has several significant benefits over carrying on business through an unincorporated structure.

2.2.1.1 Corporate personality

The primary advantage, from which many other advantages flow, is that the company acquires corporate (or separate, or legal) personality. This means that the company is regarded by the law as a person. Whereas humans are classed as natural persons, the company is a legal person and can therefore do many things that humans can. As corporate personality is so fundamental, it is discussed in more detail later in this chapter at 2.3.

2.2.1.2 Limited liability

As the company is a separate entity, it follows that the members are not usually personally liable for its debts and liabilities—the company itself is liable. However, this does not mean that the members are not liable to contribute anything. Where a company is unlimited, the members' liability will also be unlimited. However, the overwhelming majority of companies are limited, and so the liability of the members will also be limited, with the methods of limitation having already been discussed at 1.4.2.

 LOOKING FOR EXTRA MARKS?

Limited liability is a powerful incentive to incorporate, but for many smaller companies it may not provide as substantial a benefit in practice. When lending to a smaller company, banks will often require that the directors/members sign personal guarantees, thereby ensuring that, should the company default on the loan, the relevant directors/members may become personally liable to pay to the bank any part of the loan unpaid by the company. Further, limited companies pay for limited liability in the form of increased regulation (e.g. disclosure requirements). Students are usually aware of the advantages of limited liability, but are often unaware of its disadvantages. For an account of the advantages and disadvantages of limited liability, see Brian R Cheffins, *Company Law: Theory, Structure and Operation* (Clarendon, 1997) 497–508.

There is little doubt that limited liability minimizes the risk faced by the members and encourages investment in companies. The problem with limited liability is that, whilst it protects the members, it arguably weakens the position of the company's creditors. In a sole proprietorship or ordinary partnership, the creditors can obtain satisfaction of the debt from the personal assets of the sole proprietor or partners. In a company, the creditors of the company can only usually look to the company for payment. It has therefore been argued that limited liability does not so much minimize the members' risk, but instead shifts it from them and onto the company's creditors.

LOOKING FOR EXTRA MARKS?

Does limited liability really shift the risk from the members onto the creditors? The answer is undoubtedly yes, but it has been argued that the creditor is fully compensated for the increased risk by the interest charged on the loan. However, smaller creditors may not be powerful enough to negotiate increased interest rates with the company. Further, some creditors are unable to negotiate with the company at all (e.g. persons who are owed compensation from the company as a result of the company's tortious acts or omissions). For a detailed discussion, see Frank H Easterbrook and Daniel R Fischel, 'Limited Liability and the Corporation' (1985) 52 Uni Chi LR 89.

2.2.1.3 Perpetual succession

Companies are not subject to the physical weaknesses that natural persons are subject to. Accordingly, companies can continue forever and there are numerous existing companies that are centuries old. Members and directors can come and go, but the company remains (see the Australian case of *Re Noel Tedman Holdings Pty Ltd* **[1967]** for a stark example of this). Compare this to a sole proprietorship which, upon the death of the sole proprietor, will be dissolved.

2.2.1.4 Contractual capacity

As the company is a person, it can enter into contracts with persons inside and outside the company.

Lee v Lee's Air Farming Ltd **[1961] AC 12 (PC)**

Facts: Lee was employed as a pilot by a company. He was the only director and held 2,999 of the 3,000 shares that had been issued. Whilst engaged on company business, his plane crashed and he was killed. His widow sought compensation for his death from the company, which, under the relevant legislation, was payable only to the widows of deceased employees. The company's insurers argued that Lee was not an employee of the company, on the basis that he was synonymous with the company and had therefore made a contract with himself (which is not permitted by the law, as agreement requires two parties).

Held: Lee's widow was entitled to compensation. Lee had not made a contract with himself; rather, he had made a contract with the company, which was a separate entity. The fact that he owned almost all the shares and was the only director did not change that fact that the company was the employer and he was its employee.

The extent of a company's ability to enter into contracts (i.e. its contractual capacity) is discussed at 3.3.

2.2.1.5 Ownership of assets

The assets of the company belong to it as a legal person. This allows for a clear separation between the property of the company and the property of the members, and the members have no proprietary interest in the company's assets.

Macaura v Northern Assurance Co Ltd [1925] AC 619 (HL)

Facts: Macaura owned a timber yard. He created a company and transferred the timber to this new company, in return for which he obtained shares in the company. He then insured the timber, in his own name, against loss caused by fire. Subsequently, the timber was destroyed in a fire, but the insurance company refused to pay out.

Held: The insurance company was entitled to refuse payment as, whilst the timber was insured in Macaura's name, it did not belong to him—it belonged to the company he created. Accordingly, Macaura had no insurable interest in the timber and so could not claim on the insurance policy.

It is important to be able to determine which property belongs to the company because any capital borrowed by the company will usually be secured against the company's assets, not the assets of the members/directors. In such a case, if the company fails to repay the loan, the creditors can bring claims against the assets of the company, but cannot generally claim against the assets of the members/directors (unless personal guarantees have been entered into).

2.2.1.6 Creating and participating in other business structures

Being a person, a company is generally free to form other business structures. A company can incorporate another company (**CA 2006, s 7(1)**) or LLP (**LLPA 2000, s 2(1)**), or form a partnership with other persons. However, a company cannot be a sole proprietor. A company can also participate in other businesses. A company can be a member of another company, although a subsidiary cannot generally be a member of its holding company (**CA 2006, s 136(1)**). A company can act as a company secretary and, at the time of writing, a company can act as director but this will change when **s 156A of the CA 2006** comes into force (discussed at 4.1). A company can be a partner in a partnership or a member of an LLP.

2.2.1.7 Commencing legal proceedings

Determining who can sue in cases involving unincorporated businesses (especially partnerships) has historically proven to be an extremely difficult issue. No such difficulty exists in relation to companies, as where a company is wronged, it is the company, as a person, who is usually the proper claimant. However, in certain cases, the members can commence proceedings for a wrong done to the company via what is known as a derivative claim (discussed at 8.3).

2.2.1.8 Transferable shares

In a partnership, the transfer of one partner's interest to another can be an extremely complex process and can adversely affect the operation of the partnership. Conversely, transferring interests in a company with a share capital is straightforward, due to the transferable nature of the share. A shareholder who wishes to transfer his interest in the company need only sell his shares and his interest in the company will come to an end.

2.2.1.9 Floating charges

Incorporated bodies have access to a specific form of security known as a 'floating charge' (discussed at 7.3.1.2). Currently, sole proprietors and ordinary partnerships are not permitted to grant floating charges. Access to this form of security makes it easier for companies to borrow money, when compared to sole proprietors and ordinary partnerships which, despite their unlimited liability, often find it difficult to raise significant amounts of debt capital.

2.2.1.10 Human rights

As a company is a person, it follows that certain pieces of law that protect persons can also apply to companies. For example, the **European Convention on Human Rights** not only protects natural persons, but several its provisions also offer protection to legal persons too (accordingly, the word 'human' in the title could be regarded as inaccurate). For example, **Art 1 of the First Protocol** of the Convention provides that 'every natural or legal person is entitled to the peaceful enjoyment of his possessions'.

2.2.2 Disadvantages

Whilst incorporation carries some notable benefits, a promoter considering incorporating their business should also be aware of several disadvantages.

2.2.2.1 Increased formality, regulation, and publicity

Companies are subject to significantly more formality and regulation than unincorporated businesses. Setting up a company is a more complex task than setting up a sole proprietorship or ordinary partnership and complex rules can apply throughout the company's existence (e.g. the rules relating to the calling and running of general meetings, which are discussed at 5.3). Directors are subject to a raft of statutory duties (discussed at 4.4) that sole proprietors and partners are not subject to. Incorporation also results in a loss of privacy, as most companies are required to make certain information (e.g. financial accounts) publicly available throughout their existence. Further, almost all information on Companies House's public register is available online free of charge.

LOOKING FOR EXTRA MARKS?

You should be aware of why companies are subject to so much regulation. Put simply, corporate regulation (especially the rules relating to disclosure of information) is the price the company pays for having the benefits of corporate personality and for being able to offer its members limited liability. Creditors, knowing that they will normally be unable to look to the company's members for satisfaction of their debt, will understandably want to investigate the financial affairs of the company to decide whether to loan the company capital, or on what terms the capital will be loaned. This is easily done, as limited companies are required to publicly disclose their financial accounts.

Companies can only be held accountable if information on their business activities is readily available. Accordingly, promoting corporate transparency is a key feature of the UK company law system, resulting in companies being subject to extensive disclosure requirements. Companies are required to disclose significant amounts of financial information (e.g. annual accounts). Companies are required, every year, to prepare a series of annual reports with quoted companies having to produce additional reports (i.e. the directors' remuneration report) and comply with disclosure obligations under the **FCA Handbook**. Companies also have to keep certain information in a series of statutory registers (e.g. the register of members), which specified persons can inspect. Over time, these disclosure obligations only tend to increase (e.g. via the creation of new statutory registers such as register for people with significant control and the register of overseas entities).

LOOKING FOR EXTRA MARKS?

It has been argued that the disclosure requirements placed upon companies are overly burdensome, especially for private companies. Unfortunately, the trend is to increase disclosure obligations placed upon companies, but the **SBEEA 2015** does aid private companies by allowing them to choose between (i) maintaining certain registers themselves, and (ii) keeping the required information on the public register maintained by Companies House (although they must notify Companies House of any relevant changes). Given that the public register is now available online free of charge, this should improve access to information on companies.

2.2.2.2 Civil and criminal liability

As discussed earlier, if a company has been wronged, it can commence legal proceedings to redress that wrong. Similarly, if a company commits a civil wrong, it can be sued and a remedy awarded against it (e.g. required to pay compensation, ordered to stop or to engage in a specified act). A company can also be found guilty of committing a crime. However, in the case of *R v ICR Haulage Ltd* **[1944]**, it was held that, as a company cannot be imprisoned, it cannot be found guilty of any crime for which the only punishment is imprisonment (e.g. murder).

As the company can only operate through the actions of others, the imposition of civil and criminal liability on a company does result in additional complexities. These are discussed more at 2.4.

2.3 Corporate personality

Upon incorporation, the company becomes a person in its own right and can do many things that a natural person can do. Corporate personality was available to unregistered companies, but with the passing of the **Joint Stock Companies Act 1844** and the ability to incorporate a company by registration, corporate personality took on a new-found importance. However, despite this, it was over fifty years later, in the following landmark case, that the courts finally appreciated the true significance of corporate personality.

Salomon v A Salomon & Co Ltd [1897] AC 22 (HL)

Facts: Salomon was a sole trader engaged in the business of bootmaking. He created a new company and sold the bootmaking business to this new company, in return for which Salomon received shares and £10,000 worth of **debentures**, secured by a floating charge. Salomon held 20,001 shares and six members of his family held one share each (the **Companies Act 1862** required companies to have a minimum of seven members), although they took no part in the business. The business soon found itself unable to pay its debts. Broderip loaned £5,000 to Salomon, which Salomon then lent to the company. In return for this, Broderip was granted debentures in the company. The company failed to pay the interest on these debentures and so Broderip exercised his right to appoint a receiver and recover the money owed. The company was later placed into liquidation at the insistence of the unsecured creditors. The company's assets were used to repay Broderip, with the remainder going to Salomon. As a result, there was no money left to pay the company's unsecured creditors. The liquidator argued, *inter alia*, that Salomon should be personally liable for the company's debts, as the company was his agent or trustee.

Held: Salomon was not personally liable for the company's debts. The company was not an agent or trustee for Salomon—it was a separate entity, with which the creditors had contracted. Accordingly, its debts were not Salomon's debts and, as his debt outranked the debts of the unsecured creditors (due to the floating charge), he was entitled to the money that was paid to him.

 LOOKING FOR EXTRA MARKS?

Be aware of the true significance of *Salomon*. Many students incorrectly believe that *Salomon* created the concept of corporate personality, but this is not the case (for a discussion of the history and origins of corporate personality, see Paddy Ireland, 'The Conceptual Foundations of Modern Company Law' (1987) 14 J Law & Soc 149). *Salomon* is regarded by many as one of the most important cases in company law for three reasons:

1. it recognized that a company could legitimately be set up to shield its members and directors from liability;

2. it implicitly recognized the validity of the 'one-man company' (i.e. a company run by one person, with a number of dormant nominee members) nearly a century before single-member companies could formally be created; and

3. the fact that a person holds shares (even all the shares) is not enough to create a relationship of agency or trusteeship.

There is no doubt that *Salomon* is the one of the most important company law cases. However, the ability to set up a company to shield oneself from liability is clearly open to abuse. Accordingly, both Parliament and the courts can disregard a company's corporate personality and impose liability upon those behind the company's corporate personality. This disregarding of a company's corporate personality is often known as 'piercing the veil'—referring to the 'corporate veil' that hides the company's members and directors from liability (although the use of these terms was criticized by Lord Neuberger in *VTB Capital plc v Nutritek International Corp* **[2013]**).

REVISION TIP

The law relating to corporate personality is a popular exam topic. Essay questions typically focus on *Salomon* or the validity and clarity of those instances where the courts will disregard a company's corporate personality (an area which has undergone substantial change, as is discussed at 2.3.2). Problem questions tend to require students to determine if a company's corporate personality will be upheld or disregarded.

2.3.1 Disregarding corporate personality under statute

As companies are granted corporate personality by statute (namely, **s 16(2) of the CA 2006**), it follows that statute can set aside corporate personality and impose liability on those behind the veil. Notable examples include:

- If a public company carries on business, or exercises any borrowing powers, prior to being issued with a trading certificate, then the directors will commit an offence and can be made liable if the company fails to comply with the terms of any transactions entered while it has no trading certificate (**CA 2006, s 767**).

- The directors of a company can be required to contribute to the company's assets if they cause the company to engage in fraudulent trading (**Insolvency Act 1986, s 213**, discussed at 9.2.3.2) or wrongful trading (**Insolvency Act 1986, s 213**, discussed at 9.2.3.3).

- The officers of a company can be guilty of an offence if the company trades with the enemy (**Trading with the Enemy Act 1939, s 10**).

2.3.2 Disregarding corporate personality under the common law

As corporate personality is bestowed by statute, it follows that the courts are reluctant to disregard a company's corporate personality in the absence of statutory authority, as the following case demonstrates.

Adams v Cape Industries plc [1990] Ch 433 (CA)

Facts: Cape Industries plc was incorporated in the UK. A **subsidiary** of Cape was based in South Africa where it mined asbestos. The asbestos was sold by other subsidiaries, one of which was based in Illinois, USA. The asbestos was sold to a factory in Texas and a number of the factory's employees developed asbestos-related medical conditions. A US court ordered that $15 million be paid in damages, but this could only be enforced in the UK against Cape if the claimants could show that Cape was present in the USA. Accordingly, the claimants argued that Cape was present in the USA through its Illinois subsidiary. For this argument to succeed, the separate personalities of the various companies would need to be ignored.

Held: The Court refused to disregard the corporate personality of the companies involved and held that the US subsidiary was separate and distinct from its UK parent. Accordingly, Cape was not present in the USA and the judgment of the US court could not be enforced against it. *Salomon* allowed a parent to use its subsidiaries to avoid liability in this way, and the Court was of the opinion that, on the facts, there were no grounds to avoid following *Salomon*.

In *Adams*, the claimants put forward several arguments for disregarding corporate personality. All of these arguments failed, and the Court strongly reaffirmed the principle in *Salomon* and indicated that corporate personality will not be lightly cast aside. This is especially important in corporate groups, where each company in the group will rely on the fact that its debts and liabilities are isolated from other companies within the group by virtue of their separate personalities. Fortunately, in *The Albazero* [1977], Roskill LJ stated that it is 'long established and now unchallengeable by judicial decision . . . that each company in a group of companies . . . is a separate legal entity possessed of separate legal rights and liabilities'.

The modern approach to disregarding corporate personality was established in the case of *Petrodel Resources Ltd v Prest* [2013]. Prior to this case, the two principal common law instances in which the courts would disregard corporate personality were where (i) a relationship of agency existed, or (ii) the company was used to perpetrate fraud, or was a façade or a sham. To fully understand how *Prest* has significantly altered the law in this area, these two instances must be discussed first.

2.3.2.1 Agency

A relationship of agency usually arises where one person (known as the principal) appoints another person (known as the agent) to act on their behalf. Where two parties are involved in an agency relationship, the principal is normally legally responsible for the acts of the agent. In the corporate context, a relationship of agency can arise in two situations:

1. The company could be regarded as an agent of a member, so that the member, as principal, is liable for the acts of the company (i.e. the company's corporate personality is disregarded and the member made liable). However, as discussed earlier, *Salomon* established that the mere fact of incorporation does not cause a relationship of agency to be created between the company and its members, although an agency relationship between the company and its members can arise on the particular facts of a case (see e.g. *Gramophone & Typewriter Ltd v Stanley* [1908]).

2. Where two companies are in an agency relationship, the principal (normally the parent or holding company) can be liable for the acts of its agent (normally a subsidiary company). In effect, the corporate personality of the subsidiary is disregarded and the parent company is made liable for the subsidiary's acts. The following case provides an example of when such an agency relationship arose.

Smith, Stone and Knight Ltd v Birmingham Corporation [1939] 4 All ER 116 (QB)

Facts: Smith, Stone and Knight Ltd ('SSK') purchased a business, and set up a new subsidiary company to run this business. However, SSK never transferred ownership of the business to the newly created subsidiary. The land upon which the subsidiary conducted business was compulsorily purchased by Birmingham Corporation, which planned to pay compensation to the subsidiary for loss of business. SSK contended that it was entitled to the compensation.

Held: The subsidiary was the agent of SSK and, therefore, the corporate personality of the subsidiary was ignored and SSK obtained the compensation. The crucial factor was that the newly acquired business and the land on which it operated still belonged to SSK.

Cases such as *Smith, Stone and Knight Ltd* are rare. In most cases, in the absence of an express agency agreement, a relationship of agency will not exist between a parent and its subsidiaries (even if the parent owns 100 per cent of the subsidiary's shares). However, as noted, a relationship of agency may exist based on the facts of a case, but exactly what type of facts will cause an agency relationship to arise is unclear. It should also be noted that, following *Prest*, the finding of an agency relationship and the subsequent imposition of liability on a parent will likely no longer be regarded as an example of disregarding a company's corporate personality.

2.3.2.2 Fraud, sham, or cloak

In *Adams*, Slade LJ stated that 'there is one well recognised exception to the rule prohibiting the piercing of the "corporate veil"'. This was where the company was used to perpetrate a fraud, was a façade or a sham, or was used to carry out some form of wrongdoing. A common theme amongst such cases is that the company was used to evade some form of existing contractual provision or obligation, as the following case demonstrates.

Gilford Motor Co Ltd v Horne [1933] Ch 935 (CA)

Facts: Horne was the managing director of Gilford Motor Co Ltd ('Gilford'). His employment contract provided that, should he leave the company, he would not attempt to solicit any of its customers. His employment was terminated and his wife set up a new company, which competed directly with Gilford. It was clear that this new company was set up at Horne's behest and was under Horne's control.

Held: The Court granted an injunction preventing Horne (and the new company) from soliciting Gilford's customers. Lord Hanworth MR stated that the new company was 'formed as a device, a stratagem, in order to mask the effective carrying on of a business of [the defendant]' and to avoid the restrictive covenant.

2.3.2.3 The current approach: Petrodel Resources Ltd v Prest

The decision of the Court of Appeal in *Adams v Cape Industries plc* clearly indicates that the courts are not quick to disregard corporate personality and the number of grounds upon which corporate personality would be disregarded was limited. The Supreme Court case of *Petrodel Resources Ltd v Prest* [2013] has further limited this by stating that there is only one instance in which a company's corporate personality can be disregarded and, even in that instance, it will only be disregarded if it is necessary to do so. *Prest* is now the leading case in this area, but as will be seen, it has not been universally accepted.

Petrodel Resources Ltd v Prest [2013] UKSC 34

Facts: The case involved a divorce settlement between Mr and Mrs Prest. The High Court had awarded Mrs Prest a divorce settlement totalling £17.5 million, but much of Mr Prest's assets were tied up in companies that were solely controlled by him. **Section 24(1)(a) of the Matrimonial Causes Act 1973** grants courts the power to 'order that a party to the marriage shall transfer to the other party . . . property to which the first mentioned party is entitled'. The High Court utilized this power to disregard the corporate personalities of these companies and order the relevant properties to be transferred to Mrs Prest. Mr Prest appealed, questioning whether the Court had the power to do this given that the properties did not belong to Mr ➡

➡ Prest, but to his companies. The Court of Appeal, in allowing Mr Prest's appeal, held that the companies' corporate personalities could not be disregarded in these circumstances and so the High Court had no jurisdiction to make the order under s 24(1)(a). Mrs Prest appealed.

Held: The appeal was unanimously allowed, but not on the ground that the corporate personality of the companies was disregarded. The Supreme Court held that the properties were held on trust by the companies for the benefit of Mr Prest and, as such, they could form part of the divorce settlement. More importantly for present purposes, the Court unanimously refused to disregard the companies' corporate personality, with Lord Sumption JSC stating that there was only one instance where corporate personality would be disregarded, namely where 'a person is under an existing legal obligation or liability or subject to an existing legal restriction which he deliberately evades or whose enforcement he deliberately frustrates by interposing a company under his control'. Further, a court could only disregard corporate personality in this instance if 'all other, more conventional, remedies have proved to be no assistance'.

The leading judgment of Lord Sumption JSC began by looking at what 'piercing the corporate veil' actually means:

> Properly speaking, it means disregarding the separate personality of the company. There is a range of situations in which the law attributes the acts or property of a company to those who control it, without disregarding its separate legal personality. The controller may be personally liable, generally in addition to the company, for something that he has done as its agent or as a joint actor. Property legally vested in a company may belong beneficially to the controller, if the arrangements in relation to the property are such as to make the company its controller's nominee or trustee for that purpose. . . . But when we speak of piercing the corporate veil, we are not (or should not be) speaking of any of these situations, but only of those cases which are true exceptions to the rule in Salomon . . . i.e. where a person who owns and controls a company is said in certain circumstances to be identified with it in law by virtue of that ownership and control.

Accordingly, Lord Sumption JSC does not regard many of the pre-**Prest** cases as true situations in which corporate personality was disregarded. *Prest* has redefined what disregarding corporate personality actually means, with the result that many cases that were previously thought to be instances of disregarding corporate personality (e.g. agency) must no longer be regarded as such. This is perhaps most evident in relation to cases where the company is being used as a façade (discussed at 2.3.2.2), where Lord Neuberger JSC stated that such cases often did not involve disregarding corporate personality. Lord Sumption JSC stated that many of these cases were examples of what he called the 'concealment principle', which states that:

> the interposition of a company or perhaps several companies so as to conceal the identity of the real actors will not deter the courts from identifying them, assuming that their identity is legally relevant. In these cases the court is not disregarding the 'façade', but only looking behind it to discover the facts which the corporate structure is concealing.

For Lords Sumption and Neuberger JJSC, the concealment principle is 'legally banal and does not involve piercing the veil at all'. The court is simply looking behind the corporate veil to discover the facts hidden behind the company's corporate personality.

The only true instance in which a company's corporate personality could be disregarded is in relation to the 'evasion principle', which occurs where 'a person is under an existing legal obligation or liability or subject to an existing legal restriction which he deliberately evades or whose enforcement he deliberately frustrates by interposing a company under his control'. From this, it is clear that, for a company's corporate personality to be disregarded and liability to be imposed on a person (X), three conditions must be satisfied:

1. there must be an existing legal obligation, liability, or restriction that is placed upon X;

2. X must interpose a company in order to evade or frustrate the obligation, liability, or restriction in question; and

3. the company being interposed must be under X's control.

Even where such conditions are satisfied, Lord Neuberger JSC was of the opinion that many cases that could be regarded as examples of the evasion principle (e.g. **Gilford Motor Co Ltd v Horne**, discussed at 2.3.2.2) could actually have been decided without resorting to disregarding corporate personality. He even went so far as to state that 'there is not a single instance in this jurisdiction where the doctrine [of the court piercing the corporate veil] has been invoked properly and successfully'.

 LOOKING FOR EXTRA MARKS?

It is vital that you appreciate the importance of *Prest* and the effect that it has had upon the law. The statements in *Prest* relating to disregarding corporate personality did not form part of the reasoning behind the Court's decision and so are *obiter* only. Despite this, Lord Sumption JSC's approach has been followed in subsequent cases. The result is that the instances in which corporate personality can be disregarded have been much reduced. Indeed, it was argued that, following **Prest**, the courts' ability to disregard corporate personality 'may be considered a vacant power because the circumstances are unlikely to arise that would allow the court to exercise that power' (Laura Stockin, 'Piercing the Corporate Veil: Reconciling *R v Sale*, *Prest v Petrodel Resources Ltd* and *VTB Capital plc v Nutritek International Corp*' (2014) 35 Co Law 363, 365). Whilst it is certainly true that most post-*Prest* cases have not resulted in corporate personality being disregarded (see e.g. *R v Sale* [2013]; *R v Boyle Transport (Northern Ireland) Ltd* [2016]; *Persad v Singh* [2017]), the courts have disregarded corporate personality using the evasion principle in a number of cases (see e.g. **Pennyfeathers Ltd v Pennyfeathers Property Co Ltd** [2013]; **Wood v Baker** [2015]). For more discussion of *Prest*, see Ernest Lim, 'Salomon Reigns' (2013) 129 LQR 480.

However, it should be noted that Supreme Court approval of the approach adopted by Lord Sumption has not been universal, for two reasons:

1. Whilst the Supreme Court in **Prest** was unanimous in its decision, the Justices did not agree on the approach to disregarding corporate personality. For example, Lords Sumption and Neuberger JJSC stated that the evasion principle is the only instance in which the courts should disregard corporate personality. However, other Justices (namely Lords Mance and Clarke JJSC) were open to the possibility that there may be other instances in which the

courts could disregard corporate personality, albeit with Lord Mance JSC stating that such instances would be 'novel and very rare'.

2. In the Supreme Court case of **Hurstwood Properties (A) Ltd v Rossendale Borough Council [2021]**, Lords Briggs and Leggatt JJSC stated '[w]hether the evasion principle is needed or provides the best justification for cases such as *Gilford Motor* . . . is itself open to debate.' Whilst the Court's comments on **Prest** were merely *obiter*, they do indicate that if a corporate personality case were to come before the Supreme Court, the Court may adopt an approach different to that set out in **Prest**.

2.3.2.4 A direct duty of care

In **Prest**, Lords Sumption and Neuberger JJSC were clearly of the opinion that many of the cases that were traditionally regarded as examples of disregarding corporate personality did not in fact involve disregarding corporate personality, and that the same result could be achieved in some other way. The result is that, in certain cases, the courts can, by alternative means, achieve the same result as if they disregarded corporate personality without actually having to disregard a company's corporate personality. The following provides a good example of a case where the Court was able to impose liability on a parent company for the acts of a subsidiary, not by disregarding the companies' corporate personality, but by holding that the parent owed a duty of care.

Chandler v Cape plc [2012] EWCA Civ 525

Facts: Chandler was, for periods between 1959 and 1962, an employee of Cape Building Products Ltd ('CBP'), a subsidiary of Cape plc. In 2007, Chandler discovered that he had contracted asbestosis as a result of being exposed to asbestos whilst working for CBP. He sought to obtain compensation, but CBP had been dissolved many years before and, during Chandler's period of employment, CBP had no insurance policy in place that would indemnify Chandler for his loss. Accordingly, Chandler commenced proceedings against the parent, Cape plc.

Held: The Court held that Cape plc assumed responsibility towards Chandler and so owed him a duty of care, which it had breached. Accordingly, Cape plc was ordered to pay damages to Chandler. Arden LJ highlighted four factors that could indicate the presence of a duty of care:

> (1) the businesses of the parent and subsidiary are in a relevant respect the same; (2) the parent has, or ought to have, superior knowledge on some relevant aspect of health and safety in the particular industry; (3) the subsidiary's system of work is unsafe as the parent company knew, or ought to have known; and (4) the parent knew or ought to have foreseen that the subsidiary or its employees would rely on its using that superior knowledge for the employees' protection.

 LOOKING FOR EXTRA MARKS?

Chandler is an important case, but it is important to understand its current impact. The Court emphatically rejected any suggestion that the imposition of liability on Cape plc involved disregarding its corporate personality. The Court stated clearly that the duty was based on Cape assuming a responsibility ➔

→ towards Chandler, which it had breached. The Court was also keen to stress that the duty of care owed by a parent company to the employees of its subsidiaries did not arise automatically and would only occur where the three-stage test in *Caparo Industries plc v Dickman* [1990] was met. Accordingly, whilst *Chandler* is not an example of the courts disregarding corporate personality, it does demonstrate that liability can be imposed on a parent for the actions of its subsidiary by using conventional legal principles (e.g. the duty of care) and without having to disregard corporate personality. Indeed, one might argue that, following *Prest*, the courts might rely more on such conventional legal principles, rather than disregarding corporate personality.

Since *Chandler*, there have been two notable Supreme Court cases with similar facts to *Chandler*. In both cases, the issue was whether a UK-registered parent company could owe a duty of care to persons harmed by the acts of its overseas subsidiary:

- In *Vedanta Resources plc v Lungowe* [2019], the claimants alleged that Vedanta was liable for the damage caused by the discharge of toxic materials from a Zambian mine run by one of Vedanta's subsidiaries. The Supreme Court held that there was an arguable case that Vedanta owed the claimants a duty of care and so held that the case could proceed to trial in the UK.

- In *Okpabi v Royal Dutch Shell plc* [2021], the claimants alleged that Shell was liable for the damage caused by oil leaks resulting from the negligence of one of Shell's Nigerian-based subsidiaries. The Supreme Court held that the level of control that Shell exercised over the subsidiaries' meant that there was an arguable case to answer, and so the case was allowed to proceed to trial.

Most cases to date have focused on whether a duty of care is owed by a parent company to someone harmed by the act of one of its subsidiaries. However, in *Shah v L3 Commercial Training Solutions Ltd* [2021], the court stated that there is no need to establish a parent–subsidiary relationship and all models of management and control that may exist between groups of companies could result in a duty of care arising.

2.4 Corporate liability

The company, as a person, can be liable for civil wrongs and can be convicted for committing criminal offences. However, the company as a person cannot act on its own and requires others to act on its behalf, and this leads us to ask who is liable when breaches of the law occur—the company and/or those who act on its behalf. In many cases, no difficulty will arise as statute will expressly identify who is to be personally liable. However, in other cases, the issue may not be so clear and so the law has devised three further methods of liability, namely (i) strict liability, (ii) vicarious liability, and (iii) liability imposed via attribution. All forms of liability will be discussed.

2.4.1 Personal liability

In many cases, the law expressly states who can be liable by imposing personal liability on the company and/or other relevant persons (e.g. criminal offences established under the **CA 2006** almost always expressly state who can be convicted). In situations where it is not expressly stated who is to be liable, the approach adopted depends upon the type of liability.

2.4.1.1 Contractual liability

A company has contractual capacity, so can be held personally liable on contracts. However, the company does require others to contract on its behalf and the issue is whether those who contract on behalf of the company can also be liable. The issue is largely determined by reference to the law of agency—in a typical agency relationship, the agent (e.g. a director) effects a contract between his principal (the company) and a third party and then drops out of the transaction. Accordingly, it generally follows that agents of the company are generally not liable for the contracts they enter into on behalf of the company—the company itself is liable. Due to **s 40 of the CA 2006** (discussed at 3.3.2), this is usually the case even if the director had no authority to commit the company to a contract. However, there are instances where a third party can enforce the contract against the agent (e.g. where the director has not disclosed that he is acting on behalf of the company) (***Sims v Bond*** (1835)).

2.4.2.2 Tortious liability

As discussed at 2.4.4, in many cases, there is no need to establish personal liability in tort because a company will be vicariously liable for the tortious acts of its employees and agents. However, in some cases, vicarious liability cannot be imposed or commencing proceedings against the company will be of no aid (e.g. because it is insolvent). The question is, can the person who caused the company to commit the tort (usually a director) be found liable?

The starting point is that a director who, in acting on behalf of the company, causes it to commit a tort, will not automatically be liable for that tort (***C Evans & Sons Ltd v Spritebrand Ltd*** [1985]). However, if the director engages in tortious conduct in some personal capacity, then he can be liable (***Standard Chartered Bank v Pakistan National Shipping Corp (No 2)*** [2002]), provided that the requirements of the tort can be established. Where this requires establishing the existence of a duty of care, this can be difficult.

> ***Williams v Natural Life Health Foods Ltd*** [1998] 1 WLR 830 (HL)
>
> **Facts:** Mistlin was the sole director and principal shareholder in Natural Life Health Foods Ltd ('NLHF'), which was set up to franchise retail health food shops. Williams and Reid (the claimants) wished to acquire a franchise and so NLHF sent them favourable details regarding the franchise's projected financial performance, along with a brochure advertising Mistlin's expertise in the health food trade. The claimants entered into a franchise agreement with NLHF (the claimants dealt with an employee of NLHF and had no direct dealings with Mistlin), but their franchise's turnover was significantly less than what was projected and it soon ceased trading after incurring substantial losses. The claimants sued NLHF, arguing that the financial projections ➡

➡ were negligently produced (which was the case). However, NLHF was liquidated shortly thereafter, so the claimants made Mistlin a defendant to the action, claiming negligent misstatement.

Held: Mistlin was not liable. Lord Steyn stated that the fact that NLHF was a one-man company did not, in itself, mean that Mistlin was personally answerable to NLHF's customers. In claims for negligent misstatement, the claimant needs to establish that the defendant assumed a responsibility towards the claimant when making the statement in question. On the facts, the House held that such an assumption was not present, stating that, as the claimants had no personal dealings with Mistlin, then '[t]here were no exchanges or conduct crossing the line which could have conveyed to the plaintiffs that Mr Mistlin was willing to assume personal responsibility to them'.

2.4.2 Criminal liability

A company can be convicted of many criminal offences and, in most cases, statute will identify who can be convicted. Where statute does not expressly state that a company can be convicted of an offence, the courts will determine this (*R v P&O European Ferries (Dover) Ltd* [1991]).

Establishing guilt for certain offences has proven problematic and, in certain cases, Parliament's response has been to create a version of that offence specific to companies. For example, whilst a company could be convicted of manslaughter, convictions were extremely rare (especially in larger companies), as the prosecution had to prove that the deaths were the result of the actions and gross negligence of an identifiable member of the directing mind and will within the company. The response to this was the creation of the offence of corporate manslaughter under the **Corporate Manslaughter and Corporate Homicide Act 2007**. Despite the Act making it easier in theory to obtain convictions against companies, the first conviction only occurred in 2011. Since then, although the number of prosecutions has increased year-on-year, the number of successful convictions has been low, and they have all been against small and medium-sized companies—not the larger companies that the Act was designed to make it easier to prosecute. Despite the low number of cases, corporate manslaughter cases can be important due to the media exposure they receive. For example, at the time of writing, the CPS is considering whether corporate manslaughter charges should be brought against the council and management company responsible for the safety of the residents of Grenfell Tower.

2.4.3 Strict liability

Strict liability can occur in relation to civil wrongs and criminal offences, but it tends to arise most commonly in relation to criminal liability. Many criminal offences require the prosecution to prove that a specific mental element was present (e.g. the defendant intended to commit the crime) and this is known as the '*mens rea*' ('guilty mind'). Strict liability offences have no *mens rea* requirement and are committed simply by engaging in the prohibited act.

The statutory provisions creating the offence will indicate whether *mens rea* is required or whether it is strict liability. Many criminal offences under the **CA 2006** impose strict liability (e.g. if the articles are amended, the company will commit an offence if a copy of the amended articles is not sent to Companies House within fifteen days (**CA 2006, s 26**)).

2.4.4 Vicarious liability

Personal liability and vicarious liability often overlap in that an employee or agent who commits an unlawful act may be found personally liable, whilst the company may be found vicariously liable.

2.4.4.1 Civil liability

A company can be vicariously liable for civil wrongs committed by other persons. In relation to contractual liability, vicarious liability is rarely established as the matter can usually be dealt with using the law of agency. Vicarious liability becomes much more relevant when dealing with tortious liability and, for a company to be vicariously liable, three conditions must be satisfied:

1. the tortfeasor (i.e. the person who committed the tort) and the company must be in a relationship capable of giving rise to the imposition of vicarious liability on the company (e.g. a relationship of agency or employment);

2. the tortfeasor must have committed a tort; and

3. the tort must have been committed in the course of the relationship in question.

It is the third requirement that has proven difficult to apply in practice. The courts will ask whether the tortfeasor's torts were so closely connected to the relationship in question that it would be fair and just to hold the company vicariously liable (**Lister v Hesley Hall Ltd [2001]**). The use of this 'close connection' test did make it easier to establish vicarious liability (see e.g. **Mohamud v WM Morrison Supermarkets plc [2016]**), but a more recent Supreme Court case has halted the expansion of vicarious liability and sought to introduce more certainty into this area of the law.

WM Morrison Supermarkets plc v Various Claimants [2020] UKSC 12

Facts: Skelton was employed by Morrison on its internal audit team and part of his job involved transferring payroll data to the company's auditor. He was found to have engaged in misconduct, after which he bore a grievance against the company. He took a copy of the company's payroll data and leaked it to a file-sharing website and several UK newspapers. Morrison discovered this and Skelton was subsequently imprisoned. The employees of Morrison who had their payroll data leaked sued Morrison alleging that it was vicariously liable for Skelton's unlawful conduct.

Held: Morrison was not vicariously liable for Skelton's acts. The Court stated that two issues had to be considered: (i) what functions or field of activities have been entrusted to the employee by the employer; and (ii) whether there was sufficient connection between the position which the employee was employed in and his wrongful conduct to make it right that the employer should be vicariously liable. Applying this, the Court held that Skelton's leaking of the payroll data did not form part of his employment or field of activities. Even if it had, there was not a sufficiently close connection as Skelton was not engaged in furthering Morrison's business when he leaked the data—on the contrary, he was pursuing a personal vendetta. That his employment gave him the opportunity to commit the wrongdoing was not enough to establish vicarious liability.

2.4.4.2 Criminal liability

In relation to criminal liability, vicarious liability has had a much more limited role to play, largely due to the court's reluctance to hold that an employee's/agent's criminal activity falls within the scope of his employment/agency. Vicarious liability can be imposed where statute expressly provides for the company to be criminally liable for the acts of others. Where statute does not provide for this, the courts will determine if the offence is one of vicarious liability, and this is more likely to occur in offences involving strict liability (*National Rivers Authority v Alfred McAlpine Homes East Ltd* [1994]).

2.4.5 Liability imposed via attribution

Establishing *mens rea* or any other mental element is problematic as the company does not have a mind of its own. One solution to this is to utilize what is known as '**identification theory**', which states that the knowledge of certain persons will be attributed to the company (i.e. the knowledge of such persons will be regarded as the knowledge of the company). Historically, the courts would only attribute to the company the knowledge of persons who constitute the 'directing mind and will' of the company (*Lennard's Carrying Co Ltd v Asiatic Petroleum Co Ltd* [1915]) which, in most cases, will be limited to the directors and senior officers of the company and to persons in management to whom the directors have delegated managerial functions (*Tesco Supermarkets Ltd v Nattrass* [1972]). However, a more purposive and contextual approach was adopted in *Meridian Global Funds Management Asia Ltd v Securities Commission* [1995]. Here, Lord Hoffmann stated that a company's primary rules of attribution (which are usually found in its constitution), along with general principles of agency and vicarious liability, will usually be enough to determine the company's rights and obligations. However, in some cases, these will not be enough and so the courts may need to determine how a particular rule is to apply to a company. The answer might be that the rule was not intended to apply to a company at all, or that the rule could only apply if the act giving rise to liability is one that was authorized by the company's constitution. But there will be instances where these solutions are unsatisfactory and so the court will need to 'fashion a special rule of attribution for the particular substantive rule'. Such a rule will need to bear in mind certain questions, such as was the law in question meant to apply to a company and whose acts or knowledge were for this purpose intended to count as the act or knowledge of the company. To answer these questions, Lord Hoffmann stated that the court must apply 'the usual canons of interpretation, taking into account the language of the rule (if it is a statute) and its content and policy'. In some cases, the 'directing mind and will' approach might be appropriate, but in other cases, it might not be. The following case demonstrates this more purposive approach in action.

Morris v Bank of India [2005] EWCA Civ 693

Facts: BCCI collapsed in 1991 after being found to have engaged in large-scale fraud. BCCI's liquidator alleged that the Bank of India ('BoI') knew that, by entering into certain transactions with BCCI, it was defrauding BCCI's creditors, and it had therefore engaged in fraudulent trading under **s 213 of the IA 1986.** Liability under **s 213** can only be established if it can be shown that the defendant 'knowingly' was a party to fraudulent trading. BoI argued that the employee who was responsible for entering into the transactions on its behalf (namely Samant) was not a board member and so was not part of its directing mind and will. Accordingly, his knowledge could not be attributed to BoI and so BoI was not a knowing party to the fraud.

Held: In most companies, there is a chain of command and delegation of authority and so it is likely that a fraudulent transaction will be dealt with by someone below board level. It would therefore be 'inappropriate, in the case of a company, to limit attribution for its purposes to the board, or those specifically authorised by a resolution of the board. To limit it in such a way would be to ignore reality, and risk emasculating the effect of the provision.' The question was who had authority in BoI to deal with BCCI in relation to the relevant transactions. Here, that person was Samant. He had a senior position in BoI, had brought the transactions to BoI, was given a free hand to negotiate them, and did not question the transactions, despite their suspiciousness. Accordingly, it was proper that BoI should take responsibility for the consequences and so it was found liable under **s 213.**

In relation to civil liability, the approach established in *Meridian* is now the generally accepted approach and has been applied to numerous civil wrongs. However, in relation to criminal liability, it has not gained the same support and the 'directing mind and will' approach still appears to be the primary one used. It appears that in criminal cases, the courts will first apply the 'directing mind and will' test and, if that does not establish guilt, the courts will apply the *Meridian* approach.

 LOOKING FOR EXTRA MARKS?

Keep an eye on this area of the law as the Law Commission has recently published an options paper on corporate criminal liability that could lead to reform in this area (Law Commission, 'Corporate Criminal Liability: An Options Paper' (Law Commission, 2022)). This paper discusses whether identification theory is a satisfactory basis for establishing corporate criminal liability and sets out some alternative methods for attributing liability. The government is currently reviewing and considering the options paper.

2.4.5.1 Attribution as a defence

The above discussion has focused on attribution as a means of establishing liability. One interesting issue that has arisen is whether the actions of certain persons can be attributed to the company for the purposes of establishing a defence to a claim brought by the company. Cases in this area typically involve the defence of *ex turpi causa non oritur actio* (or the 'illegality defence' as it is usually known), which provides that a claimant cannot recover compensation for loss which he suffered in consequence of his own criminal act. So, for example, if a company brought a claim against its directors, could the directors attribute their wrongdoing to the company and then argue that the company's loss is a result of its own wrongdoing? The following case provides that the answer is generally no.

Bilta (UK) Ltd v Nazir [2015] UKSC 23

Facts: Chopra and Nazir were the only directors of Bilta (UK) Ltd. Bilta was wound up in November 2009, whilst owing HMRC around £38 million in unpaid VAT. It was alleged that Chopra and Nazir entered into a 'carousel fraud' with several other parties (including Jetivia SA), the effect of which was to leave Bilta insolvent and unable to pay its VAT liability. Bilta, via its liquidator, commenced proceedings against Chopra, Nazir, Jetivia, and Jetivia's CEO. The defendants sought to strike out the claims on the ground that Chopra's and Nazir's wrongdoing should be attributed to Bilta itself, and therefore Bilta should not be able to bring a claim based on its own illegal acts.

Held: The strike-out application was rejected, with Lord Neuberger stating that 'where a company has been the victim of wrong-doing by its directors, or of which its directors had notice, then the wrongdoing, or knowledge, of the directors cannot be attributed to the company as a defence to a claim brought against the directors by the company's liquidator . . . '.

LOOKING FOR EXTRA MARKS?

It should be noted that *Bilta* does not state that a director's wrongdoing can never be attributed to the company, and the Supreme Court has since stated that it will be relevant to consider the context and the purpose of the attribution (*Singularis Holdings Ltd v Daiwa Capital Markets Europe Ltd* [2019]). Lord Neuberger in *Bilta* stated that where a director's wrongdoing led to the company incurring loss via being liable to third parties, then the wrongdoing can be attributed to the company. Further, it is not yet clear whether the *ratio* established in *Bilta* will have an application in relation to solvent companies. In fact, whilst the seven Justices involved agreed that the wrongdoing could not be attributed to *Bilta*, their reasoning did differ, resulting in a notable amount of confusion. Lord Neuberger acknowledged this by stating that 'the proper approach to the defence of illegality needs to be addressed by this court (certainly with a panel of seven and conceivably with a panel of nine Justices) as soon as appropriately possible, [but] this is not the case in which it should be decided'. The illegality defence was examined again by the Court in *Patel v Mirza* [2016], but it did not focus on corporate liability, so the law is still not fully clear. For more, see William Day, 'Attributing Illegalities' (2015) 74 CLJ 409.

The Supreme Court in *CPS v Aquila Advisory Ltd* [2021] has since stated that the principle in *Bilta* can apply not only where a company is seeking to recover a loss due to a director's breach of duty (as in *Bilta*), but also to a company seeking to recover a profit made by a director in breach of duty.

KEY CASES

CASE	FACTS	PRINCIPLE
Adams v Cape Industries plc [1990] Ch 433 (Ch)	A US court held that a US subsidiary was liable to pay damages to the US claimants. The claimants wanted to enforce the judgment against the English parent company in an English court, but could only do this if the parent was present in the USA. To do this, the separate personality of the subsidiary had to be ignored.	Each company in a group has its own separate corporate personality. The US subsidiary was separate and distinct from its English parent and the claimants could not therefore enforce the US judgment in an English court.
Bilta (UK) Ltd v Nazir [2015] UKSC 23	Two directors of a company engaged in fraud, leaving the company insolvent and unable to pay its debts.	Generally, where a company has been a victim of wrongdoing by its directors, the directors' wrongdoing cannot be attributed to the company for the purpose of raising the illegality defence.
Chandler v Cape plc [2012] EWCA Civ 525	The claimant contracted asbestosis whilst working for a subsidiary of the defendant. When the claimant discovered his condition, the subsidiary had long since been dissolved, so the claimant commenced proceedings against the subsidiary's parent.	A parent company can owe a duty of care directly to an employee of its subsidiary, providing that the three-stage test for establishing duty has been satisfied. This does not involve piercing the corporate veil.
Gilford Motor Co Ltd v Horne [1933] Ch 935 (CA)	The defendant attempted to avoid a restrictive covenant by conducting business through a company set up by his wife.	Corporate personality will be cast aside where a company is a sham or is used to evade a contractual obligation.
Lee v Lee's Air Farming Ltd [1961] AC 12 (PC)	The sole director (and majority shareholder) of a company entered into a contract of employment with that company. He was killed whilst working for the company, but the insurance company refused to pay compensation to his widow.	As the company is a legal person, it can enter into binding contracts, with persons inside the company, as well as those outside the company.
Macaura v Northern Assurance Co Ltd [1925] AC 619 (HL)	The claimant transferred his stock of timber to a company and took out, in his own name, an insurance policy insuring against loss caused to the timber by fire.	The assets of the company are separate from the assets of its members and the members have no proprietary interest in the company's assets.

CASE	FACTS	PRINCIPLE
Petrodel Resources Ltd v Prest [2013] UKSC 34	Mrs Prest was awarded a divorce settlement of £17.5 million, but most of Mr Prest's assets were tied up in companies that he controlled. Mrs Prest argued that the corporate personalities of these companies should be pierced.	The veil will only be pierced where (i) a person interposes a company in order to evade, or frustrate the enforcement of, an existing legal obligation or restriction, and (ii) other conventional remedies have been exhausted.
Salomon v A Salomon & Co Ltd [1897] AC 2 (HL)	Salomon sold his business to a company that he created, in return for shares and a debenture, secured by floating charge. The company failed and Salomon enforced the charge and recovered the monies owed to him. As a result, the company's other creditors went unpaid. The liquidator argued that Salomon should be personally liable.	Setting up a company to shield the directors or members from liability is a legitimate use of the corporate form. Holding shares in a company does not create a relationship of agency or trusteeship.

 KEY DEBATES

Topic	Limited liability
Author/Academic	Frank H Easterbrook and Daniel R Fischel
Viewpoint	Argues that limited liability does not eliminate the risk of business failure, but rather shifts it from the company's members onto its creditors.
Source	'Limited Liability and the Corporation' (1985) 52 Uni Chi LR 89

Topic	Corporate personality
Author/Academic	Tan Cheng-Han
Viewpoint	Discusses in detail the case of *Petrodel Resources Ltd v Prest*. Argues that *Prest* is a welcome decision and discusses the underlying basis in which veil-piercing cases should be based.
Source	'Veil Piercing—A Fresh Start' [2015] JBL 20

Topic	Attribution of directors' wrongdoing to the company
Author/Academic	William Day
Viewpoint	Discusses the Supreme Court decision in *Jetivia SA v Bilta (UK) Ltd*. Argues that the case clears up the law relating to attribution of directors' wrongdoing, but questions remain regarding the defence of illegality.
Source	'Attributing Illegalities' (2015) 74 CLJ 409

 EXAM QUESTIONS

Essay question

Otto Khan-Freund famously described *Salomon v A Salomon & Co Ltd* as 'a calamitous decision'. Discuss the impact and importance of the case and the justifications behind the decisions of the various courts. Do you agree with Khan-Freund's statement?

See the Outline answers section in the endmatter for help with this question.

Problem question

DriveTech plc is engaged in the business of designing and manufacturing high-performance racing cars. It wishes to build a racetrack upon which it can test its prototype models and, to that end, it creates a subsidiary company called TrackBuild Ltd. A suitable piece of land on which to build the testing track is located and TrackBuild purchases it using capital borrowed from DriveTech. However, shortly thereafter, the directors of TrackBuild (all of whom are also directors of DriveTech) discover that the land does not have planning permission and so TrackBuild agrees to sell the land to BuildCorp Ltd, a local construction company. However, several days later, a member of the local council indicates to the directors of TrackBuild that, should it apply for planning permission, it would certainly be granted. Accordingly, before sale of the land to BuildCorp is completed, TrackBuild transfers ownership of the land to DriveTech, and argues that the contract with BuildCorp is no longer valid as it no longer owns the land. TrackBuild successfully applies for planning permission.

DriveTech decides that it wishes to expand into the consumer car market and, to this end, it creates another subsidiary called GearShift Ltd. The articles of GearShift provide that only directors nominated by DriveTech may sit on its board and, accordingly, all the directors of GearShift are either persons nominated by DriveTech or are actually also directors of DriveTech. GearShift engages in research and development on a new car and this is funded exclusively by issuing shares that are purchased by DriveTech (with the result that GearShift becomes a wholly owned subsidiary). However, more capital is required, but the directors of DriveTech refuse to provide GearShift with any more capital and instead order the board of GearShift to cut back on its research and development. Accordingly, the directors of GearShift agree to cut back on research into the car's safety features. GearShift finishes designing a new car and it is manufactured and sold to the public. However, the car turns out to be unsafe due to a defect in the car's brakes and numerous accidents occur. Those who suffered injury and loss due to the defective cars initiate proceedings against GearShift but, by this time, GearShift has entered insolvent liquidation and has insufficient funds to meet any liability.

Advise the parties of any potential liability they might face.

Online resources

For an outline answer to this problem question, as well as multiple-choice questions, interactive key cases, and further reading, please visit: www.oup.com/he/roach-concentrate7e.

The constitution of the company

3

- A company's constitution consists primarily of the articles of association and agreements and resolutions affecting the company's constitution.

- The Companies Act 2006 has significantly reduced the importance of the memorandum of association, and the articles now form the company's principal constitutional document.

- The constitution forms a statutory contract between the company and its members, and between the members themselves, but only those provisions relating to membership rights will constitute terms of the statutory contract.

- A company that acts outside the scope of its objects clause will be acting *ultra vires.*

- Companies incorporated under the Companies Act 2006 have unrestricted objects by default.

- A company can alter its articles by passing a special resolution, although statute and the common law restrict a company's ability to alter its articles.

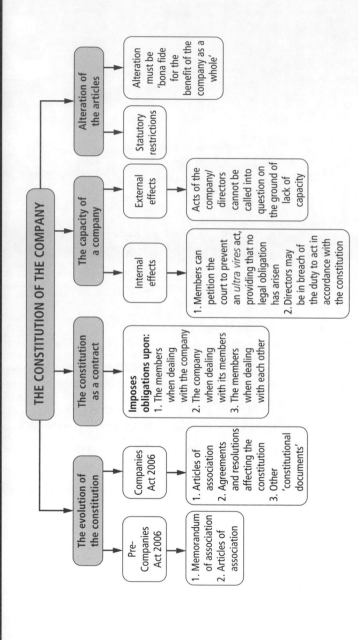

THE CONSTITUTION OF THE COMPANY

The evolution of the constitution

Pre-Companies Act 2006
1. Memorandum of association
2. Articles of association

Companies Act 2006
1. Articles of association
2. Agreements and resolutions affecting the constitution
3. Other 'constitutional documents'

The constitution as a contract

Imposes obligations upon:
1. The members when dealing with the company
2. The company when dealing with its members
3. The members when dealing with each other

The capacity of a company

Internal effects
1. Members can petition the court to prevent an *ultra vires* act, providing that no legal obligation has arisen
2. Directors may be in breach of the duty to act in accordance with the constitution

External effects
Acts of the company/directors cannot be called into question on the ground of lack of capacity

Alteration of the articles

Statutory restrictions

Alteration must be 'bona fide for the benefit of the company as a whole'

Introduction

Despite being one of the largest pieces of legislation ever passed, the **CA 2006** does not seek to exhaustively regulate the internal affairs of companies. Much is left to the companies themselves who will usually create their own internal rules via the company's constitution. A company's constitution largely fulfils the same function as the constitution of a country, namely to set out the powers, rights, and obligations of those who are subject to the constitution. Accordingly, a company's constitution aims to set out the powers, rights, and obligations of the company's members and directors, and also to lay down certain processes regarding how the company is to be run.

3.1 The evolution of the corporate constitution

The **CA 2006** has altered significantly the form and content of the corporate constitution. Prior to the passing of the **CA 2006**, a company's constitution consisted primarily of the **memorandum of association** and the **articles of association**. Section 17 of the CA 2006 now provides that a company's constitution will include:

1. the company's articles, and

2. resolutions and agreements affecting the company's constitution.

Accordingly, the memorandum no longer forms a principal component of the constitution (indeed, it is unclear whether it forms part of the constitution at all) and, as is discussed, its importance and content are greatly diminished. As **s 17** uses the word 'include', it does not provide an exhaustive definition of the constitution and other documents will also form part of a company's constitution. For example, **s 32 of the CA 2006** provides the members with a right to request 'constitutional documents', which will include the documents referred to in **s 17**, but will also include a copy of the company's certificate of incorporation and, in the case of a limited company, a statement of capital or guarantee.

3.1.1 The memorandum of association

Prior to the **CA 2006**'s enactment, the memorandum was of fundamental importance and formed one of the two principal documents that formed a company's constitution. To simplify company formation and to make it easier to discover the constitutional workings of a company, the Company Law Review Steering Group originally proposed that the memorandum and articles should be merged to create one single constitutional document. The government disagreed and recommended retaining both the memorandum and articles, and **s 7(1)(a) of the CA 2006** provides that all companies must have a memorandum. However, under the **CA 2006**, the content and importance of the memorandum have been reduced

Table 3.1 The evolution of the memorandum

COMPANIES ACT 1985	COMPANIES ACT 2006
Sections 1(3)(a) and 2 of the CA 1985 (now re-pealed) provided that the memorandum must state: • if the company is public, the memorandum must state that the company is public; • the name of the company; • whether the company is to be situated in England and Wales, or in Scotland; • the objects of the company; • whether or not the liability of the members is limited, and the method of limitation; and • details concerning the company's share capital and the subscribers of the company's first shares.	Section 8 of the CA 2006 provides that the memorandum must state that the subscribers: • wish to form a company under the Act; and • agree to become members of the company and, in the case of a company with a share capital, to take at least one share each.

significantly. Table 3.1 demonstrates clearly the reduced importance of the memorandum under the **CA 2006**.

It can therefore be seen that, under the **CA 2006**, all that the memorandum does is to provide a 'historical snapshot' that indicates the company's state of affairs at the time it was created.

3.1.2 The articles of association

With the emasculation of the memorandum, the articles now form a company's principal constitutional document. The articles tend to regulate the internal workings of the company and typically cover issues such as the balance of power between the members and the directors, the conduct of general meetings, and certain issues pertaining to shares and the distribution of assets. If a company chooses to limit its objects, the objects clause will also form part of the articles (the objects clause is discussed later in this chapter at 3.3).

Every company must have a set of articles (**CA 2006, s 18(1)**) and promoters are free to draft their own articles that suit the needs of their particular business requirements and submit them upon registration. However, drafting articles is a complex and technical task and many promoters (especially promoters of smaller companies) will lack the knowledge required to draft suitable articles. Accordingly, statute has long provided a set of model articles that companies may adopt if they so choose. **The Companies (Model Articles) Regulations 2008** provide model articles for private limited companies limited by shares (found in **Sch 1**), private companies limited by guarantee (found in **Sch 2**), and public companies (found in **Sch 3**). Unlimited companies, being very rare, are not provided with a set of model articles and promoters of such companies will need to draft and register their own articles.

LOOKING FOR EXTRA MARKS?

Be aware of the differences between the model articles found under the **CA 1985** and the **CA 2006**. Prior Companies Acts only provided model articles for companies limited by shares (these model articles were known as **Table A**). Conversely, the **2008 Regulations** provide model articles for a wider range of companies (notably for different types of private company).

Where the promoters of a limited company do not submit their own articles upon registration, the applicable model articles will form the company's articles (**CA 2006, s 20(1)**). Even if the promoters do register their own articles, the relevant model articles will still form part of the company's articles, unless its registered articles modify or exclude them (**CA 2006, s 20(1)(b)**). Companies incorporated under prior Companies Acts will not be governed by the new model articles, but can adopt them if they so choose.

REVISION TIP

Certain provisions of the **CA 2006** can be modified, or even disapplied, by the articles. The **CA 2006** is silent on many aspects of running a company, preferring to allow the company to determine such aspects via the articles. It is therefore vital that you are aware of what a company's articles state. Where a problem question does not provide details regarding a company's articles, it is reasonable to proceed on the basis that the model articles found in the **2008 Regulations** form the basis of the company's articles (although it is common for larger companies to expressly exclude the model articles). Unfortunately, whilst many students are aware of the provisions of the **CA 2006**, students tend to neglect the provisions of the model articles—this is a major mistake.

Should a dispute arise, the courts may be required to interpret the provisions of the articles in order to resolve the dispute. The courts have stated, on numerous occasions, that 'the articles of association of the company should be regarded as a business document and should be construed so as to give them reasonable business efficacy' (*Holmes v Keyes* [1959]). The courts have even stated that the words of the articles are not to be given their plain and obvious meaning if such an interpretation would produce a commercial absurdity (*Thompson v Goblin Hill Hotels Ltd* [2011]).

3.1.3 Resolutions and agreements affecting the company's constitution

Certain resolutions and agreements will also form part of the company's constitution. These are listed in **s 29 of the CA 2006** and are referred to as 'resolutions and agreements affecting a company's constitution'. However, the list of such resolutions and agreements is much wider than this definition suggests and appears to go beyond agreements and resolutions that affect the company's constitution. For example, **s 29(1)(a)** provides that any special resolution will form part of the company's constitution, even though many special resolutions will involve decisions that have no bearing on the company's constitution.

3.2 The constitution as a contract

The courts have long held that a company's articles form a contract between a company and its members, and between the members themselves (*Re Tavarone Mining Co (Pritchard's Case)* *(1873)*). **Section 33(1) of the CA 2006** expands upon this by stating that:

> The provisions of a company's constitution bind the company and its members to the same extent as if there were covenants on the part of the company and of each member to observe those provisions.

Accordingly, the company's constitution forms what is known as the 'statutory contract' and imposes obligations upon:

- the company when dealing with its members,
- the members when dealing with the company, and
- the members when dealing with each other.

Breach of certain provisions of the company's constitution may therefore constitute breach of contract, thereby allowing the non-breaching party to commence a personal action and obtain a remedy. However, as will be discussed, not all of the constitution's provisions will amount to terms of the statutory contract.

Before discussing the extent to which the statutory contract can be enforced, it is important for students to realize the ways in which the statutory contract differs from a standard contract.

3.2.1 The statutory contract

The statutory contract created by **s 33** is a highly unusual one and, in several important ways, it differs from a standard contract and is not subject to certain standard contractual rules. Table 3.2 demonstrates the principal differences between a standard contract and the statutory contract.

One cardinal rule of contract law that does apply to the statutory contract is the doctrine of privity of contract. The statutory contract is formed between a company and its members— persons not party to the statutory contract (known as 'outsiders') are therefore not permitted to enforce the provisions of the constitution, as *Eley* demonstrates below.

Eley v Positive Government Security Life Assurance Co (1876) LR 1 Ex D 88 (CA)

Facts: Eley, a solicitor, drafted the defendant company's articles, which were duly registered. The articles provided that Eley would act as the company's solicitor and could not be removed unless he engaged in some form of misconduct. Soon thereafter, the company ceased to employ Eley and engaged another firm of solicitors. Eley alleged that the company had breached the terms of the articles.

Held: Eley's action failed. The company might very well have breached the articles, but as Eley was not party to the statutory contract, he could not sue for such a breach.

Table 3.2 Differences between a standard contract and the s 33 statutory contract

	A STANDARD CONTRACT	THE S 33 STATUTORY CONTRACT
Source of binding force	Derives its binding force from the agreement between the parties	Derives its binding force from **s 33 of the CA 2006**
Alteration of terms against a party's wishes	Terms cannot usually be altered against the wishes of the parties	As the articles can be altered by passing a special resolution, the majority can alter the terms of the statutory contract against the wishes of the minority
Enforcement by a third party	Generally, third parties cannot enforce a standard contract, but can do so where **s 1(1) of the Contracts (Rights of Third Parties) Act 1999** applies	Third parties cannot enforce the statutory contract and the statutory contract is not subject to **s 1 of the Contracts (Rights of Third Parties) Act 1999**
Action for breach of contract	If any term of a standard contract is breached, it can give rise to an action for breach of contract	Only those terms of the constitution that relate to membership rights can form the basis for an action for breach of the statutory contract
Rectification of contract	The courts may be willing to rectify a standard contract if it fails to give effect to the parties' intentions, or if it contains a mistake	The courts will not rectify the statutory contract if it fails to give effect to the parties' intentions, or if it contains a mistake (*Scott v Frank F Scott (London) Ltd* [1940])
Defeasible on certain grounds	Standard contracts can be defeated on the grounds of mistake, misrepresentation, duress, or undue influence	The statutory contract cannot be defeated on the grounds of mistake, misrepresentation, duress, or undue influence (*Bratton Seymour Service Co Ltd v Oxborough* [1992])

REVISION TIP

Section 1(1) of the Contracts (Rights of Third Parties) Act 1999 provides that a third party can enforce a term of a contract if it purports to confer a benefit on him. One might have assumed that a claimant in a similar position to the claimant in *Eley* could therefore argue that the term of the articles confers a benefit on him, and so can be enforced by him. However, s 6(2) of the 1999 Act provides that s 1 will not apply to the statutory contract created by s 33 of the CA 2006, meaning that the statutory contract cannot be enforced by a third party.

3.2.2 The contract between the company and its members

As the constitution forms a contract between the company and its members, it follows that both parties can enforce compliance with the terms of the constitution against the other. In the following case, the company enforced the constitution against one of its members.

Hickman v Kent or Romney Marsh Sheepbreeders' Association [1915] 1 Ch 881 (Ch)

Facts: The company's articles provided that any dispute between it and a member should be referred to arbitration before any legal proceedings were initiated. The company purported to expel one of its members (Hickman) from its organization but, instead of referring the dispute to arbitration, Hickman petitioned the High Court for an injunction restraining his expulsion.

Held: The articles formed a contract between the company and its members. The company was therefore permitted to enforce the term of the articles and require disputes to be referred to arbitration. The High Court therefore stayed Hickman's legal proceedings and he was subsequently expelled.

A member can enforce compliance of a term of the constitution against the company, as occurred in the following case.

Pender v Lushington (1877) 6 ChD 70 (Ch)

Facts: The company's articles provided that its members would have one vote for every ten shares, up to a maximum of 100 votes. Consequently, members with over 1,000 shares would not have voting power commensurate to their shares. To avoid this, members with over 1,000 shares (of which Pender was one) transferred some of their excess shares to several nominees, thereby unlocking the votes within them. The company's chairman (Lushington) refused to accept the nominees' votes and Pender alleged that his votes were improperly rejected.

Held: Pender's action succeeded. The shares were properly transferred and registered to the nominees, so refusing to accept their votes constituted a breach of the articles. The court therefore issued an injunction restraining the rejection of the nominees' votes.

It is important to note, however, that not all the terms of the constitution can be enforced in this way. As Buckley LJ stated in *Bisgood v Henderson's Transvaal Estates Ltd* [1908], '[t]he purpose of the [constitution] is to define the position of the shareholder as shareholder, and not to bind him in his capacity as an individual'. It follows that only the terms of the constitution that relate to membership rights will form part of the statutory contract and members must bring their claim in their capacity as members (case law uses the phrase 'member *qua* member' with *qua* meaning 'in the capacity of').

Beattie v E and F Beattie Ltd [1938] Ch 708 (CA)

Facts: The company's articles provided that any disputes between it and its members should be referred to arbitration. Ernest Beattie ('EB', a director and member) was alleged to have improperly drawn his director's salary without the authorization of the company or its members. Margaret Beattie, a member of the company, therefore initiated legal proceedings to recover this payment. EB alleged that, because he was a member, the article provision applied and the dispute should be referred to arbitration. He therefore sought to enforce the provision of the constitution.

Held: EB was relying on the articles in his capacity as a director, not in his capacity as a member. Accordingly, EB could not enforce the relevant provision of the articles and the legal proceedings were permitted to go ahead.

Accordingly, provisions of the constitution that relate to the rights of directors will not normally form part of the statutory contract. However, in a certain type of company known as a 'quasi-partnership' (discussed at 8.5.2), the dividing line between a member and director is blurred and the members will usually expect to be involved in management. In such companies, rights conferred upon directors may also be regarded as membership rights (**Rayfield v Hands [1960]**, discussed in the next section).

 REVISION TIP

In problem questions, it is vital that you can determine whether or not a provision of the constitution concerns a membership right. Common membership rights contained in the constitution include:

- the right to attend, speak, and vote at general meetings;
- the method of counting votes at general meetings;
- rights relating to the transfer and transmission of shares;
- the right to a dividend, once it has been validly declared;
- in the case of a quasi-partnership company, the right to manage the company.

3.2.3 The contract between the members themselves

Just as the constitution forms a contract between the company and its members, so too does it form a contract amongst the members themselves. Accordingly, a breach of the statutory contract by a member can be enforced by another member, providing that the provision breached concerns a membership right.

Rayfield v Hands [1960] Ch 1 (Ch)

Facts: The company's articles provided that, if a member wished to sell his shares, he should inform the directors, who would then purchase the shares between them. Rayfield wished to sell his shares and so notified the directors, but the directors refused to purchase his shares. The directors were all members of the company, and so Rayfield sought an order requiring the directors to purchase his shares.

Held: The High Court ordered that the directors should purchase Rayfield's shares. As the company was a quasi-partnership, the article provision affected the directors in their capacity as members. Accordingly, the provision concerned a membership right and formed part of the statutory contract.

3.3 The capacity of a company

As the company is a legal person, it can enter into contracts in much the same way as natural persons can. However, historically, the company's ability to enter into contracts was subject to a significant limitation. Prior to the passing of the **CA 2006**, all companies were required to state in their memoranda the objects or purposes for which the company was set up (this is known as the '**objects clause**'). The objects clause serves to limit the contractual capacity of the company and if a company entered into a contract that was outside the scope of its objects clause, the company would be acting *ultra vires* ('beyond one's powers') and the contract would be void *ab initio* (***Ashbury Railway Carriage and Iron Co Ltd v Riche* (1875)**).

This restriction on a company's capacity was introduced to protect persons who provided a company with capital, namely members and creditors. Such persons provided capital on the expectation that the company would pursue the lines of business for which it was set up and would not expend capital on frolics outside the company's stated purposes. The problem was that the rules relating to *ultra vires* were overly complex, technical, and vague, and served to harm third parties who had innocently contracted with the company. The *ultra vires* doctrine also served to inhibit a company's ability to diversify into other areas of business that could prove profitable. Accordingly, successive Companies Acts have weakened the *ultra vires* doctrine, with the **CA 2006** significantly curtailing its scope, especially in relation to companies incorporated under the **CA 2006** and third parties, for whom the doctrine is now largely irrelevant.

REVISION TIP

Be prepared to discuss the evolution of the law relating to *ultra vires*. There is no doubt that the **CA 1985** and **CA 2006** have substantially weakened the doctrine of *ultra vires*, but it has not been abolished (despite what some sources might state). Do you think the doctrine of *ultra vires* should be completely abolished?

3.3.1 Abolition of the objects clause requirement

The requirement of an objects clause has been abolished by the **CA 2006** (although companies can still include an objects clause if they so wish) and such companies will accordingly have unrestricted objects (**CA 2006, s 31(1)**). For such companies, the *ultra vires* doctrine will be of little relevance as the company's contractual capacity will not be limited. This is the default position for companies incorporated under the **CA 2006**. Of course, companies incorporated under previous Companies Acts will still have an objects clause but, as a result of the **CA 2006**'s reforms relating to the memorandum (discussed at 3.1.1), such an objects clause will now be regarded as forming part of the company's articles and not its memorandum. As the articles can be altered by passing a special resolution (**CA 2006, s 21(1)**), such companies can accordingly delete the objects clause by passing a special resolution to that effect, and in doing so will acquire unrestricted capacity.

3.3.2 Inclusion/retention of the objects clause

The objects clause and the doctrine of *ultra vires* are still relevant in two instances:

1. Although companies incorporated under the **CA 2006** do not need to include an objects clause in their articles, they may do so if they wish. It is anticipated that very few companies incorporated under the **CA 2006** will include an objects clause.

2. Companies incorporated under prior Companies Acts will retain their objects clause, unless they decide to remove it.

In both cases, the objects clause will serve to limit the company's capacity and the directors' authority, and the *ultra vires* doctrine will still be of relevance, although, as will be discussed, it has lost much of its force. As was noted, historically, if a company entered into an *ultra vires* contract, then that contract would be rendered void *ab initio*. Unfortunately, this served to harm the innocent third party who contracted with the company and who often had no idea of the scope of the company's objects clause. This is no longer the case as **s 39(1) of the CA 2006** provides that '[t]he validity of an act done by a company shall not be called into question on the ground of lack of capacity by reason of anything in the company's constitution'.

It may be the case that a transaction is within the capacity of the company, but the director who caused the company to enter into the transaction lacked the authority to do so. In such a case, the issue is not one of corporate capacity, but of directors' authority. Again, the Act seeks to protect third parties, with **s 40(1) of the CA 2006** stating '[i]n favour of a person dealing with a company in good faith, the power of the directors to bind the company, or authorize others to do so, is deemed to be free of any limitation under the company's constitution'.

The result of **ss 39(1)** and **40(1)** is that if a company or director enters into an *ultra vires* contract with a third party, then the contract cannot be attacked on the ground that it is *ultra vires*. Therefore, from the point of view of a third party, the *ultra vires* doctrine is of little relevance, which is why it is often stated that the **CA 2006** abolishes *ultra vires* externally, because it is of little concern to external third parties.

However, whilst the **CA 2006** may have rendered the *ultra vires* doctrine largely irrelevant to persons outside the company, it remains relevant to persons inside the company for two reasons:

1. If a member of a company discovers that the directors are acting beyond their powers, the member has a personal right to petition the court for an order restraining the directors' action. However, this right only arises if a legal obligation has yet to arise **(CA 2006, s 40(4))**—the right is lost once the company has entered into the contract. In practice, most members will only become aware of a contract once the company has entered into it and so this right will be of little use.

2. Where the directors of a company cause the company to enter into an *ultra vires* transaction, or where the directors exceed the authority bestowed upon them by the constitution, then they will likely be in breach of the statutory duty to act in accordance with the company's constitution **(CA 2006, s 171(a)**—discussed at 4.4.2.1).

+ LOOKING FOR EXTRA MARKS?

That an *ultra vires* act can result in a breach of directors' duties demonstrates that this area of company law can overlap with other areas. You will want to be aware of other potential overlaps, including the following:

- As the constitution forms a contract between the company and its members, acting *ultra vires* might place the company in breach of the statutory contract created by s **33 of the CA 2006** (discussed earlier at 3.2). →

■ As acting *ultra vires* can amount to a breach of duty, the members may be able to bring a derivative claim (discussed at 8.3) on behalf of the company against the directors who have acted *ultra vires*.

■ If the company acts *ultra vires* because it has become impossible for it to fulfil the purposes for which it was set up, it may be wound up on just and equitable grounds (discussed at 8.5).

3.4 Alteration of the articles

As a company, or the market within which it operates, evolves, it may become necessary for it to alter its articles. **Section 21(1) of the CA 2006** provides that a company may amend its articles by passing a special resolution, and, in certain cases, the courts also have the power to amend the articles. The courts have also provided that if all the members agree to an amendment of the articles, this will be effective even if no resolution was passed (*Cane v Jones* **[1980]**). It has even been held that agreement to amend can be inferred from the members' conduct (*Re Sherlock Holmes International Society Ltd* **[2016]**).

 REVISION TIP

The rules relating to the alteration of the articles are also important in relation to the statutory contract formed by the articles as part of the company's constitution. Normally a contract can only be altered with the consent of all parties to it (unless the contract states otherwise). The fact that the articles can be altered by special resolution means that (i) generally only the members can alter the content of the statutory contract and (ii) some members may be bound by article provisions to which they object.

The ability to alter the articles is not limitless and both statute and the common law impose restrictions on a company's ability to alter its articles.

3.4.1 Statutory restrictions

Statute may limit a company's ability to alter its articles. Examples of such limitations include the following:

- The ability to alter the articles is limited by the provisions of the Companies Acts (*Allen v Gold Reefs of West Africa Ltd* **[1900]**).

- A member is not bound by any change in the articles made after he became a member if the effect of the change is to require him to take or subscribe for more shares than the amount he had at the date of the alteration, unless he expressly agrees in writing to the change (**CA 2006, s 25**).

- In certain situations, statute empowers the court to prohibit a company from altering its articles without the court's permission (e.g. where the members of a public company object to it re-registering as private (**CA 2006, ss 97 and 98(6)**)).

3.4.2 Common law restrictions

Perhaps the most important limitation on a company's ability to alter its articles was laid down by Lindley MR in *Allen v Gold Reefs of West Africa Ltd* **[1900]**, who stated that the power to alter the articles must:

> like all other powers, be exercised subject to those general principles of law and equity which are applicable to all powers conferred on majorities and enabling them to bind minorities. It must be exercised, not only in the manner required by law, but also bona fide for the benefit of the company as a whole . . ..

The test imposed by Lindley MR, whilst flexible enough to grant the court a wide discretion, is rather vague, to the extent that the High Court of Australia described it in one case as 'almost meaningless' (*Peters' American Delicacy Co Ltd v Heath* **[1939]**). Accordingly, in the following case, the Court of Appeal aimed to provide some much-needed guidance.

Shuttleworth v Cox Brothers & Co (Maidenhead) Ltd [1927] 2 KB 9 (CA)

Facts: The company's articles provided that its directors (one of whom was Shuttleworth) would hold office for as long as they wished, unless they became disqualified by virtue of one of six specified events. Shuttleworth engaged in a financial irregularity, but it did not fall within one of the six specified events. The other directors therefore used their majority shareholding to pass a special resolution altering the articles by adding a seventh event, namely that a director must resign if all the other directors required him to. Following the alteration, Shuttleworth's co-directors demanded his resignation. Shuttleworth challenged the alteration.

Held: The test imposed by Lindley MR is predominantly subjective, meaning that if the majority shareholders honestly believed that the alteration was for the company's benefit as a whole, then the alteration would be valid, even if the court disagrees with the majority's assessment. On this basis, the Court held that the alteration was valid, as the other directors did believe that it was for the company's benefit. The Court did, however, impose an objective requirement, namely that an alteration would not be valid if 'no reasonable man could consider it for the benefit of the company'.

It is therefore apparent that a minority shareholder who wishes to challenge an alteration on this ground will face a difficult task. As our system of company law is based heavily on the principle of majority rule, the courts are reluctant to invalidate alterations of the articles. This has led to accusations that the courts now focus more on the effect that the amendment has on the members, with the following case often cited as an example of this.

Greenhalgh v Arderne Cinemas Ltd [1951] CH 286 (CA)

Facts: Greenhalgh was a minority shareholder of Arderne Cinemas Ltd ('Arderne'), the articles of which provided that a shareholder should not sell his shares to an outsider if an existing shareholder was willing to purchase them. The managing director, who was also Arderne's majority shareholder, wished to sell his shares to an outsider. He therefore (in his capacity as a shareholder) altered the articles to permit the selling of shares to an outsider, provided that it was approved by an ordinary resolution (which would be a certainty, given that he owned the majority of Arderne's shares). Greenhalgh challenged the alteration, on the ground that it was not for the benefit of Arderne as a whole. ➡

> **Held:** The phrase 'the company as a whole' meant the shareholders as a body and the court should take the case of a hypothetical member and ask whether the alteration was for his benefit. On this basis, if an outsider was to wish to purchase the shares of a hypothetical member, it might well be in that member's benefit to sell his shares directly to an outsider. Further, the advantage obtained by the majority shareholder was also obtained by all the other shareholders, so the alteration was not discriminatory. Accordingly, the alteration was deemed valid.

A useful summary of the case law principles relating to altering the articles was set out by Sir Terence Etherton in *Re Charterhouse Capital Ltd* **[2015] [90]**.

3.4.3 Entrenched article provisions

A company cannot make its articles unalterable (***Walker v London Tramways Co* (1879)**). However, the **CA 2006** introduced the ability to entrench article provisions, thereby making them more difficult to alter (**s 22 of the CA 2006**). This could be done by requiring additional conditions to be met (e.g. by requiring unanimity instead of the normal special resolution) or by imposing restrictive procedures to be adhered to (e.g. by requiring the alteration to be approved by certain specified members). In order to prevent abuse, the Act does impose several safeguards:

- Entrenchment will not prevent alteration where all of the members agree to an alteration, or where the court orders an alteration be made (**s 22(3)**).
- **Section 22(2)** provides that a company may only entrench an article provision (i) in the company's articles on formation, or (ii) by an amendment of the company's articles agreed to by all the members of the company. Note, however, that **s 22(2)** has not yet been brought into force, largely due to the fear that it could prevent the creation or amendment of class rights.

 KEY CASES

CASE	FACTS	PRINCIPLE
Allen v Gold Reefs of West Africa Ltd [1900] 1 Ch 656 (CA)	The company's articles granted it a lien over partly paid shares. The articles were amended to extend the lien to cover fully paid-up shares.	An alteration to the articles will only be valid if it is bona fide for the benefit of the company as a whole.
Beattie v E and F Beattie Ltd [1938] Ch 708 (CA)	A company initiated legal proceedings against one of its directors. The director sought to rely on a provision of the articles, which stated that disputes would first be referred to arbitration.	A member seeking to enforce the constitution must be acting in his capacity as a member. Constitution provisions that do not relate to membership rights will not normally form part of the statutory contract.

CASE	FACTS	PRINCIPLE
Eley v Positive Government Security Life Assurance Co (1876) LR 1 Ex D 88 (CA)	The company's solicitor attempted to enforce a provision in the company's articles in order to prevent his removal.	Outsiders are not party to the statutory contract created by the constitution and so cannot enforce its provisions.
Greenhalgh v Arderne Cinemas Ltd [1951] Ch 286 (CA)	The company's managing director and majority shareholder sought to alter the articles to remove the members' pre-emption rights, and allow them to sell shares to an outsider, without first offering them to existing members.	The phrase 'the company as a whole' refers to the shareholders as a body. The court should ask whether or not the alteration was for the benefit of a hypothetical member.
Hickman v Kent or Romney March Sheepbreeders' Association [1915] 1 Ch 881 (Ch)	A member initiated legal proceedings against the company, even though the company's articles stated that disputes would first be referred to arbitration.	The constitution forms a contract between the company and its members. Accordingly, the company could enforce the constitution and the legal proceedings were stayed.
Pender v Lushington (1877) 6 Ch D 70 (Ch)	The articles limited the voting power of members who held a large amount of shares. These members transferred their shares to nominees in order to circumvent the limitation. The company's chairman rejected the nominees' votes.	The shares were validly transferred. Therefore, the company had no right to reject the nominees' votes. The nominee members were therefore permitted to enforce the constitution against the company.
Rayfield v Hands [1960] Ch 1 (Ch)	The articles provided that if a member wished to sell his shares, the directors would purchase them. The directors refused to purchase a member's shares.	The constitution forms a contract between the members themselves, which can be enforced by a member, providing that the provision breached concerns a membership right. In quasi-partnership companies, rights conferred upon the directors will likely be regarded as membership rights.
Shuttleworth v Cox Brothers & Co (Maidenhead) Ltd [1927] 2 KB 9 (CA)	The company wished to alter its articles in order to remove a director who had engaged in financial irregularities.	The test imposed in *Allen* was primarily subjective, although an alteration would not be valid if no reasonable man could consider it to be for the benefit of the company.

KEY DEBATES

Topic	The constitution as a contract
Author/Academic	Robert R Drury
Viewpoint	Reviews a number of academic viewpoints regarding a member's ability to enforce the constitution.
Source	'The Relative Nature of a Shareholder's Right to Enforce the Company Contract' [1986] CLJ 219

Topic	Alteration of the articles
Author/Academic	FG Rixon
Viewpoint	Provides an in-depth analysis of the power to alter the articles and examines the limitations upon this power. It also discusses what remedies are available to a person who wishes to challenge an alteration of the articles.
Source	'Competing Interests and Conflicting Principles: An Examination of the Power of Alteration of Articles of Association' (1986) 49 MLR 446

Topic	Entrenched article provisions
Author/Academic	Rita Cheung
Viewpoint	An interesting piece that discusses the entrenched article provisions under the **CA 2006** and compares them to US and Canadian statutory unanimous shareholder agreements.
Source	'The Use of Statutory Unanimous Shareholder Agreements and Entrenched Articles in Reserving Minority Shareholders' Rights: A Comparative Analysis' (2008) 29 Co Law 234

 EXAM QUESTIONS

Essay question

'The contract created by the company's constitution is a highly unusual one, but the ability to enforce the constitution provides the members with a powerful source of protection.'

Discuss.

See the Outline answers section in the endmatter for help with this question.

Problem question

The objects clause of Covenant Ltd, a company incorporated in 2010, provides that the business of the company is to design and create websites for charities. The company's two directors, Mike and Paul, own 25 per cent of the company's shares, with the remaining shares split equally between three private investors (Ceri, Jo, and Deborah). Ceri, Jo, and Deborah are concerned that the company could become burdened by debt, so they pass a special resolution directing the board not to borrow any capital unless first approved by an ordinary resolution.

Covenant's business prospects are not good and the directors believe that the company will need an injection of capital if it is to continue trading. Ceri argues that the company should expand its business by designing and creating websites for any corporate client, not just charities, and if the directors agree to this, she will lend the company £100,000. A meeting is convened, but Jo and Deborah do not believe that the company should take on more debt, although Jo does believe that the company should not limit its client base to charities. Accordingly, Jo and Deborah vote against the loan. Believing the loan to be in the interests of the company, the board accepts the loan and uses it to expand their business by taking on corporate clients. The expansion of the business is a success and Covenant begins to make a profit. However, Deborah believes that the company should stick to its original aim of only designing websites for charities, and argues that, in not doing so, it is acting outside the scope of its constitution. The board, Ceri, and Jo become tired of Deborah's complaints and insert a provision in the articles, which provides the majority with the power to compulsorily purchase the shares of any minority member. They exercise this power and expel Deborah as a member.

Advise Deborah.

 Online resources

For an outline answer to this problem question, as well as multiple-choice questions and further reading, please visit the online resources.

4 Directors

KEY FACTS

- Every private company must have at least one director and every public company must have at least two directors.

- The power to manage the company is initially vested in the members, but is usually delegated to the directors by the articles.

- Directors' duties are now found in the Companies Act 2006, which provides for seven general duties that directors owe to the company.

- The general duties are based on prior common law duties, so pre-2006 case law will remain relevant.

- Certain types of transaction involving directors will only be valid if authorized by a resolution of the members.

- A director's term of office can terminate in several ways including resignation, retirement, or removal. Additionally, the courts can disqualify a person from acting as director.

CHAPTER OVERVIEW

THE BOARD OF DIRECTORS

Types of director
There are a number of different types of director, including:
- *de facto* directors
- *de jure* directors
- executive directors
- non-executive directors
- shadow directors

Directors' duties

General duties
- **Section 171**: Duty to act within the company's powers
- **Section 172**: Duty to promote the success of the company for the benefit of its members as a whole
- **Section 173**: Duty to exercise independent judgment
- **Section 174**: Duty to act with reasonable skill, care, and diligence
- **Section 175**: Duty to avoid conflicts of interest
- **Section 176**: Duty not to accept benefits from third parties
- **Section 177**: Duty to declare interest in proposed transactions or arrangements (the criminal offence for failing to declare an interest in an existing transaction or arrangement is found in s 182)

Specific duties to obtain approval of the members
- **Sections 188 and 189**: Duty to obtain approval for certain service contracts
- **Sections 190–196**: Duty to obtain approval for substantial property transactions
- **Sections 197–214**: Duty to obtain approval for loans, quasi-loans, and credit transactions
- **Sections 215–222**: Duty to obtain approval for certain payments for loss of office

Termination of office
There are a number of different ways in which a director might vacate office, including:
- termination upon the director's resignation
- termination upon the occurrence of an event specified in the articles
- termination upon retirement by rotation
- termination upon removal under s 168 of the CA 2006, or via a power in the articles
- disqualification under the **Company Directors Disqualification Act 1986**

4.1 What is a 'director'?

A company may be run by persons who call themselves 'governors' or 'managers' and, increasingly, persons not involved in management at board level are called 'directors'. Are such persons actually directors?

REVISION TIP

Many provisions of the **CA 2006** apply solely to directors. It may therefore be crucial, especially in problem questions, that you correctly determine whether or not the persons concerned are actually directors. Do not forget that a person may legally be regarded as a director, even though he has not been formally appointed as such.

The **CA 2006** does not define what a director is. Rather, it states who is included within the office of director with **s 250 of the CA 2006** providing that a director 'includes any person occupying the position of director, by whatever name called'. This broad formulation will cover those who have been validly appointed to the office of director (known as *de jure* ('in law') directors), but will also cover persons who have not been validly appointed, but who act as directors (known as *de facto* ('in fact') directors). *De facto* directors, although not validly appointed, are therefore directors under the Act and subject to the relevant provisions (e.g. the general duties discussed later in this chapter at 4.4).

LOOKING FOR EXTRA MARKS?

There is little doubt that the courts have, over time, notably expanded the types of person who can be classified as a *de facto* director. For an account of the history of the law relating to *de facto* directors and how the breadth of the office has been expanded, see the judgment of Lord Collins in *Commissioners of HM Revenue and Customs v Holland* [2010], especially [58]–[93]. A useful summary of the authorities in this area was provided by Hacon J in *Popely v Popely* [2019], notably paras [78]–[88].

The word 'person' in **s 250** indicates that a director can be a natural person or a body corporate, but concerns arose regarding the use of corporate directors and it was argued by the government that:

> [c]orporate directors can bring about a lack of transparency and accountability with respect to the individuals influencing the company. A person's details and relationship to the company can be challenging to identify, which, among other consequences, can hinder law enforcement investigations. Even when they are identifiable, there may be no legal route to holding these individuals to account. More broadly, a company acting as a director, instead of an accountable individual, could suggest the potential for a deficit in corporate governance and oversight.

LOOKING FOR EXTRA MARKS?

For an example of a case that demonstrates the issues that arise with establishing liability in cases involving corporate directors, see *Revenue and Customs Commissioners v Holland* [2010], in which the defendant was able to avoid liability through a complex web of forty-two companies, all of which had one common corporate director.

Accordingly, the **SBEEA 2015** largely abolishes corporate directors by inserting a new **s 156A** into the **CA 2006**, which provides that '[a] person may not be appointed a director of a company unless the person is a natural person'. However, **s 156B** does allow for exceptions to this prohibition to be created and the government has spent a considerable period consulting on what these exceptions are, with the result that the **s 156A** prohibition is still not in force. Finally, a 2022 White Paper indicated that only one exception will exist, namely that a company may be appointed as a director where (i) all of its directors are natural persons, and; (ii) those natural persons had, prior to the company being appointed as a director, their identities verified by the Companies House verification identity programme (BEIS, *Corporate Transparency and Register Reform White Paper* (CP 638, 2022) Annex 3).

LOOKING FOR EXTRA MARKS?

For a more detailed discussion of the government's rationale behind the prohibition on corporate directors, see BIS, 'Transparency and Trust: Enhancing the Transparency of UK Company Ownership and Increasing Trust in UK Businesses: Government Response' (BIS, 2014) 44–6.

4.1.1 Shadow directors

A person who has neither been appointed a director, nor acts as a director, may be treated as a director if he is 'a person in accordance with whose directions or instructions the directors of the company are accustomed to act' **(CA 2006, s 251(1))**, other than where that advice is given in a professional capacity **(CA 2006, s 251(2))**. Such a person is known as a 'shadow director'.

REVISION TIP

It is important that you are aware of how to identify a shadow director as not all provisions in the **CA 2006** that apply to directors will apply to shadow directors. Often, the **CA 2006** will expressly state that a particular duty or obligation is imposed upon shadow directors. For example, in relation to the rules concerning directorial transactions that require member approval (discussed later in this chapter at 4.4.3), a shadow director is to be treated as a director **(CA 2006, s 223(1))**.

In practice, determining whether a person is a shadow director can be difficult. Accordingly, in several cases (of which the two most important are *Secretary of State for Trade and Industry v Deverell* [2001] and *Ultraframe (UK) Ltd v Fielding* [2005]), the courts sought to provide guidance, which is summarized as follows:

- it is not necessary for the shadow director to give directions/instructions over the whole field of the company's activities;
- whether a communication amounts to a direction/instruction is to be determined objectively;
- it is not necessary to show that the *de jure* directors acted in a subservient manner;
- it is insufficient that some of the *de jure* directors follow the directions/instructions—it must be demonstrated that a governing majority of the board were accustomed to following the directions/instructions;
- as the *de jure* directors must be *accustomed* to the directions/instructions, it follows that, initially, a person who gives directions/instructions will not be a shadow director; and
- the mere giving of directions/instructions is insufficient—it must also be shown that the directors acted on such directions/instructions.

Historically, the courts held that a shadow director could not also be a *de facto* director and vice versa. However, the courts have now acknowledged that a person can be both a *de facto* director and shadow director (*Secretary of State for Business, Innovation and Skills v Chohan* [2013]).

4.2 Appointment

Every private company must have at least one director and every public company must have at least two directors (**CA 2006, s 154**). The proposed directors of the company will become its directors officially upon successful incorporation. Thereafter, the power to appoint directors is a matter for the articles, but where the articles are silent on this issue, the power to appoint directors is vested in the members (*Worcester Corsetry Ltd v Witting* [1936]) and is usually exercised by passing an ordinary resolution. The model articles for private companies limited by shares and the model articles for public companies provide that directors may be appointed by an ordinary resolution of the members, or by a decision of the directors.

LOOKING FOR EXTRA MARKS?

Should you be required to discuss the appointment of directors in a listed company, it is worth noting that **Provision 17 of the UK Corporate Code** states that the appointment of directors should be led by a nomination committee, consisting predominantly of independent non-executive directors. These committees were introduced to combat the perception of the 'old boys' network' that many believed operated in larger public companies. Sadly, there remains significant doubt about the effectiveness of nomination committees. Grant Thornton's 2019 Corporate Governance Review noted that nomination committee reporting lags behind that of the audit and remuneration committees, and that ➡

→ nomination committees meet less (with some companies having no meetings at all). However, more recent evidence does seem to indicate that nomination committees are meeting more often and that reporting on their activity is getting better, but there is still considerable scope for improvement (see e.g. Grant Thornton, Corporate Governance Review 2021 (Grant Thornton, 2021) 41; 'FRC, 'Review of Corporate Governance Reporting' (FRC 2022)).

Whilst generally anyone can be appointed as a director, certain types of person are prohibited by statute from acting as a director (e.g. the **Economic Crime and Corporate Transparency Bill** will amend the **CA 2006** to provide that an individual cannot act as a director unless their identity has been verified).

Once appointed, directors may be required to be periodically re-elected by the members (known as 'retirement by rotation') in order to remain in office. The **2016 UK Corporate Governance Code** stated that all directors should submit to re-election at regular intervals, with FTSE 350 directors having to face re-election every year. **Provision 18 of the 2018 Code** now states that all directors should be subject to annual re-election. The model articles for public companies also establish rules that require a director to submit himself for re-election at least every three years.

LOOKING FOR EXTRA MARKS?

The 2016 Code's statement that FTSE 350 directors should face annual re-election was extremely controversial, with many directors fearing that it would lead to a short-termist approach and less stable boards. This does not appear to have been the case and annual re-election is now an accepted practice (as evidenced by the fact that the 2018 Code extends it to all companies subject to the Code), with almost all FTSE 350 companies subjecting their directors to annual re-election.

4.2.1 Board diversity

The need to improve board diversity has been recognized amongst larger companies for some time. Despite this, it was only with the publication of Lord Davies' 2011 report entitled *Women on Boards* that the topic gained the prominence it deserved. This report recommended that FTSE 100 companies should aim for a minimum of 25 per cent female representation by 2015. This 25 per cent goal was successfully reached (although the number of women in prominent executive roles is still disappointingly low) and a new voluntary goal was set by the Hampton–Alexander Review (the successor to Lord Davies' review), namely that FTSE 350 companies should aim for 33 per cent female representation by the end of 2020. This goal was also reached and the FTSE Women Leaders' Review (the successor to the Hampton–Alexander Review) now recommends that FTSE 350 boards and FTSE 350 leadership teams should consist of at least 40 per cent women by the end of 2025.

Although the above initiatives have primarily been aimed at FTSE 350 companies, their recommendations can be relevant to other companies. First, the FTSE Women Leaders' review now states that it will also cover the largest 50 UK private companies in terms of sales. Second, the guidance of **Principle Two of the Wates Corporate Governance Principles** states that a company's diversity policy should consider targets promoted by government and industry initiatives or expert reviews, with the Hampton–Alexander Review cited as an example.

There is strong disagreement over how greater diversity can be achieved. The UK clearly favours a voluntary business-led approach but other countries adopt a legislative quota that requires a certain level of boardroom diversity. In December 2022, the EU passed a directive that will require Member States to ensure that all listed companies are subject to one of two objectives, which must be reached by 30 June 2026, namely (i) members of the under-represented sex must hold at least 40 per cent of non-executive director positions, or; (ii) members of the under-represented sex must hold at least 33 per cent of all director positions, including both executive and non-executive directors. Of course, as the UK is no longer a Member State, UK listed companies are not subject to this quota.

It is clear that gender diversity within the boardroom is a highly prominent and developing topic and one that you should stay abreast of. The best source of statistics on board diversity is the annual Female FTSE Board Reports published by Cranfield University and the FTSE Women Leaders' Review annual update reports.

LOOKING FOR EXTRA MARKS?

Be aware of how the diversity debate is evolving. The debate has largely focused on gender diversity, but this is starting to change. In October 2017, the Parker Review published a report into ethnic diversity and put forward voluntary goals for FTSE 350 companies regarding increasing the number of directors of colour on their boards (these were updated in 2023). That the concept of diversity is broadening is also evident in **Principle J of the UK Corporate Governance Code**, which provides that board appointments should promote 'diversity of gender, social and ethnic backgrounds, cognitive and personal strengths'.

4.3 The board of directors

Collectively, the directors of a company are referred to as the 'board'. Much of a company's power is concentrated in its board, which exercises its powers via board meetings (not to be confused with general meetings of the company). The procedures relating to board meetings are a matter for the company's articles and decisions of directors are only valid if made at a board meeting, unless all the directors agree to, or acquiesce to, a decision (*Charterhouse Investment Trust Ltd v Tempest Diesels Ltd* [1986]). The law does not require that all the directors must be present at a board meeting, but decisions of board meetings will only be valid if a **quorum** can be obtained. The model articles set the quorum at two (unless the company is private and only has one director, in which case, it will be one), and decisions taken at a meeting that lacks a quorum (such meetings are said to be 'inquorate') are invalid.

4.3.1 Powers of management

A company, being a legal person, can only be run through human intermediaries, which leads us to ask, who has the power to run the company? The power to run a company is initially vested in its members. However, in all but the smallest private companies (where the directors and members are usually the same persons), it is impractical for the members to exercise day-to-day control over the company's affairs. Accordingly, the members' powers are usually delegated to the company's directors via the articles, but who has the ultimate right to manage the company: the members or the directors?

The directors have only such power as is delegated to them by the members, with most companies having a provision in their articles that delegates day-to-day management of the company to the directors. In such cases, the power to manage is vested in the directors and the members have no right to interfere in the company's management, unless such a power has been reserved to the members via the articles or statute.

Automatic Self-Cleansing Filter Syndicate Co Ltd v Cuninghame [1906] 2 Ch 34 (CA)

Facts: The articles of a company conferred general powers of management upon its directors and provided that they could sell any property of the company on such terms as they deemed fit. The members passed an ordinary resolution resolving to sell the company's assets and undertakings, but the directors did not believe that such a sale was in the interests of the company and so refused to proceed with the sale.

Held: The right to manage the company and the right to determine which property to sell was vested in the directors. Accordingly, the directors were not required to comply with the resolution, unless the articles so provided.

Article 3 of both the **model articles for private companies limited by shares** and the **model articles for public companies** provides that '[s]ubject to the articles, the directors of the company are responsible for the management of the company's business, for which purpose they may exercise all the powers of the company'. Clearly, this vests considerable powers in the directors, but, as it is 'subject to the articles', provisions can be inserted into the articles that affect the balance of power, as the following case demonstrates.

Salmon v Quin & Axtens Ltd [1909] AC 442 (HL)

Facts: The company's articles conferred general powers of management upon the directors, but such powers were subject to the articles. Article 80 provided that decisions of the directors relating to the acquisition of certain properties would be invalid if either of the company's two managing directors (who were also members) were to dissent. The directors decided to acquire such property, but one of the managing directors vetoed the decision. An extraordinary meeting was called and the members passed an ordinary resolution resolving to acquire the property. The managing director who vetoed the decision sought an injunction to restrain the property acquisition. ➡

> ➡ **Held:** Whilst the directors had a general power of management, it was subject to the articles. Accordingly, the veto exercised by the managing director was valid and the company could not override it by passing an ordinary resolution. The House therefore granted an injunction restraining the acquisition.

In both *Automatic Self-Cleansing* and *Salmon*, ordinary resolutions passed by the members could not affect the powers conferred by the articles, as this would permit the members to alter the articles indirectly by ordinary resolution and, as noted at 3.4, an alteration of the articles requires a special resolution. It follows from this that a direction from the members passed by special resolution should be valid, and this is reflected in **art 4(1)** of the model articles, which states that '[t]he members may, by special resolution, direct the directors to take, or refrain from taking, specified action'. Accordingly, whilst general power is vested in the directors, the members retain a specific statutory supervisory power exercisable by passing a special resolution (providing that **art 4(1)** forms part of the company's articles).

Finally, it should be noted that where the directors are unable or unwilling to exercise the powers of management conferred by the articles, then the general powers of management revert back to the members (***Barron v Potter* [1914]**).

REVISION TIP

Exam questions discussing the powers of directors, especially in relation to the powers of members, are popular. Be prepared to discuss the powers of management of the directors and the balance of power within a company. In problem questions, be mindful of companies with article provisions that affect the balance of power between the directors and the members.

4.4 Directors' duties

The problem with having such a concentration of power vested in the directors is that they might be tempted to use their powers to benefit themselves, or to engage in acts that are not in the company's interests. The law aims to discourage such behaviour in several ways, with the principal method being the imposition upon directors of a number of legal duties.

REVISION TIP

Questions on directors' duties arise commonly in exams (in fact, it would be unusual for directors' duties to not feature in an exam). Essays tend to focus on the scope or effectiveness of the duties (or the effectiveness of a single duty) or require a discussion of how the **CA 2006** has reformed directors' duties (therefore, you should pay particular attention to those duties that have been substantially reformed by the 2006 ➡

→ Act, such as the duty found in s 172). Problem questions usually require you to discuss whether the directors involved have committed a breach of their duties. Given the pervasiveness of directors' duties, it is common for directors' duties to feature in problem questions concerning other areas of company law.

4.4.1 Codification

Historically, the duties of directors were set out in a mass of case law spanning several centuries that was based on the common law of negligence and equitable duties analogous to those imposed on trustees. The result was that the law was unclear, inaccessible, and out of date, and, to obtain a clear understanding of the duties imposed upon them, directors would need to read through this mass of case law and statute or obtain costly legal advice. It was therefore decided that the law relating to directors' duties should be collected and set out in statute (this is known as '**codification**'), thereby providing an authoritative, accessible, and more modern statement of directors' duties. Accordingly, the common law duties have been abolished (although as is discussed, the case law remains very relevant) and replaced by the duties found in **ss 171–177 of the CA 2006**. The law relating to director transactions that require member approval has also been restated in **ss 188–226**. Figure 4.1 sets out the duties as imposed by the **CA 2006**.

 LOOKING FOR EXTRA MARKS?

An exam question may require you to discuss whether or not codification was a worthwhile reform. For a detailed yet clear discussion of the advantages and disadvantages of codifying the law relating to directors' duties, see the Law Commission Report entitled *Company Directors: Regulating Conflicts of Interest and Formulating a Statement of Directors' Duties* (Law Com No 261, 1999) and the consultation documents of the Company Law Review Steering Group entitled *Developing the Framework* (2000) and *Completing the Structure* (2000).

4.4.2 The general duties

The **CA 2006** refers to the newly codified duties as the 'general duties' and provides that they are 'based on certain common law rules and equitable principles as they apply in relation to directors' (**CA 2006, s 170(3)**). This makes clear the fact that codification has not radically altered the content of the duties, but has merely restated them in a more appropriate manner (although notable reforms have been made). The lack of change ensures that the significant and authoritative pre-2006 body of case law that exists will remain relevant—a fact backed up by s **170(4)**, which provides that 'regard shall be had to the corresponding common law rules and equitable principles in interpreting and applying the general duties'. Accordingly, you should not ignore case law simply because it was decided under the common law duties, especially as the **CA 2006** does not specify what remedies can be ordered for breach of the various duties, but simply provides that the remedies under the common law will continue to apply to their statutory successors (**CA 2006, s 178(1)**).

Figure 4.1 Directors' duties

```
                    ┌─────────────────────┐
                    │  DIRECTORS' DUTIES  │
                    └─────────────────────┘
```

THE GENERAL DUTIES

- **Section 171**—Duty to act within the company's powers.
- **Section 172**—Duty to promote the success of the company for the benefit of its members as a whole.
- **Section 173**—Duty to exercise independent judgment.
- **Section 174**—Duty to exercise reasonable care, skill, and diligence.
- **Section 175**—Duty to avoid conflicts of interest.
- **Section 176**—Duty not to accept benefits from third parties.
- **Section 177**—Duty to declare interest in proposed transactions or arrangements (the criminal offence for failing to declare an interest in an existing transaction or arrangement is found in **s 182**).

TRANSACTIONS INVOLVING DIRECTORS REQUIRING APPROVAL OF THE MEMBERS

- **Sections 188 and 189**—Duty to obtain approval for certain service contracts.
- **Sections 190–196**—Duty to obtain approval for substantial property transactions.
- **Sections 197–214**—Duty to obtain approval for loans, quasi-loans, and credit transactions.
- **Sections 215–222**—Duty to obtain approval for payments for loss of office.

LOOKING FOR EXTRA MARKS?

It would not have been unduly burdensome for Parliament to set out in the **CA 2006** what remedies are available for breach of the general duties, but it chose not to. Setting out the remedies would have made the law clearer and more accessible, but by preserving the remedies already set out in case law, the law remains flexible as the courts can continue to develop existing case law in a way that would not have been possible if the remedies had been set out in statute. By not setting the remedies out in statute, do you think the statutory statement of directors' duties is incomplete or lacks the clarity that it should have had?

The general duties are 'owed by a director of a company to the company' (**CA 2006, s 170(1)**). Accordingly:

- As the directors owe their duties to the company, they do not generally owe their duties to members, creditors, employees, or anyone else. The result is that generally only the company itself can commence proceedings to remedy a breach of the directors' duties, although in some cases the members might be able to commence proceedings via a derivative claim (discussed at 8.3).

- Although the general duties are 'owed by a director', it is clear that they can also be owed by other persons in certain situations (e.g. the duties in ss 175 and 176 can apply to former directors). Directors continue to owe general duties to the company, even if the company is in administration or a creditors' voluntary liquidation (*Re System Building Services Group Ltd* [2020]).

The courts have struggled to clearly and consistently articulate what duties shadow directors are subject to. A new s 170(5) of the CA 2006 now provides that the general duties apply to a shadow director 'where and to the extent that they are capable of so applying', with the SBEEA 2015's Explanatory Notes stating that this means that the general duties will apply to shadow directors unless they are not capable of so applying. In addition, s 89(2) of the SBEEA 2015 empowers the Secretary of State to make regulations setting out which general duties do, and do not, apply to shadow directors. At the time of writing, no such regulations have been made. A useful summary of the relevant law was provided by Trower J in *Standish v Royal Bank of Scotland plc* [2019], paras 50–65.

Sections 171–177 of the CA 2006 provide for seven general duties (with a supplementary criminal offence found in s 182) and you should ensure that you are familiar with them all.

 REVISION TIP

It is important to note that the general duties discussed below do not exist in isolation and they are not mutually exclusive—a point emphasized by s 179 which provides that '[e]xcept as otherwise provided, more than one of the general duties may apply in any given case'. For example, in *Joint Liquidators of CS Properties (Sales) Ltd* [2018], the defendant directors were found to have breached five of the seven general duties. Likely overlaps between general duties are discussed below.

4.4.2.1 Duty to act within the company's powers

The first general duty, which is an amalgam of two prior common law duties, is found in s 171 which imposes upon directors:

(a) a duty to act in accordance with the company's constitution, and

(b) a duty to exercise powers only for the purposes for which they are conferred.

As is discussed at 3.3, the powers of the company are predominantly set out in the company's articles, and the default position is that companies created under the CA 2006 will have unrestricted objects. However, it is common for companies to impose some form of limitation on the directors' power and directors who breach such limitations (e.g. by acting *ultra vires*) will likely breach the duty found in s 171(a). A director who breaches the duty found in s 171(a) is liable to account for any gains made and to indemnify the company for any losses resulting from the breach.

Whilst the duty to act in accordance with the company's constitution is important, it is the second strand of the s 171 duty that is arguably the more important. This strand is based on the common law 'proper purpose' doctrine and provides that directors must exercise their powers only for the purposes for which they are conferred.

 REVISION TIP

The duty found in **s 171(b)** is a wide-ranging one and applies to all the powers of a director. However, much of the case law in relation to the proper purpose doctrine concerns the directors' power to allot shares (discussed at 7.1.2.1), or the extent to which the directors can act to frustrate a takeover bid. Should you face a problem question involving either of these situations, do not forget to consider whether or not the directors have used their powers for a proper purpose. If the directors have acted for the dominant purpose of maintaining themselves in office, manipulating voting power, or benefiting themselves financially, the duty will likely have been breached.

The problem that arises is that directors will often exercise their powers for several purposes, some of which are proper and others improper. The approach taken by the courts in such instances was established in the following case.

Howard Smith Ltd v Ampol Petroleum Ltd [1974] AC 821 (PC)

Facts: Ampol Petroleum Ltd ('Ampol') controlled 55 per cent of shares in RW Miller (Holdings) Ltd ('Miller') and wanted to take it over. Howard Smith Ltd ('HS') made a rival bid which was rejected by Miller's majority shareholder, namely Ampol. Miller's directors favoured HS's bid, but this bid could not succeed so long as Ampol was the majority shareholder. Accordingly, Miller's directors allotted a batch of shares and issued them to HS. The purpose of the share allotment was (i) to raise capital to purchase a new oil tanker and (ii) to reduce Ampol's shareholding to 37 per cent, thereby preventing it from rejecting HS's bid. Ampol alleged that the allotment of shares was for an improper purpose.

Held: Where the directors exercise their powers for several purposes, the court should objectively determine what is the dominant purpose. If the dominant purpose is proper, no breach of duty will occur, even though subservient improper purposes might exist, and vice versa. Applying this, the court held that the dominant purpose of the share issue was to relegate Ampol to the status of minority shareholder. This was unsurprisingly deemed to be an improper purpose and so Miller's directors had breached their duty to act for a proper purpose.

In *Extrasure Travel Insurances Ltd v Scattergood* **[2003]**, it was stated that the test in *Howard Smith* involves four parts under which the court will determine:

1. what power is being exercised;

2. the proper purpose for which that power was delegated to the directors;

3. the substantial purpose for which the power was in fact exercised; and

4. whether that substantial purpose was proper.

Further guidance was provided in the following Supreme Court case. Whilst the Justices unanimously agreed that the duty had been breached, the opinions advanced by Lord Sumption do leave some questions unanswered.

Eclairs Group Ltd v JKX Oil & Gas plc [2015] UKSC 71

Facts: The board of JKX Oil & Gas plc ('JKX') believed that JKX was the target of a 'corporate raid' under which two minority shareholders (Eclairs and Glengary) would seek to obtain control of JKX. **Section 793 of the CA 2006** allows a company to issue a notice upon a person, requiring that person to disclose certain information regarding their shares. Article 42 of JKX's articles provided that if a **s 793** notice was not complied with, JKX could place restrictions upon the non-complying party, including disenfranchising that party's shares. JKX issued a **s 793** notice to Eclairs and Glengary, but was not satisfied with the information received. Accordingly, the directors exercised the power under art 42, thereby preventing Eclairs and Glengary from voting at the upcoming AGM (Eclairs and Glengary planned to vote against a number of resolutions tabled by the board of JKX). Eclairs and Glengary stated that the board of JKX had exercised this power for an improper purpose. At first instance, it was held that the disenfranchisement of Eclairs and Glengary was invalid as the directors of JKX exercised the power in art 42 in order to ensure that their resolutions passed at the upcoming AGM, and this was clearly an improper purpose. On appeal, the Court of Appeal held that, when determining the validity of restrictions imposed under the articles following a breach of **s 793**, the purpose behind those restrictions was immaterial and so the disenfranchisement of Eclairs and Glengary was valid. Eclairs and Glengary appealed.

Held: The Supreme Court allowed the appeal and restored the first instance decision. The Court held that the proper purpose rule did apply to art 42. Lord Sumption went on to state that 'a battle for control of the company is probably the one in which the proper purpose rule has the most valuable part to play'. The Court agreed with the first instance decision and held that the exercise of art 42 was for an improper purpose. Accordingly, the disenfranchisement of Eclairs and Glengary was invalid and the votes of these companies would count (resulting in two resolutions not being passed at the AGM)

LOOKING FOR EXTRA MARKS?

Be prepared to discuss this case and the lack of clarity exhibited. Lord Sumption (with whom Lord Hodge agreed) gave the leading judgment. He appeared to move away from *Howard Smith* somewhat by stating that the **s 171(b)** duty provides that directors should exercise their powers 'only' for the purposes for which they are conferred and, therefore, '[t]hat duty is broken if they allow themselves to be influenced by any improper purpose'. However, Lord Mance disagreed and the other two Justices declined to express a view on this point, leaving the scope of the duty in a slightly unclear state (although it is likely that the traditional view in *Howard Smith* remains good law), especially where a director acts based on several concurrent purposes.

Any agreement entered into in breach of **s 171(b)** is voidable at the company's instance, but a third party may be able to enforce the agreement against the company if the director had authority to enter into it (**Criterion Properties plc v Stratford UK Properties LLC [2004]**). The directors in question may be required to compensate the company for any loss sustained. However, both consequences can be avoided if the members ratify the breach of duty (**Hogg v Cramphorn [1967]**).

4.4.2.2 Duty to promote the success of the company

The second general duty can be found in **s 172** and is a reformulation of the common law duty to act *bona fide* in the interests of the company (**Re Smith and Fawcett Ltd [1942]**). **Section 172** provides that a director must 'act in the way he considers, in good faith, would be most likely to promote the success of the company for the benefit of its members as a whole'.

REVISION TIP

The duty found in s 172 is arguably the most important general duty and is the duty that has undergone most change as a result of codification. Be prepared to discuss how the s 172 duty differs from its common law predecessor, the rationale behind the changes, and the extent to which the reforms encourage a more stakeholder-orientated approach. Numerous articles have been written on s 172, so there is a wealth of academic analysis available.

The phrase 'act in the way he considers' clearly indicates that the duty is subjective, meaning that what matters is what the directors honestly believed would promote the success of the company. It is not the court's place to substitute its views for those of the directors. Accordingly, providing that the decision of the directors was honest, it does not matter that it was unreasonable (*Extrasure Travel Insurance Ltd v Scattergood* [2003]). However, there are limits on the subjectivity of the duty. In *Hutton v West Cork Rly Co* (1883), Bowen LJ stated that if the duty was entirely subjective then 'you might have a lunatic conducting the affairs of the company, and paying away its money with both hands in a manner perfectly *bona fide* yet perfectly irrational'. Accordingly, the courts will closely examine the evidence and try to determine whether or not the directors honestly believed that their actions were designed to promote the success of the company for the benefit of its members. Where a director's act or omission causes the company harm, the court will not be easily persuaded that the director honestly believed his actions to be in the company's interest (*Regentcrest plc v Cohen* [2001]). There is little doubt that where the evidence does not provide a conclusive answer, the courts will temper the subjective test with an objective examination, but the test still remains primarily subjective.

REVISION TIP

What if the director in question has not considered whether his act or omission will promote the success of the company for the benefit of its members? In such a case, a subjective test will be of little use. In *Charterbridge Corporation Ltd v Lloyds Bank Ltd* [1970], Pennycuick J stated that, in such cases, the proper test would be 'whether an intelligent and honest man in the position of the director of the company concerned, could . . . have reasonably believed that the transaction was for the benefit of the company'. Accordingly, in such cases, the duty becomes primarily objective. However, this approach has been criticized, with some academics (e.g. Rosemary Teele Langford and Ian M Ramsay, 'Directors' Duty to Act in the Interests of the Company—Subjective or Objective?' [2015] JBL 173) arguing that a director who fails to consider whether his act or omission promotes the success of the company should be held in breach of s 172. Pennycuick J in *Charterbridge* stated that such an approach was 'unduly stringent' and could result in a breach of s 172 even where the director's act benefitted the company.

The phrase 'promote the success of the company for the benefit of its members' is interesting, but the Act does not indicate how the success of the company is to be measured. Parliamentary debate in Hansard indicates that success should be measured in terms of long-term share-holder value. In many cases, the interests of the company and its members will align, so no problem arises. However, this will not always be the case and, in some instances, the interests of the company and its members may conflict. The following case indicates that where the in-terests of the company and part of its membership conflict, preference should be given to the interests of the company. Whether the directors can favour the company over the members as a whole is unclear.

Mutual Life Insurance Co of New York v Rank Organisation Ltd [1985] BCLC 11 (Ch)

Facts: Rank Organisation Ltd issued 20 million shares, half of which were made available, on preferential terms, to existing shareholders. However, existing shareholders in the USA and Canada were excluded from this offer on the ground that to include them would require the company to comply with complex legislation in those countries, which would prove costly and therefore would not be in the company's interests. Mutual Life Insurance Co of New York (an organization acting on behalf of a number of Rank's American shareholders) objected to the exclusion.

Held: Rank's directors had exercised their powers in the interest of the company, and so, in favouring the company over some part of the shareholders, they had not breached their duty.

The duty imposed by **s 172** is a broad one and can impact upon other duties. In *Item Software (UK) Ltd v Fassihi* **[2004]**, the Court held that a director who breaches a fiduciary duty will be required to disclose that breach of duty to the company if the duty to act in the interests of the company requires such disclosure. The Court in *British Midland Tool Ltd v Midland International Tooling Ltd* **[2003]** held that this obligation extends to disclosing the breaches of fellow directors. In keeping with the subjective nature of this duty, the key factor is whether the director honestly considers that it is in the company's interest to know about the breach (*Fulham Football Club (1987) Ltd v Tigana* **[2004]**). Clearly, disclosure of a breach of duty will usually be in the company's interests and a failure to do so might result in a breach of **s 172**, in addition to a breach of the original duty. In *GHLM Trading Ltd v Maroo* **[2012]**, Newey J went further and stated, *obiter*, that this duty of disclosure could extend to disclosing matters other than wrongdoing and that disclosure might be justified to a person other than a board member. A failure to disclose can result in a loss of employment benefits (e.g. share options or certain employment rights) and may provide a justification for sum-mary dismissal (*Tesco Stores Ltd v Pook* **[2003]**). The obligation upon a director to disclose his own breaches of duty and those of his fellow directors is a controversial and developing area of the law. For more, see Alan Berg, 'Fiduciary Duties: A Director's Duty to Disclose his Own Misconduct' (2005) 121 LQR 213.

A common criticism levelled at the previous common law duty was that it overly prioritized the interests of members and failed to acknowledge the effect that the directors' actions can have on other constituents, such as employees, creditors, or the environment. To remedy this, the Company Law Review Steering Group recommended the adoption of the 'enlightened shareholder value approach', under which the interests of the members would retain priority, but the directors would also be required to take into account wider factors.

LOOKING FOR EXTRA MARKS?

The other approach considered by the Company Law Review Steering Group was the 'pluralist approach', which provided that the members' interests would not have priority and the company would be required to equally balance the interests of all stakeholders. In a discussion of **s 172**, be prepared to discuss why the Company Law Review Steering Group rejected the pluralist approach (on this, see the consultation document entitled *The Strategic Framework* (1999)), and whether you think it was right to do so.

Parliament accepted the Company Law Review Steering Group's recommendation and so **s 172(1)** provides that when directors are considering what would promote the success of the company for the benefit of its members, regard must be had (amongst other things) to the following:

- The likely consequences of any decision in the long term. The White Paper *Company Law Reform* (Cm 6456, 2005) recommended that the directors should be required to consider the short-term and long-term impacts of their actions—that Parliament chose to remove the reference to short-term impacts clearly indicates that it considers the long-term well-being of the company to be more important. This is noteworthy, as a common criticism of our system of company law was that it took an overly short-term approach.
- The interests of the company's employees.
- The need to foster the company's business relationships with suppliers, customers, and others.
- The impact of the company's operation on the community and the environment.
- The desirability of the company maintaining a reputation for high standards of business conduct.
- The need to act fairly as between members of the company.

There is one group that is notably absent, namely the creditors (although, of course, suppliers, customers, and employees may be creditors). Prior to the 2006 Act, there were several notable *dicta* requiring the directors to take into account the interests of creditors when the company neared insolvency (see e.g. ***West Mercia Safetywear Ltd v Dodd*** **[1988]**). **Section 172(3)** preserves these principles by stating that **s 172** 'has effect subject to any enactment or rule of law requiring directors, in certain circumstances, to consider or act in the interests of creditors of the company'. However, for decades the courts have struggled to establish exactly when directors must consider the interests of creditors. The Supreme Court finally sought to provide clarity in the following case.

BTI 2014 LLC v Sequana SA [2022] UKSC 25

Facts: In 2009, the directors of AWA caused it to pay out a dividend of €135 million to its only shareholder, Sequana SA. At the time of the payment, AWA was solvent and could pay its debts, but it had a number of contingent liabilities of an uncertain amount that did create a real risk that the company could become insolvent in the future, although this risk was neither probable nor imminent. That risk came to pass, albeit not until 2018, when AWA entered insolvent administration.

AWA's legal claims had been assigned to BTI, which brought proceedings to recover from AWA's directors the amount of the 2009 dividend. BTI claimed that, when paying out the dividend, the directors had not taken into account the interests of AWA's creditors. Both the High Court and the Court of Appeal rejected BTI's claim. BTI appealed.

Held: The Court agreed that the existence of a 'creditor duty' should be affirmed, but it was not a free-standing duty—instead it is simply an aspect or modification of the **s 172** duty. The majority held that the duty would become engaged when the directors know, or ought to know, that the company is insolvent or bordering on insolvency, or that an insolvent liquidation or administration is probable. What the duty requires of the directors depends upon the likelihood of insolvency:

- Where the company is insolvent or bordering on insolvency, but insolvent liquidation/administration is not inevitable, the company should consider the interests of its creditors, balancing them against the interests of the members where they conflict.

- The greater the company's financial difficulties, the more the directors should prioritize the interests of its creditors. Where insolvent liquidation/administration is inevitable, the creditors' interests become paramount as the members no longer have any valuable interest in the company.

Applying this, BTI's appeal was dismissed. At the time the dividend was paid, AWA was not insolvent nor was insolvency imminent or probable. The creditor duty is not engaged merely because there is real and not remote risk of insolvency.

LOOKING FOR EXTRA MARKS?

To what extent does **s 172** provide a more stakeholder-friendly duty? The non-exhaustive list of factors contained in **s 172(1)** is welcome, but the directors are only required to 'have regard' to these factors. The phrase 'have regard' was used in **s 309 of the CA 1985**, which imposed a duty on directors to have regard to the interests of employees, but it was universally acknowledged that this duty was extremely weak. What **s 172** does not clearly state is whether the directors are free to subordinate the interests of the members to the interests stated in **s 172(1)**, although Lord Goldsmith, a former Attorney General, stated in Hansard that the list of factors in **s 172(1)** was subordinate to the overall duty imposed by **s 172**. For an excellent discussion of the common law predecessor to **s 172**, and the extent to which **s 172** changes the law, see David Kershaw, *Company Law in Context: Text and Materials* (2nd edn, OUP, 2012) ch 10.

Where a director acts in a manner that breaches **s 172**, that act is voidable at the company's instance. Where the act also causes the company to sustain loss, those directors in breach will be required to indemnify the company for such loss. Given the breadth of the duty found in **s 172**, it can be difficult for the members to determine whether or not the directors have breached the **s 172** duty. Accordingly, **s 414A** of the **CA 2006** places a duty on the directors to prepare a strategic report for each financial year. **Section 414C** goes on to state that '[t]he purpose of the strategic report is to inform members of the company and help them assess how the directors have performed their duty under section 172 . . . '. **Section 414C** then goes on to state what information must be contained within the strategic report, with **s 414CZA** stating that certain companies must include in the strategic report a 'section 172(1) statement' that sets out how the directors have had regard to the matters set out in **s 172(1)(a)–(f)**.

4.4.2.3 Duty to exercise independent judgment

The third general duty, namely the duty to exercise independent judgment found in **s 173**, is a reformulation and encapsulation of the common law duty placed upon directors not to fetter their discretion when exercising their powers. However, this duty was not absolute and the courts recognized that directors could fetter their discretion and bind themselves to act in a certain way if they *bona fide* believed such an action to be in the interests of the company (**Fulham Football Club Ltd v Cabra Estates plc** [1992]). This principle has been preserved by **s 173(2)(a)** which provides that the duty to exercise independent judgment will not be breached where the directors act 'in accordance with an agreement duly entered into by the company that restricts the future exercise of discretion by its directors'. Additionally, **s 173(2) (b)** provides that the duty will not be breached where the director acts in a way that is authorized by the company's constitution (e.g. where the articles provide that a nominee director must follow the instructions of the person who nominated him).

REVISION TIP

Note that s 173 does not require a director to be independent. A director who lacks independence (e.g. because he has a conflict of interest under ss 175, 176, or 177) will not be in breach of the s 173 duty as a result of his lack of independence. The s 173 duty requires the director to exercise independent judgment. An example of this would be where a director exercises no judgment of his own and blindly follows the instructions of another person. Note, however, that reliance upon advice will not generally amount to a breach of the s 173 duty.

Any agreement entered into that contravenes **s 173** will be voidable at the company's instance. Any directors in breach will also be required to account for any gains made and indemnify the company for any losses sustained as a result of the breach.

LOOKING FOR EXTRA MARKS?

If you are required to discuss the s 173 duty, an excellent analysis of the duty, together with a discussion of its common law predecessor, can be found in Andrew Keay, 'The Duty of Directors to Exercise Independent Judgment' (2008) 29 Co Law 290.

4.4.2.4 Duty to exercise reasonable care, skill, and diligence

The fourth general duty can be found in s 174 and places a duty on directors to 'exercise reasonable care, skill and diligence'. The common law had imposed a similar duty on directors long before the CA 2006 was passed (*Re City Equitable Fire Insurance Co Ltd* [1925]), but the common law duty was heavily subjective and based on the skills and experience that the director actually had. Accordingly, a director with little skill or experience would be subject to an extremely low standard of care (see e.g. *Re Cardiff Savings Bank* [1892]; *Re Brazilian Rubber Plantations and Estates Ltd* [1911]).

The effect of the subjective duty was to allow unskilled, inexperienced, and incompetent directors to use their deficiencies as a shield against liability. Accordingly, the courts added an objective element to the duty and this dual subjective/objective test has now been incorporated into the s 174 duty. Section 174(2) provides that the standard of care, skill, and diligence expected of a director is based on that of a reasonably diligent person with:

(a) the general knowledge, skill, and experience that may reasonably be expected of a person carrying out the functions carried out by the director in relation to the company, and

(b) the general knowledge, skill, and experience that the director actually has.

The test found in (a) imposes an objective minimum standard of care that will apply to all directors, irrespective of their individual capabilities. Accordingly, directors can no longer use their lack of skill or experience as a means of lowering the standard of care. However, this standard will take into account the functions of the director, so the standard will likely vary from director to director (e.g. the standard imposed on a director of a small private company will likely differ from the standard imposed on a director of a listed company), thereby providing the courts with a measure of flexibility. The test found in (b) imposes a subjective standard that will apply where the director has some special skill, qualification, or ability (e.g. they are a lawyer or an accountant), and will serve to raise the standard expected of the director.

LOOKING FOR EXTRA MARKS?

Be prepared to critically evaluate this dual test. Imposing higher subjective standards is a controversial issue. The rationale behind it is that such qualified persons are employed to bring their special skills or knowledge to bear (and are likely to be paid more as a result), so the imposition of a higher standard requires them to use such skills. The counter-argument is that the higher standard might deter such qualified persons from undertaking directorial office.

Section 174 establishes the test the courts must use, but does not provide any guidance as to how to apply the test, or what sort of factors will be relevant in determining whether or not a breach has occurred. Accordingly, case law will remain highly relevant (although much of it is first instance) with the following leading case providing an especially useful series of principles that have been widely cited by subsequent courts.

Re Barings plc (No 5) [2000] 1 BCLC 523 (CA)

Facts: Barings Bank collapsed in 1995 following the unauthorized trading activities of a trader named Nick Leeson, which resulted in the bank sustaining losses of £827 million. The case concerned three of the bank's directors who, it was alleged, had made serious errors of management in relation to Leeson's activities. At first instance, Jonathan-Parker J held that the three directors should be disqualified.

Held: The Court of Appeal upheld the disqualifications and, more importantly, it affirmed a series of principles laid down at first instance by Jonathan-Parker J in relation to the duty of skill and care, namely:

- Directors have a continuing duty to acquire and maintain a sufficient knowledge and understanding of the company's business to enable them properly to discharge their duties.
- Whilst directors are entitled to delegate particular functions to those below them, and to trust their competence and integrity to a reasonable degree, such delegation will not absolve the director of the duty to supervise the discharge of the delegated functions.
- The extent of the duty, and the question as to whether it has been discharged, must depend on the facts of each particular case, including the director's role in the company's management.

A director who causes his company to sustain a loss due to a failure to exercise reasonable care, skill, and diligence will be liable to compensate the company for such loss. However, obtaining compensation for a breach of **s 174** is not easy, as the claimant will need to prove that the acts of the director(s) in question were the cause of the company's loss. This explains why many cases involving director negligence are not brought under **s 174**, but are brought under the **Company Directors Disqualification Act 1986**.

4.4.2.5 Duty to avoid conflicts of interest

Section 175 contains the first of several duties relating to conflicts of interest and provides that '[a] director of a company must avoid a situation in which he has, or can have, a direct or indirect interest that conflicts, or possibly may conflict, with the interests of the company'. Examples of conduct that may (although not necessarily will) constitute a breach of **s 175** include:

- a director helps a competing company (e.g. by sitting on its board, or by providing it with consultancy services);
- a director learns of a business opportunity, or acquires information, whilst director of a company, and then exploits that opportunity/information to benefit himself personally (referred to as 'the corporate opportunity doctrine');
- a director uses the company's property to benefit himself financially;
- a director of a company is also a major customer, supplier, or creditor of that company.

Section 175(2) provides that this duty applies in particular to 'the exploitation of any property, information or opportunity' and it is irrelevant whether or not the company wishes or is able to take advantage of the property, information, or opportunity. The fact that the profit made by the director is negligible is also irrelevant (*Towers v Premier Waste Management Ltd* [2011]). **Section 175(3)** states that **s 175** does not apply to transactions between a director and the company—where the transaction is with the company, then **ss 177** and **182** will instead be applicable. The **s 175** duty is extremely strict as can be seen in the following case.

Bhullar v Bhullar [2003] EWCA Civ 424

Facts: For over fifty years, the families of two brothers (M and S) had run a company that let commercial property. Following an argument, it was decided that the families would part ways. M's family proposed that the company should not acquire any further properties and S's family agreed. A director, who was part of S's family, discovered, by chance and not whilst acting in the course of the company's business, a piece of property near to a piece of property owned by the company. Through another company that they owned, S's family acquired this property without informing M's family. M's family alleged that S's family had acted in conflict with the interests of the company.

Held: Although S's family acquired knowledge of the property in a 'private' capacity, the opportunity to purchase the property was one that belonged to the company. Whether or not the company could have or would have acquired the property (because it was in the process of being wound up) was irrelevant.

 LOOKING FOR EXTRA MARKS?

Bhullar has been heavily criticized, largely because the company agreed, at the behest of M's family, not to acquire any more properties. The Court, in effect, allowed M's family to change their minds opportunistically at the moment an attractive commercial opportunity arose. For a detailed discussion of this case, see Hans C Hirt, 'The Law on Corporate Opportunities in the Court of Appeal: *Re Bhullar Bros Ltd*' [2005] JBL 669. See also the case of *Regal (Hastings) Ltd v Gulliver* [1967].

Section 175 preserves the strict and inflexible position evidenced in *Bhullar* and there is little doubt that the case would be decided the same way under **s 175**. However, pre-**CA 2006** law did mitigate the harshness of the rule in one important respect, namely that the duty would not be breached if the director disclosed the nature of the conflict and obtained authorization.

Section 175(5) preserves this rule, but amends the requirement of authorization. Under pre-2006 law, the director could disclose the conflict and obtain authorization from the company in a general meeting, but companies could provide, in their articles, that disclosure and authorization from the board would be sufficient. Under the **CA 2006**, where the company is private, authorization from the directors alone will suffice unless the constitution provides otherwise (the model articles contain no such prohibition), therefore avoiding the need to organize a general meeting. The directors of public companies can provide authorization, but only if the constitution so provides (the model articles do not contain a provision allowing the directors to authorize a conflict). A director's power to authorize a conflict must, like all other powers, be exercised in accordance with the general duties, notably **ss 171, 172,** and **174**.

Where a director breaches s 175, any resulting contract is voidable at the company's instance, provided that the third party involved had notice of the director's breach (*Hely-Hutchinson & Co Ltd v Brayhead Ltd* [1968]). In addition, the company can require the director to account for any profit made as a result of the conflict (*Aberdeen Railway Co v Blaikie Bros* (1854)). These consequences can be avoided if the members ratify the director's breach.

REVISION TIP

As noted, the general duties are not mutually exclusive and a single act may breach several duties. In *Industrial Development Consultants Ltd v Cooley* [1972], the court held that a director who fails to disclose the existence of a conflict may, in addition to breaching a duty involving a conflict of interest, also breach the duty to act in the interests of the company—it is likely that this will continue to apply to the successor duty found in s 172.

4.4.2.6 Duty not to accept benefits from a third party

The sixth general duty can be found in s 176 and provides that a director must not accept from a third party a benefit conferred by reason of his being a director, or by doing (or not doing) anything as a director. An obvious example of such a benefit would be a payment made to a director to influence his decision (e.g. X pays a bribe or a commission payment to a director if that director's company agrees to do business with X).

As with s 175, motive is irrelevant and it will be no defence for the director to argue that he acted in good faith. However, the s 176 duty will not be breached where 'the acceptance of the benefit cannot reasonably be regarded as likely to give rise to a conflict of interest' (CA 2006, s 176(4)). Accordingly, the duty only arises in relation to benefits that are likely to give rise to a conflict of interest.

REVISION TIP

Given that the s 176 duty only arises in relation to benefits that are likely to cause a conflict, it might be thought that the s 176 duty is irrelevant as s 175 would cover such cases. Certainly, there is a significant overlap between ss 175 and 176, but there is a key difference. A conflict under s 175 can be authorized by the directors, whereas a conflict under s 176 can only be authorized by the members (this is not expressly stated, but is a consequence of s 180(4)(a) of the CA 2006, which preserves the common law rules relating to authorization). This clearly indicates that the receipt of benefits from third parties constitutes a greater danger to board impartiality than the conflicts covered solely by s 175. For an example of a conflict that fell within s 176, but not s 175, see *Parr v Keystone Healthcare Ltd* [2019].

Should a director accept an unauthorized third-party benefit, the company can rescind the contract and the benefit can be recovered (**Shipway v Broadwood [1899]**). Instead of recovering the benefit, the company can claim damages in fraud from either the director in breach or the third party. In addition, the company can summarily dismiss the director (**Boston Deep Sea Fishing Co v Ansell (1888)**). If the benefit amounts to a bribe, then under agency principles, other consequences may follow (e.g. the director may lose any right to remuneration (**Andrews v Ramsay & Co [1903]**)). Receipt of a bribe is also a criminal offence (**Bribery Act 2010, s 2**).

4.4.2.7 Duty to declare interest in transactions or arrangements

The seventh and final general duty can be found in **s 177**, which provides that '[i]f a director of a company is in any way, directly or indirectly, interested in a proposed transaction or arrangement with the company, he must declare the nature and extent of that interest to the other directors'. An example of this would be where company A is proposing to enter into a transaction with a person who has links to a director of company A.

Guidance on what information must be included in the declaration can be found in **Fairford Water Ski Club Ltd v Cohoon [2021]**, paras 25–32 and 42–50 (although the case is concerned with **s 317 of the CA 1985** (the predecessor to **s 177**), the points made appear to be applicable to **s 177** also, unless otherwise stated). The declaration must be made before the company enters into the transaction or arrangement (**CA 2006, s 177(4)**). Two points should be noted:

- the **s 177** duty only applies to transactions/arrangements that are likely to give rise to a conflict of interest, and

- as the duty covers indirect transactions/arrangements, the director does not actually need to be a party to the transaction/arrangement for the **s 177** duty to be relevant.

Following the declaration, the other directors can then decide whether to proceed with the proposed transaction/arrangement. Note that under the model articles, the director who made the declaration cannot generally participate in the board resolution, nor will he generally count towards the quorum during that resolution.

REVISION TIP

In problem questions involving a conflict of interest, students are often unsure whether to apply **s 175** or **s 177**. It is important that you understand the differences between the two duties as applying the incorrect section will result in a loss of marks. The key difference is in the scope of the two duties. **Section 175(3)** states that **s 175** does not apply to transactions between a director and the company. Conversely, **s 177** does apply to transactions between the director and the company. Also note that, unlike **s 175**, **s 177** only requires disclosure (and not authorization). Understanding the different scope of the duties will better enable you to identify which section should be applied to the facts of the question.

The **s 177** duty relates to *proposed* transactions or arrangements only. *Existing* transactions or arrangements are covered by **s 182**, which provides that where a director is interested in an existing transaction or arrangement that has been entered into by the company, he must declare the nature and extent of that interest to the directors.

Where a director enters into a transaction in contravention of **s 177**, the transaction is voidable at the company's instance. Where a director enters into a transaction in contravention of **s 182**, he commits an either way offence (**CA 2006, s 183**). A director can be liable under both sections if he does not disclose his interest in a proposed transaction, and then does not disclose once the same transaction has been entered into by the company.

LOOKING FOR EXTRA MARKS?

That no liability is placed upon a director for a breach of **s 177** has been heavily criticized for three reasons. First, it appears that a director who has breached **s 177** can keep any profit acquired if the transaction or arrangement proceeds. Second, if rescission is not available (e.g. because a third party's rights would be affected), then there will be no consequences for the director's breach of duty. Third, it has been argued that there is no justification for imposing criminal liability for breach of **s 182**, but not imposing criminal liability for breach of **s 177** (indeed, **s 317(7) of the Companies Act 1985** (now repealed) imposed criminal liability on directors who failed to disclose an interest in proposed or existing contracts).

A failure to comply with **s 182** will not invalidate the transaction/arrangement, nor can the director involved be made to account for any gains made or indemnify the company for losses sustained (***Coleman Taymar Ltd v Oakes* [2001]**), although such remedies may be obtained if a breach of any other general duties has occurred.

REVISION TIP

Sections 175, 176, 177, and 182 all relate to conflicts of interest. A single or continuing act or omission can often result in breaches of multiple duties. For example, a director may fail to disclose an interest in a proposed transaction, thereby causing a breach of the duty contained in **s 177**. Once the company enters into the transaction, if the director does not disclose the interest as soon as is reasonably practicable, he will also commit the offence in **s 182**. The non-disclosure and his failure to disclose his own breach of duty may also amount to a breach of **s 172**. Ensure that you are aware of the differences between the various provisions, and the ways in which they can overlap. Table 4.1 demonstrates the differences between the various conflict of interest duties in relation to disclosure and authorization.

Table 4.1 Disclosure and authorization of conflicts of interest

DUTY	DISCLOSURE REQUIRED?	WHEN IS DISCLO-SURE REQUIRED?	IS AUTHORIZATION REQUIRED?
Section 175—Duty to avoid conflicts of interest	The **CA 2006** does not expressly require the director to disclose the conflict/benefit. However, as authorization is required, the director will, in practice, need to disclose the existence of the conflict/benefit prior to obtaining authorization. Further, the courts have made clear that a director should disclose the existence of a conflict/benefit in order to comply with the duty to act in the interests of the company (*Industrial Development Consultants Ltd v Cooley* [1972]) and it is likely that this will continue to apply in relation to the duty imposed by s **172**		Yes. In private companies, the directors can authorize the interest, provided that the constitution does not prohibit such authorization. In public companies, the directors can authorize the interest only if the constitution so provides
Section 176—Duty not to accept benefits from third parties	Yes. The benefit must be authorized by the members in general meeting		
Section 177—Duty to declare interest in proposed transactions or arrangements with the company	Yes. The director must disclose the nature and extent of the interest to the other directors	Disclosure must be made prior to the company entering into the transaction or arrangement	No, but if the directors do not approve of the transaction/arrangement, they will likely prevent the company from entering into it
Section 182—Declaring interest in existing transactions or arrangements entered into by the company	Yes. The director must disclose the nature and extent of the interest to the other directors	Disclosure must be made as soon as is reasonably practicable	No

4.4.3 Transactions requiring member approval

In addition to the general duties, the law imposes more specific 'duties' in relation to certain transactions or arrangements the directors enter into with the company (as these transactions are between the company and the director, they could be regarded as specific cases involving a conflict of interest). In relation to such transactions or arrangements, compliance with the general duties is insufficient (**CA 2006, s 180(3)**) and member approval is also generally required.

4.4.3.1 Service contracts

Historically, directors would try and make it prohibitively expensive to remove them from office by negotiating lengthy service contracts. For example, if a company sought to remove a director five years before his service contract is to end, and he was being paid £2 million per year, the company may need to pay the director £10 million in compensation for early termination of his contract.

This practice is now regulated by **s 188 of the CA 2006**, which provides that a director cannot have a guaranteed term of employment of over two years, unless it has been approved by a resolution of the members. Where **s 188** is breached, the relevant contractual provision will be void and the contract will be deemed to contain a term allowing the company to terminate it at any time by giving reasonable notice (**CA 2006, s 189**).

 REVISION TIP

Students frequently misunderstand **s 189** by stating that if member approval is not obtained, the director's employment contract will be void. This is not the case—only the term relating to the director's length of employment will be void.

Note that, in relation to companies with a premium listing, **Provision 39 of the UK Corporate Governance Code** states that contract or notice periods should be one year or less, meaning that **s 188** is rarely relevant in such companies.

4.4.3.2 Substantial property transactions

Under the general duties, a director with a conflict of interest can avoid committing a breach of duty if he discloses that interest to the other directors (although **ss 175 and 176** also require authorization). However, where the arrangement constitutes a 'substantial property transaction', disclosure alone is insufficient and the company must not enter into the arrangement unless it has first been approved by a resolution of the members, or is conditional upon such approval being obtained (**CA 2006, s 190(1)**). Two types of arrangement require such approval:

1. where a director of a company, or a person connected with the director, acquires, or is to acquire, a substantial non-cash asset, or

2. where the company acquires, or is to acquire, a substantial non-cash asset from such a director or person so connected.

A 'non-cash asset' is 'any property or interest in property, other than cash' (**CA 2006, s 1163(1)**) and it will be substantial if it is (i) over £100,000, or (ii) exceeds 10 per cent of the company's asset value and is more than £5,000 (**CA 2006, s 191(2)**).

A substantial property transaction entered into without member approval is voidable at the company's instance, unless (i) restitution is impossible, (ii) the company has been indemnified, or (iii) a third party's rights would be affected (**CA 2006, s 195(2)**). Additionally, any director or connected person involved in the arrangement will be liable to account for any gains made and will be liable to indemnify the company for any losses sustained as a result of the arrangement. For an example of these above rules in action, see *Re Duckwari plc* **[1995]**.

4.4.3.3 Loans, quasi-loans, and credit transactions

Under the **CA 1985**, companies were generally prohibited from making any form of loan to their directors, and breach of this prohibition constituted a criminal offence.

The **CA 2006** takes a very different approach that is dependent upon the type of transaction in question:

- No company can make a loan to a director unless the transaction has been approved by a resolution of the members (**CA 2006, s 197(1)**).

- A public company cannot make a quasi-loan to a director unless the transaction has been approved by a resolution of the members (**CA 2006, s 198(2)**). A quasi-loan occurs where a company agrees to pay a sum on behalf of the director, or where it reimburses expenses incurred by another due to the actions of the director.

- A public company cannot enter into a credit transaction (e.g. hire purchase or conditional sale agreements, the leasing or hiring of goods) with a director unless it has been approved by a resolution of the members (**CA 2006, s 201(2)**).

It should be noted that the requirement for member approval will not apply in certain cases (e.g. loans or quasi-loans that do not exceed £10,000 do not require approval). Where approval is needed, a failure to obtain such approval will result in the same remedies as failure to obtain approval for a substantial property transaction.

4.4.3.4 Payments for loss of office

The law requires that the members approve certain voluntary payments made by the company to directors leaving office, with such payments being defined by **s 215(1) of the CA 2006**. The rules differ depending on whether the company is quoted or unquoted:

- An unquoted company cannot make a loss of office payment to a director unless the payment has been approved by a resolution of the members (**CA 2006, s 217(1)**).

- A quoted company or an unquoted traded company cannot make a loss of office payment to a director unless (i) the payment is consistent with the approved directors' remuneration policy, or (ii) the payment has been approved by a resolution of the members of the company (**CA 2006, s 226C(1)**).

LOOKING FOR EXTRA MARKS?

Be aware of why certain topics are current and controversial. Payments made to departing directors are a controversial issue, especially where the payment has been made to a director who is regarded as ineffective. The government originally recommended that loss of office payments made to directors of quoted companies should be subject to a binding shareholder vote but, following consultation, this was dropped and **s 226C** was enacted instead. Do you think such payments should always be subject to member approval?

Where member approval is required and is not obtained, the recipient will hold the payment on trust for the company and any director who authorized the payment is jointly and severally liable to indemnify the company for any loss resulting from the payment (**CA 2006, ss 222(1) and 226E(1)**).

4.4.4 Relief from liability

A director who has committed a breach of duty may attempt, or be able, to obtain relief from liability in several ways:

- A director's service contract or the company's articles may contain a provision excluding liability for negligence, default, breach of duty, or breach of trust. Such provisions are void (**CA 2006, s 232(1)**). Similarly, provisions requiring the company to indemnify the director for losses sustained due to his breach of duty are also generally void (**CA 2006, s 233**).

- **Section 239 of the CA 2006** puts in place, for the first time, a statutory scheme concerning ratification of acts committed by directors that amount to negligence, default, breach of duty, or breach of trust (it will be noted that these are the grounds for a derivative claim, as discussed at 8.3.2). Accordingly, ratification can serve to prevent a derivative claim from being brought (indeed, **s 263(2)(c)** provides that permission to continue a derivative claim will be refused where the act has been ratified). Ratification requires a resolution to be passed. Where ratification occurs, any cause of action is extinguished, but acts that cannot be ratified under pre-2006 law (e.g. acts not *bona fide* in the interests of the company) cannot be ratified under **s 239**.

- Where an officer of the company is found liable for negligence, default, breach of duty, or breach of trust, then **s 1157 of the CA 2006** allows a court to grant that officer, either wholly or partly, relief from liability on such terms as it sees fit. An officer of the company can also petition the court for such relief. For an example of **s 1157** in action, see *Re Duomatic Ltd* **[1969]**.

4.5 Vacation of office

A director's term of office may be vacated in numerous ways:

- The director can relinquish office at any time by giving notice to the company and the company must accept his resignation. The director's employment contract will normally provide for a notice period, but where it does not, a term requiring reasonable notice will be implied into the contract (***CMS Dolphin Ltd v Simonet* [2002]**).

- The articles may provide that a director's office will terminate upon the occurrence of a specified event. For example, the model articles provide that a person will instantly and automatically cease to be a director if he is prohibited by law from being a director (e.g. because he has been disqualified). It is common for a company's articles to provide that a director must vacate office if the other directors so require.

- The company's articles may provide for the retirement of the directors by rotation. In practice, it is only public companies that tend to require retirement by rotation (as at 4.2, 'Appointment').

Two forms of vacation of office are more complex and deserve further discussion, namely removal and disqualification.

4.5.1 Removal

There are to principal ways in which a director may be removed. First, the articles may provide for a power to remove a director. For example, it is common for a company's articles to provide that a director will be removed from office if the other directors so require (although no such power is within the model articles).

Second, **s 168(1) of the CA 2006** provides that '[a] company may by ordinary resolution at a meeting remove a director before the expiration of his period of office, notwithstanding anything in any agreement between it and him'. Despite the wording, **s 168** can be used to remove multiple directors. It should also be noted that the words 'at a meeting' indicate that the written resolution procedure cannot be used (**CA 2006, s 288(2)(a)**).

The power granted to members by **s 168** appears extremely substantial, but two factors affect its usefulness. First, a removal under **s 168** does not deprive the director of compensation payable as a result of the removal (**CA 2006, s 168(5)**). If the director's remuneration is substantial, or his service contract lengthy, this compensation may be extremely high. Second, **s 168** does not prohibit companies from including weighted voting clauses in their articles (the model articles do not provide for weighted voting rights). Such a clause usually provides that, in the event of a vote seeking to remove a director from office, the voting power of the director will be increased, usually to such an extent as to enable him to defeat any resolution seeking his removal. The case of **Bushell v Faith [1970]** provides an excellent example of how weighted voting clauses can weaken the power granted to shareholders by **s 168**.

LOOKING FOR EXTRA MARKS?

In practice, the effect of weighted voting clauses may be more limited than many realize. First, the clause in *Bushell* was justified on the ground that the company in question was a quasi-partnership, and it may be the case that such clauses are effective only in relation to such companies (although no *rationes* or *dicta* exist to this effect). Second, such clauses will breach the **Listing Rules**, and so will not be adopted by listed companies. Third, a weighted voting clause could be removed by passing a special resolution.

Section 168(5)(b) provides that **s 168** should not be construed as derogating from any power to remove a director that exists outside **s 168**. Accordingly, the power to remove a director under **s 168** exists alongside any other power (e.g. the articles may contain a provision allowing the directors to remove a board member via a board resolution). The advantage of using a power of removal contained in the articles is that it will not be subject to the procedural requirements found in **s 168** (**Browne v Panga Pty Ltd (1995)**).

4.5.2 Disqualification

The members may be able to remove a director from office but the **Company Directors Disqualification Act 1986 (CDDA 1986)** can result in a person being disqualified from promoting, forming, or taking part in the management of a company (or LLP) without the leave of the court. **Sections 2-11** set out numerous grounds for disqualification, including:

- A person can be disqualified if he commits an indictable offence in connection with the promotion, formation, or management of a company (**CDDA 1986, s 2**).

- A person can be disqualified if he is a director of a company that has become insolvent and his conduct as a director makes him unfit to be concerned in the management of the company (**CDDA 1986, s 6**). Most disqualifications occur under **s 6**.

- A director can be disqualified where he has been found to have engaged in fraudulent trading or wrongful trading (**CDDA 1986, s 10**).

LOOKING FOR EXTRA MARKS?

Be aware of how this area of the law has evolved and will continue to evolve. The disqualification regime has been slowly, but steadily, evolving over the years. New grounds for disqualification have been added and, in 2021, the regime was expanded to allow for the disqualification of directors of dissolved companies without having to restore the company.

REVISION TIP

In problem questions, you may be required to advise a director of the possible consequences of his actions. Students tend to ignore the potential for disqualification, and focus solely on the rescission of transactions, the payment of compensation, or the imposition of criminal liability. A director who could be barred from acting as a director for numerous years will clearly want to know of this potential consequence, so make sure you are aware of the grounds for disqualification.

A person can be disqualified via a disqualification order from the court, or via a disqualification undertaking, which is an undertaking from the person concerned that states that, for a specified period, they will not act as a director etc. Breach of a disqualification order or undertaking constitutes an either way offence. Further, a person who acts as a director whilst disqualified can be personally liable for the debts and liabilities of the company incurred during the duration of the contravention (**CDDA 1986, s 15**). **Sections 15A–C** empower the courts to make compensation orders against a person, providing that (i) the person is subject to a disqualification order or undertaking, and (ii) the conduct to which the order or undertaking relates has caused loss to one or more creditors of an insolvent company of which the person has at any time been a director. The order will require the disqualified person to compensate the creditors or the company. For guidance on the exercise of the powers granted by **ss 15A–C**, see the first case where a compensation order was granted, namely *Re Noble Vintners Ltd* **[2019]**.

4.5.3 Succession planning

Irrespective of how a director vacates office, a key goal of the company will be the appointment of the departing director's successor. Succession planning is now recognized as a key governance issue, with the Financial Reporting Council (FRC) stating that sound succession planning contributes to the long-term success of a company, principally because it 'ensures a continuous supply of suitable people (or a process to identify them), who are ready to take over when directors, senior staff and other key employees leave the company in a range of situations'. The UK Corporate Governance Code provides that companies should have an effective succession plan in place for board and senior management. Unfortunately, Grant Thornton's 2021 Corporate Governance Review states that only 37 per cent of FTSE 350 companies provide good or detailed accounts of their succession planning.

 KEY CASES

CASE	FACTS	PRINCIPLE
Automatic Self-Cleansing Filter Syndicate Co Ltd v Cuninghame [1906] 2 Ch 34 (CA)	The directors refused to exercise a power of sale granted to them by the articles. The members tried to exercise the power themselves by passing an ordinary resolution.	The division of power between the directors and the members is a matter for the articles, and where the articles grant a power to the directors only, then only the directors may exercise that power.
BTI 2014 LLC v Sequana SA [2022] UKSC 25	The company paid out a dividend at a time when there was a real, but not probable or imminent, risk of insolvency	The 'creditor duty' was engaged when the directors know, or ought to know, that the company is insolvent or bordering on insolvency, or that an insolvent liquidation or administration is probable.
Bushell v Faith [1970] AC 1099 (HL)	A company's articles provided that, in relation to resolutions to remove a director, the voting power of the director involved would be trebled.	The **Companies Act 1948** did not prohibit weighted voting clauses and so the clause in this case was effective.
Eclairs Group Ltd v JKX Oil & Gas plc [2015] UKSC 71	The directors used a power in the company's articles to disenfranchise a group of shareholders, who were due to vote against the company at the upcoming AGM.	The proper purpose rule would apply to provisions in the articles. Exercising a power to disenfranchise members is not a proper purpose.
Howard Smith Ltd v Ampol Petroleum Ltd [1974] AC 821 (PC)	A company issued a batch of shares to the defendant in order to relegate the claimant to the status of minority shareholder, and thereby prevent it from blocking the defendant's takeover bid.	The courts should determine the dominant purpose of the exercise of power. If proper, no breach will occur, even if subservient improper purposes exist, and vice versa.
Mutual Life Insurance Co of New York v Rank Organisation Ltd [1985] BCLC 11 (Ch)	An issue of shares on preferential terms was denied to members in certain locations, due to the cost of complying with the laws of those locations.	Where the interests of the company and some part of its members conflict, preference should be given to the interests of the company.

CASE	FACTS	PRINCIPLE
Re Barings plc (No 5) [2000] 1 BCLC 523 (CA)	Several directors were disqualified due to their failure to monitor an employee who engaged in financial transactions that caused the company's collapse.	The duty to exercise skill and care requires directors to acquire sufficient knowledge of the company's business and monitor those to whom managerial functions have been delegated. The duty will be affected by the directors' role and function.
Salmon v Quin & Axtens Ltd [1909] AC 442 (HL)	The company's articles provided that the company's ability to acquire certain properties was subject to the veto of two named members.	The director's general power of management is subject to the articles and, where the articles limit the director's powers of management, the limitation will be upheld by the courts.

KEY DEBATES

Topic	Duty to promote the success of the company for the benefit of its members
Author/Academic	Deryn Fisher
Viewpoint	Argues that the duty found in **s 172 of the CA 2006** will not make directors consider the interests of non-shareholder constituents and contends that the pluralist approach might prove more inclusive.
Source	'The Enlightened Shareholder: Leaving Stakeholders in the Dark—Will Section 172(1) of the Companies Act 2006 Make Directors Consider the Impact of Their Decisions on Third Parties?' (2009) 20 ICCLR 10

Topic	Conflicts of interest
Author/Academic	Bryan Clark
Viewpoint	Discusses the common law relating to directors who have interests that conflict with those of their companies and argues that the retention by the **CA 2006** of a strict approach is correct.
Source	'UK Company Law Reform and the Directors' Exploitation of Corporate Opportunities' (2006) 17 ICCLR 231

Topic	Boardroom diversity
Author/Academic	FTSE Women Leaders' Review
Viewpoint	Sets out the current recommendations for improving gender diversity in the boardrooms of larger companies.
Source	'Achieving Gender Balance' (2022)

EXAM QUESTIONS

Essay question

'The codification of directors' duties has done little in practice to improve the law.'

Do you agree with this statement? Provide reasons for your answers.

See the Outline answers section in the endmatter for help with this question.

Problem question

Ethos plc is a major, international graphic design company. One of Ethos's directors, Mike, is in extreme financial difficulty and is close to having to declare himself bankrupt (which would make him ineligible to act as a director of Ethos). Accordingly, to prevent this, the other directors of Ethos cause the company to lend Mike £15,000. The transaction is disclosed at a meeting of the directors and the directors unanimously agree to authorize the loan. Mike was present at this meeting, but did not vote on whether the loan should be made.

Ethos's articles of association state that 'Ethos plc may engage in any activity directly related, or incidental to, the carrying on of a graphic design business'. The directors of Ethos cause the company to lend £5,000 to Ceri, who will then pay off the loan over a two-year period. Ceri is a major client of Ethos, but aside from this has no other links with the company or its directors. A number of Ethos members hear of the loan and argue that Ceri must repay the money immediately.

The board of Ethos discover that Asset Strip plc is considering a takeover bid of Ethos. Asset Strip plans to break up the various parts of Ethos and sell them off individually and to remove the company's directors. Ethos is making a considerable profit and the directors genuinely believe that it would not be in the interests of the company or its members for Ethos to be taken over by Asset Strip. Accordingly, the directors cause the company to issue new shares to Sylvia—an existing member who is known to oppose the takeover—with the aim of preventing the takeover from succeeding.

Discuss whether or not Ethos or any of its directors have breached the law.

Online resources

For an outline answer to this problem question, as well as multiple-choice questions and further reading, please visit the online resources.

5 Members

KEY FACTS

- Members usually exercise their decision-making powers via the passing of resolutions. The two principal forms of resolution are the ordinary resolution (which requires over 50 per cent) and the special resolution (which requires a majority of not less than 75 per cent).

- Public companies must pass resolutions at general meetings. Private companies must pass resolutions at general meetings, unless the written resolution procedure is used.

- Resolutions are only valid if sufficient notice of the meeting is provided and a quorum is present. A quorum is simply the minimum number of persons required to be present in order to conduct business.

- Members can appoint a proxy to attend, speak, and vote at general meetings on their behalf.

- The general belief is that general meetings do not provide a satisfactory forum for shareholder democracy.

CHAPTER OVERVIEW

> **SIGNIFICANT DECISION-MAKING POWER IS PLACED IN THE HANDS OF THE MEMBERS, WHO CAN FORMALLY EXERCISE THIS POWER IN TWO WAYS**

Resolutions

Public companies

Private companies

General meeting

Written resolution

Unanimous assent
If all the members entitled to vote on a matter are in agreement on that matter, then that agreement will be valid even if no meeting was convened and no resolution took place (subject to exceptions)

Ordinary resolution
Requires a simple majority to pass (i.e. over 50 per cent)

Special resolution
Requires no less than a 75 per cent majority to pass

Resolution
Requires a simple majority to pass, unless the articles specify a higher majority or unanimity

Introduction

The members of a company play two vital roles. First, through the purchase of shares, they contribute capital to the company. The nature of the share and share capital is discussed in CHAPTER 7. This chapter will focus on the second vital role that the members play, namely their ability to make decisions. As will be seen, a significant amount of power is placed in the hands of members, and numerous key decisions are reserved for them alone. However, before the members' ability to exercise this power can be discussed, it is important to note the difference between a 'member' and a 'shareholder'.

5.1 Members and shareholders

Many statutes and textbooks tend to use the terms 'member' and 'shareholder' interchangeably, and, in the vast majority of cases, a member will be a shareholder and vice versa. There are differences, however, that are important to understand. The most obvious occurs in companies without a share capital—such companies will have members, but will not have shareholders.

 REVISION TIP

Although it is generally acceptable to use the terms member and shareholder interchangeably, if you are referring to a company without a share capital, make sure that you use the term 'member'. As the term 'member' is generally wider than the term 'shareholder', you may prefer to use the term 'member' in general (indeed, company law legislation uses the word 'member' significantly more than the word 'shareholder').

The distinction exists even in companies that do have a share capital. Purchasing shares will make a person a shareholder, but it will not automatically make him a member. **Section 112 of the CA 2006** sets out the two ways in which a person can become a member:

1. the subscribers of a company are deemed to have agreed to become members and, upon the company's registration, become members and their names must be entered into the register of members (although they will still be members even if their names are not so entered); and

2. every other person who agrees to become a member and whose name is entered into the register of members will be a member of the company.

5.2 Resolutions

As is discussed in CHAPTER 3, the general power to manage the company is usually vested in the directors by the company's articles. Despite this, the **CA 2006** and the **Insolvency Act 1986 (IA 1986)** place considerable decision-making power in the hands of the members, including:

- the members can alter the company's articles (see 3.4);
- if a company wishes to convert from a public company to a private company, or vice versa, or if an unlimited company wishes to convert to a private limited company, then the approval of the members will be required;
- the members can remove a director (or directors) from office (see 4.5.1);
- numerous loans and other transactions involving directors require the approval of the members (see 4.4.3); and
- the members can wind up the company.

Figure 5.1 How decisions are made by members

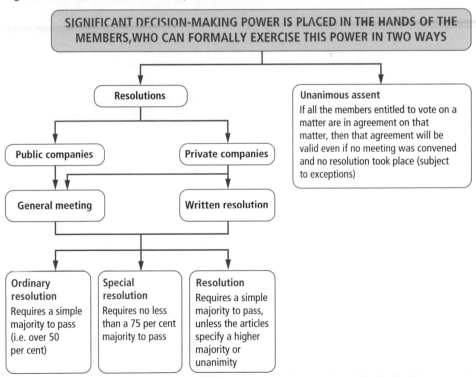

The members exercise this power in one of two ways, namely (i) through the passing of **resolutions**, or (ii) via the unanimous assent rule. This section focuses on resolutions (the unanimous assent rule is discussed at 5.4), but Figure 5.1 sets out how decisions are made by members.

A resolution is simply a more formal word for a vote, whereby the members resolve themselves or the company to a particular course of action.

5.2.1 Types of resolution

The **CA 2006** provides for three types of resolution, namely:

1. **Ordinary resolution**: an ordinary resolution of the members is one that is passed by a simple majority (**CA 2006, s 282(1)**), namely over 50 per cent—remembering that an exact 50 per cent split will mean that the resolution is lost.

2. **Special resolution**: a special resolution of the members is one passed by a majority of not less than 75 per cent (**CA 2006, s 283(1)**). Special resolutions tend to be reserved for more important decisions and constitutional changes.

3. **Resolution**: legislation may simply state that 'a resolution' is required, without specifying which type. In such a case, the resolution required will be an ordinary resolution, although the company will be free to specify a higher majority (or unanimity) by inserting a provision in the articles to that effect (**CA 2006, s 281(3)**). Where statute specifies that an ordinary or special resolution is required, the articles cannot alter the majority required.

REVISION TIP

Be accurate when stating the majorities required for ordinary and special resolutions. Students often state that an ordinary resolution requires 50 per cent, or that a special resolution requires 75 per cent. Both of these are incorrect. An ordinary resolution requires *over* 50 per cent, whereas a special resolution requires 75 per cent *or over*.

The resolutions of public companies must be passed at a meeting of the members (**CA 2006, s 281(2)**). The resolutions of private companies can be passed at a meeting, or can be passed via what is known as a written resolution (**CA 2006, s 281(1)**).

5.2.2 Written resolutions

As is discussed at 5.3, the convening of, and the passing of a formal resolution at a meeting involves compliance with a substantial body of rules and procedures that can prove burdensome and potentially costly, especially for smaller companies. Further, where the number of members is small, or where the directors are the members, convening a general meeting in order to pass a resolution seems like a rather redundant exercise. Accordingly, the **CA 2006** allows private companies to pass a written resolution in substitute for a resolution passed at a meeting (except where statute provides that a meeting must be convened (e.g. where the resolution seeks to remove an auditor or director from office)). Written resolutions require the same majorities, and have the same force, as resolutions passed at meetings (**CA 2006, s 288(5)**). However, the method of calculating majorities does differ:

- where the resolution is tabled at a meeting, the requisite majority is calculated based on the votes cast by those eligible to vote (**CA 2006, ss 282(3)–(4)** and **283(4)–(5)**) (i.e. votes are calculated based only on those who actually vote), and
- where a written resolution is used, the requisite majority is calculated based on the voting rights of the total number of members eligible to vote (**CA 2006, ss 282(2)** and **283(2)**), not just those who actually do vote.

LOOKING FOR EXTRA MARKS?

Written resolutions were permitted under the **CA 1985** but were cumbersome and difficult to pass as, irrespective of the majority required by the 1985 Act if the resolution were to be voted on at a meeting, a written resolution required unanimity to pass. The **CA 2006** has remedied this flaw and written resolutions now require the same majority as if made at a meeting. Accordingly, written resolutions now serve the purpose required of them, namely to make decision-making in private companies more efficient.

Where a written resolution has been proposed, a copy of the proposed resolution will be sent to each member along with a statement informing the member how to signify agreement and when agreement must be made by. Photocopying the resolution and posting it to the members is clearly a much quicker and cheaper method of decision-making than convening a meeting. Once a member has signified agreement, it cannot be revoked.

LOOKING FOR EXTRA MARKS?

The written resolution procedure is an example of the 'think small first' philosophy behind the **CA 2006**. The **CA 1985** was heavily criticized for catering to large companies, whilst failing to acknowledge the needs of smaller companies. If an essay requires you to discuss the extent to which the **CA 2006** caters for smaller companies, the usefulness of the written resolution procedure, and the way the 2006 Act has improved its usefulness, are topics that should be discussed.

5.3 General meetings

Except where the written resolution procedure or unanimous assent rule are used, the members will exercise their decision-making powers by passing resolutions at meetings, of which there are two types:

1. Meetings that all of the members are entitled to attend are known as 'general meetings'. The majority of meetings, including the Annual General Meeting (AGM), will constitute general meetings. It used to be the case that any meeting that was not an AGM was known as an extraordinary general meeting, but this phrase should no longer be used.

2. Meetings which only a certain class of the members are entitled to attend are known as 'class meetings'. These meetings are reserved for determining the class rights of certain members with special rights (discussed at 7.1.3).

The resolutions of public companies must be passed at meetings; resolutions of private companies must be passed at meetings unless the written resolution procedure is used (note, however, that the written resolution procedure cannot be used for certain resolutions (e.g. a resolution to remove a director under **s 168**)). Accordingly, it is possible for a private company to go its entire existence without having to call a meeting. Conversely, public companies must hold at least one general meeting every financial year that will constitute an AGM (**CA 2006, s 336(1)**).

LOOKING FOR EXTRA MARKS?

Under the **CA 1985**, public and private companies were required to hold an AGM, although private companies could opt out of this requirement. That private companies are, by default, not required to hold general meetings (unless statute requires a meeting be held) is evidence of how the **CA 2006** is better drafted to meet the needs of smaller companies when compared to the 1985 Act. In an essay discussing whether the 2006 Act provides a more suitable regulatory regime for small businesses, this is an important point to mention.

Resolutions passed at general meetings are only valid if the procedural requirements established by the **CA 2006** are complied with (**CA 2006, s 301**) and these usually cannot be excluded by the articles.

REVISION TIP

The procedural requirements laid down by the **CA 2006** are extensive and burdensome, especially for smaller companies. This is why the written resolution procedure is so potentially valuable for smaller companies, and why private companies are not generally required to hold general meetings.

5.3.1 The calling of meetings

Generally, the power to call a general meeting is vested in the directors (**CA 2006, s 302**). **Section 303 of the CA 2006** does, however, allow the members to require that the directors call a general meeting, providing that the request comes from members representing at least

5 per cent of the company's **paid-up share capital** or, in the case of a company without a share capital, members representing at least 5 per cent of the voting rights of the members.

LOOKING FOR EXTRA MARKS?

Do you think the 5 per cent threshold is a justified restriction on the members' power to request that a meeting be called? In larger companies, there is no doubt that the 5 per cent threshold will prove to be an insurmountable barrier for most private investors, so it is likely to be used only by large institutional investors (this is discussed at 6.3.1).

If the directors fail to comply with a valid request from the members, then those members, or members representing over half the total voting rights of the company, are granted the power to call a meeting themselves, at the company's expense (**CA 2006, s 305**). Where it is impracticable to call a meeting in accordance with the above provisions, the court may order a meeting to be called (**CA 2006, s 306**).

REVISION TIP

Problem questions often feature decisions taken at a general meeting, and the power to call a general meeting may also require a discussion of other areas of company law. For example, the directors are under a statutory duty to use their powers for a proper purpose (**CA 2006, s 171(b)**—discussed at 4.4.2.1) and, if the directors call a meeting for an improper purpose (or improperly refuse the members' request for a meeting), a breach of duty may have occurred which can form the basis of a derivative claim (discussed at 8.3). Similarly, if the majority shareholders call a meeting in order to adversely affect the minority, the majority's conduct may be regarded as unfairly prejudicial (discussed at 8.4).

5.3.2 Notice of meetings

Resolutions passed at general meetings are only valid if adequate notice of the meeting is provided to persons entitled to such notice (**CA 2006, s 301**), namely:

- all of the company's members (**CA 2006, s 310(1)(a)**),
- all of the company's directors (**CA 2006, s 310(1)(b)**), and
- the company's auditor (**CA 2006, s 502(2)(a)**).

The notice requirements for members and directors are subject to the articles (**CA 2006, s 310(4)(b)**), so the articles may provide that certain members or directors are not entitled to notice. The auditor's notice cannot be excluded by the articles.

Notice must be provided within a sufficient period prior to the meeting. The general rule is that notice of a meeting must be provided at least fourteen clear days prior to the meeting, rising to twenty-one clear days in the case of the AGM of a public company (**CA 2006, s 307(1)** and (2)). **The 2016 UK Corporate Governance Code** stated that companies should provide at least twenty working days' notice of an AGM, but this was removed from the 2018 Code and instead placed in para 36 of the accompanying Guidance on Board Effectiveness. The company's articles are free to specify a longer notice period (**CA 2006, s 307(3)**), but cannot specify a shorter notice period (although the members themselves can agree to a shorter notice period).

5.3.3 Quorum

A general meeting, and any decisions made at it, will only be valid if a quorum is present. In relation to general meetings, a quorum is the minimum number of 'qualifying persons' required to validly conduct business. A qualifying person is:

- a member of the company,
- a representative of a **corporate member**, or
- a **proxy** of the member (discussed later).

Where a limited company has only one member, that member will constitute a quorum (**CA 2006, s 318(1)**). In all other cases, two qualifying persons will constitute a quorum, unless the articles provide otherwise (**CA 2006, s 318(2)**).

If a quorum is not present, the meeting is said to be 'inquorate' and no business can be conducted at that meeting (although the model articles provide that an inquorate meeting can appoint a chairman for the meeting).

5.3.4 Voting

Regarding the passing of resolutions at a meeting, there are two methods of voting:

1. on a show of hands, or
2. by poll.

The method of voting is a matter for the articles and general rule is that, unless the articles provide otherwise, resolutions are voted on by a show of hands (the model articles provide that a resolution at a meeting will be decided on a show of hands, unless a poll is demanded in accordance with the articles). The members have the right to demand that a vote be taken on a poll, but the articles can stipulate that a certain number of members are required in order for such a demand to be valid (the model articles provide that two members are needed to demand a poll, and also that the chair of the meeting can demand a poll). In practice, most larger companies conduct votes on a poll because larger shareholders will want voting power commensurate with their shareholdings, and a show of hands is an imprecise method of counting.

Where a vote is taken on a show of hands, each member will have one vote. Where a vote is taken by poll, unless the articles provide otherwise, each member will have one vote per share, except where the company has no share capital, in which case each member will have one vote (**CA 2006, s 284(3)**).

5.3.4.1 Proxies

Members need not attend a meeting to exercise their voting rights. **Section 324 of the CA 2006** grants members the right to appoint another person to exercise their right to attend, speak, and vote at general meetings, and this person is known as a **'proxy'**. In large public companies, the appointment of proxies is especially important because only a small minority of the company's members will actually attend the meeting. Many other members will appoint a proxy to exercise their votes.

 LOOKING FOR EXTRA MARKS?

It is often argued that the ability to appoint a proxy emasculates the effectiveness of general meetings, especially in public companies. When such companies send out notice of a meeting, it is common for the notice to contain a document allowing the member to appoint a proxy who can exercise the member's voting rights (although the member can instruct the proxy as to how to vote and the proxy must follow such instructions (**CA 2006, s 324A**)). Unsurprisingly, the person nominated by the company to act as proxy is usually one of the directors (normally the chairman), although the member is free to appoint whomever he wishes. Accordingly, the directors will often be able to exercise the voting rights of many absent members, greatly increasing their voting power and making it difficult for members to defeat resolutions proposed by the directors.

5.3.5 The utility of meetings

As public companies are required to hold meetings, and as, in such companies, the members can only exercise many of their key decision-making powers at meetings, the general meeting as a forum for shareholder democracy is of fundamental importance. In fact, general meetings are the only formal link between the company's members and the board. Unfortunately, there is widespread dissatisfaction with the utility of general meetings as a forum for shareholder democracy, for several reasons:

- For general meetings to provide a forum for shareholder democracy, they need to be well attended. In large public companies, however, meetings tend to be poorly attended. One reason for this is that the majority of shares in listed companies are owned by persons not present in the UK (the most recent share ownership statistics released by the Office of National Statistics show that, as of 2020, 56.3 per cent of UK quoted shares are beneficially owned by overseas investors).

- For general meetings to effectively hold the directors to account, the majority of shares should not be in the hands or control of the directors. In many private companies, the directors will hold a majority of the shares, so general meetings become arguably redundant in practice (which is why private companies are not required to hold an AGM). In public companies, many members will appoint one of the directors to act as their proxy, so the directors may have control of a significant proportion of the company's shares, thereby allowing them to defeat the resolutions of those who might wish to hold them to account.

REVISION TIP

The failings mentioned here have led many to argue that the general meeting serves no useful function and companies should not be required to hold them. The Company Law Review Steering Group recommended that public companies be able to opt out of the requirement to hold an AGM, but the government disagreed. Despite these failings, general meetings are still regarded as one of the most important corporate governance mechanisms. Be prepared to discuss the effectiveness of general meetings should an essay question require you to do so. Do you think general meetings should be abolished or should they be reformed? One possible reform is to make greater use of virtual AGMs (where the entire meeting is conducted online) or hybrid AGMs (where there is a physical meeting, but members can also participate online). Some companies did use virtual or hybrid AGMs during the COVID-19 lockdown and afterwards, but most larger companies still use physical meetings. For more on this, see FRC, 'AGMs: An Opportunity for Change' (FRC, 2020).

5.4 Unanimous assent

As noted, convening meetings can be a burdensome process. Even the written resolution procedure may appear unnecessary where all the members know they are in agreement on an issue. Accordingly, the common law has long provided that if all the members entitled to vote on a matter agree on that matter, then that agreement will be valid even if no meeting was convened and no resolution took place (***Baroness Wenlock v The River Dee Co* (1883)**). This unanimous assent rule is also known as the *Duomatic* principle, named after the case of ***Re Duomatic Ltd* [1969]**, where Buckley J stated:

> where it can be shown that all the shareholders who have a right to attend and vote at a general meeting of the company assent to some matter which a general meeting of the company could carry into effect, that assent is as binding as a resolution in general meeting would be.

As this rule circumvents the rules and procedures relating to meetings and resolutions, it is unsurprising that strict rules and safeguards are in place, including:

- Nothing less than unanimity will suffice—a member holding 99 per cent of the shares cannot, by himself, take advantage of the *Duomatic* principle (***Re D'Jan of London* [1993]**).

- The *Duomatic* principle cannot be used where the decision in question could not have been taken at a meeting (***Re New Cedos Engineering Co Ltd* [1994]**).

- The *Duomatic* principle cannot apply where statute excludes its operation (***Re Oceanrose Investments Ltd* [2008]**). This usually occurs where statute provides that a resolution must be passed at a meeting (e.g. a resolution to remove a director under **s 168**).

REVISION TIP

An agreement taken by unanimous consent is likely to be classified under s **29 of the CA 2006** as an agreement that affects the company's constitution. Accordingly, such agreements may form part of the company's constitution and may be enforced by the company or its members (the company's constitution and its enforcement are discussed in CHAPTER 3). It is also likely that such agreements will need to be registered with the Registrar of Companies.

KEY DEBATES

Topic	Shareholder democracy and decision-making
Author/Academic	Richard C Nolan
Viewpoint	Examines the evolution of the law that governs shareholder decision-making and argues that the law can serve to unsatisfactorily restrict shareholder governance.
Source	'The Continuing Evolution of Shareholder Governance' [2006] CLJ 92

Topic	The annual general meeting
Author/Academic	The Company Law Review Steering Group
Viewpoint	Discusses the role and effectiveness of the AGM. Assesses a number of potential reforms, including abolishing the requirement for public companies to hold an AGM.
Source	'Modern Company Law for a Competitive Economy: Company General Meetings and Shareholder Communication' (DTI 1999)—available from http://webarchive.nationalarchives.gov.uk/20121029131934/http://www.bis.gov.uk/files/file23274.pdf

Topic	Proxy voting
Author/Academic	Financial Reporting Council
Viewpoint	Discusses whether the challenges faced during lockdown have provided lessons that can be learned to improve the operation of AGMs, including the use of virtual and hybrid AGMs.
Source	'An Opportunity for Change' (FRC 2020)

EXAM QUESTIONS

Essay question

In *Re Dorman Long & Co Ltd* [1934], Maugham J stated that, in relation to general meetings, 'the dice are loaded in favour of the views of the directors'.

Discuss the current validity of Maugham J's statement. How effective are general meetings as a forum for shareholder democracy?

See the Outline answers section in the endmatter for help with this question.

Problem question

Alyn and Helen run a successful partnership. In 2022, they incorporate their business (Coles & Wilkins Ltd) and 500 shares are issued. Alyn and Helen each take 100 shares, 200 shares are taken by Simon, and the remaining 100 shares are taken by Diane.

The company's accounts are audited by Hywel. It is apparent that Hywel has been negligently auditing the company's accounts and Alyn, Helen, Simon, and Diane all believe that Hywel should be removed before his period of office has expired. Alyn is aware of the consensus and so writes a letter to Hywel informing him that his office is terminated and he is no longer the company's auditor.

Simon and Diane rarely attend meetings and Alyn shows little interest in attending board and general meetings. Helen therefore tends to run the business by herself, and the other members appoint her to act as their proxy. She uses this power to alter the articles and to change the company's name to Wilkins Ltd.

Given that Alyn never attends board meetings, Simon and Diane are of the opinion that he should step down as a director, but Alyn refuses. Simon and Diane request that the directors call a general meeting to decide the issue, but Alyn and Helen refuse. Accordingly, Simon and Diane convene a meeting themselves (at their own expense) and invite Alyn and Helen to attend. The meeting takes place and, as Simon and Diane collectively hold 300 shares compared to the directors' 200 shares, they contend that the resolution is passed and Alyn should vacate office. Alyn points to a provision in the company's articles, which states that a director can only be removed if a special resolution is passed. Simon and Diane state that Wilkins Ltd should reimburse them for the costs of the meeting.

Discuss whether any breaches of the law have occurred and whether the decisions taken have followed the applicable procedures.

 Online resources

For an outline answer to this problem question, as well as multiple-choice questions and further reading, please visit the online resources.

Corporate governance

6

KEY FACTS

- The UK's system of corporate governance is largely voluntary, with the UK Corporate Governance Code, the Wates Corporate Governance Principles, and the UK Stewardship Code 2020 providing the main corporate governance principles.

- The UK Corporate Governance Code operates in part on a 'comply or explain' basis, whereas the Wates Corporate Governance Principles operate on an 'apply and explain' basis.

- When purchasing shares, insurance companies, pension funds, and banks, etc. are known as institutional investors. Currently, over half of the shares in UK companies are in the hands of institutional investors. The UK Stewardship Code 2020 sets out a series of Principles on how asset managers, asset owners, and service providers should discharge their stewardship functions.

- In order to prevent executive directors from determining their own pay, certain companies are encouraged to set up a remuneration committee consisting of non-executive directors.

- The Companies Act 2006 requires companies to disclose details concerning directors' remuneration and provides the members of quoted and traded companies with the right to vote on certain remuneration issues.

- Although the Companies Act 2006 does not differentiate between executive and non-executive directors, the UK Corporate Governance Code places great emphasis on the corporate governance functions of independent non-executive directors.

Introduction

Over the last thirty years, largely due to a steady stream of corporate scandals (e.g. Enron, Parmalat, BCCI, Lehman Brothers), there has been an explosion of interest in corporate governance. Whilst the term 'corporate governance' might be of relatively recent origin, the topic itself has existed since the dawn of the registered company. It is only in the last three decades or so, however, that the topic has started to receive the attention that it deserves and, in that period, it has grown significantly in scope. In fact, the topic is too large to cover comprehensively in a single text, let alone a single chapter. Accordingly, this chapter will focus on a few key governance issues, although other important issues have been covered elsewhere in this text (e.g. boardroom diversity, succession planning).

REVISION TIP

Although this chapter is entitled 'Corporate governance', it is now arguably less of a topic in its own right and instead is, alongside company law, a component of the system by which companies are run and regulated. In many areas, company law and corporate governance principles operate alongside each other, and so it is important to understand how laws and principles interact with one another. For example, there are significant provisions in the **CA 2006** relating to directors' pay (e.g. disclosure of pay, the members' 'say on pay'), but there are also numerous Principles and Provisions within the **UK Corporate Governance Code** relating to directors' pay that go far beyond what is required under the **CA 2006**.

6.1 What is 'corporate governance'?

In recent years, the phrase 'corporate governance' has become one of the most ubiquitous phrases in the business world. Despite its importance and prevalence, however, there is no accepted definition as to what corporate governance actually is. The breadth of the topic is demonstrated by the definition of the Cadbury Committee, who defined corporate governance as 'the system by which companies are directed and controlled'. Whilst this definition is doubtless correct, it is also rather broad and vague. Given the massive expansion of the topic in recent years, it is likely that the phrase is not amenable to a short, pithy definition. Instead, perhaps it is preferable not to define what corporate governance is, but what it aims to achieve. **Principle A of the 2018 UK Corporate Governance Code** sets out the goal of a governance-focused board, namely to 'promote the long-term sustainable success of the company, generating value for shareholders and contributing to wider society'.

REVISION TIP

For a useful discussion of what corporate governance is, see Jill Solomon, *Corporate Governance and Accountability* (5th edn, Wiley, 2020) ch 1. For an account of the major corporate scandals that led to the increase in the prominence of corporate governance, see Christine A Mallin, *Corporate Governance* (6th edn, OUP, 2018) ch 1.

6.2 Corporate governance codes and principles

UK company law has historically been based around a central Companies Act, with the **CA 2006** establishing the current legislative framework. Conversely, legislation is largely absent from the UK corporate governance system, with the vast majority of corporate governance principles deriving from a series of reports and codes. Within the last two decades, there have been a notable number of such reports and codes (often created as a result of some corporate scandal or emerging area of concern) and it is important that you understand how our self-regulatory system originated and has evolved. A discussion of all the codes and reports that have influenced our corporate governance system is beyond the scope of this text, but Figure 6.1 provides a timeline of the principal codes, with two being especially important, namely:

1. the **UK Corporate Governance Code**, and;

2. the **Wates Corporate Governance Principles for Large Private Companies**.

6.2.1 The UK Corporate Governance Code

The corporate governance principles for companies with a premium listing are contained in the **UK Corporate Governance Code** (formerly known as the **Combined Code on Corporate Governance**). The Combined Code was first created in 1998 and, as the UK corporate governance system has evolved and as subsequent reports have made new recommendations, the Code has been updated to reflect these changes. The Code was updated in 2000, 2003, 2006, 2008, and 2010, with the 2010 update changing the Code's name to the **UK Corporate Governance Code**. The **UK Corporate Governance Code** was updated in 2012, 2014, 2016, and 2018. The 2018 Code is applicable to all companies with a premium listing (whether incorporated in the UK or elsewhere) and applies to accounting periods beginning on or after 1 January 2019 (note that the FRC has published a proposed revised Code - this is discussed in the 'Latest News' section).

The 2018 Code is the most significant update to date, as it completely reworked the Code's structure and notably shortened the Code to provide additional clarity. The 2018 Code consists of eighteen broad Principles (numbered A to R), which are fleshed out in more detail by forty-one accompanying Provisions (with further detail being found in the accompanying 2018 document entitled Guidance on Board Effectiveness). These Principles and Provisions are grouped into five main topics, namely:

1. board leadership and company purpose;

2. division of responsibilities;

3. board composition, succession, and evaluation;

4. audit, risk, and internal control, and;

5. remuneration.

Figure 6.1 Corporate governance codes and principles

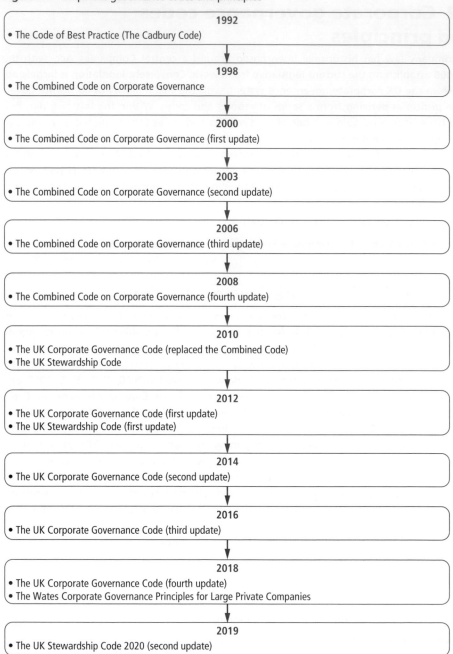

1992
- The Code of Best Practice (The Cadbury Code)

1998
- The Combined Code on Corporate Governance

2000
- The Combined Code on Corporate Governance (first update)

2003
- The Combined Code on Corporate Governance (second update)

2006
- The Combined Code on Corporate Governance (third update)

2008
- The Combined Code on Corporate Governance (fourth update)

2010
- The UK Corporate Governance Code (replaced the Combined Code)
- The UK Stewardship Code

2012
- The UK Corporate Governance Code (first update)
- The UK Stewardship Code (first update)

2014
- The UK Corporate Governance Code (second update)

2016
- The UK Corporate Governance Code (third update)

2018
- The UK Corporate Governance Code (fourth update)
- The Wates Corporate Governance Principles for Large Private Companies

2019
- The UK Stewardship Code 2020 (second update)

LOOKING FOR EXTRA MARKS?

In many cases, the Principles and Provisions contained in the Code go well beyond the requirements imposed by the **CA 2006**. Most students can effectively discuss the Act's provisions, but many students neglect the principles established by the Code, especially in problem questions. In issues of corporate governance, the Code could be just as important as the **CA 2006**, so you should ensure that you are familiar with the Code's Principles/Provisions and their impact. For a discussion of developments relating to the impact and implementation of the Code, see FRC, 'Annual Review of the UK Corporate Governance Code' (FRC 2020) and FRC, 'Review of Corporate Governance Reporting' (FRC 2022).

The Code states that it applies to companies with a premium listing. **The Listing Rules** require such companies to include within their annual report a statement setting out how the Code's Principles have been applied, and:

- a statement as to whether the company has complied with all the relevant Provisions of the Code; or
- a statement identifying which Provisions were not complied with, the period within which they were not complied with, and the reasons for non-compliance.

REVISION TIP

Students often fail to distinguish between the requirements relating to Principles and Provisions (perhaps because it is often incorrectly stated that the Code operates on a 'comply or explain' basis, whereas only the Code's Provisions operate on this basis). Companies with a premium listing must state how they have applied the Code's Principles. It is only the Code's Provisions that operate on a comply or explain basis.

A failure to comply with a Principle or Provision of the Code will not result in any legal sanction being imposed (although it may result in shareholder disapproval or damage to the company's reputation). However, if a company with a premium listing fails to include within its annual report the required statements, then that will constitute a breach of the **Listing Rules**, which can result in the imposition of a financial penalty or public censure (**Financial Services and Markets Act 2000, s 91**).

At the time of writing, the **UK Corporate Governance Code** (and the **UK Stewardship Code 2020**, discussed at 6.3.1.3) are reviewed and updated by the FRC. However, the 2018 Kingman Review was critical of the effectiveness of the FRC and recommended that it be replaced by a new regulator entitled the Audit, Reporting and Governance Authority (ARGA). The government has accepted this recommendation and the process for the FRC's replacement is well underway, although there is no timeframe for when it is expected to be completed.

6.2.1.1 The advantages and disadvantages of codes and principles

It is generally accepted that the UK's corporate governance regime is effective and there is a high level of compliance with the Code amongst larger listed companies. A number of other countries have followed the UK's lead by creating corporate governance codes of their own and an EU Green Paper resulted in strong support being expressed for the 'comply or explain' approach. Several arguments have been advanced to explain the success of our governance regime:

- *Flexibility*—Corporate governance is a constantly evolving area and regulation needs to be able to adapt quickly to emerging practices and abuses. Updating legislation can be a lengthy process, whereas codes can be quickly altered without having to wait for a gap in the crowded parliamentary timetable and without having to pass through the legislative process (as is evidenced by the regular updates to the **Combined Code/UK Corporate Governance Code**).

- *Expertise*—Codes are usually drafted and updated by, or following consultation with, the industries or entities that they are designed to apply to. In other words, they are drafted by, or with the aid of, experts in their relevant field and, as a result, the principles are more likely to be effective and are more likely to be accepted by the industry.

- *Efficiency and cost*—As the various codes are drafted and updated by experts, the drafting and updating process is likely to be achieved on a more cost-efficient basis. Further, the cost of these codes is often borne by the industry in question, whereas taxpayers bear the cost of statutory regulation.

However, the use of codes and principles can result in some notable disadvantages, including:

- *Enforcement drawbacks*—As these codes lack the direct force of law, they often lack effective sanctions. A breach of the Code brings no legal sanction in itself (although the company's reputation might suffer), but a failure to include the required statements can result in a breach of the **Listing Rules**, under which the Financial Conduct Authority can administer sanctions.

- *Bias*—As these codes are drafted by, or drafted following consultation with, the industries or persons to whom the codes are intended to apply, there is always the danger that the codes will favour those industries/persons by advocating lax standards or ineffective recommendations. However, to date, this does not appear to have been an issue, and the process of updating the codes has been open and transparent, with wide consultations taking place.

 LOOKING FOR EXTRA MARKS?

For an excellent discussion of 'comply or explain' and other related issues, see the collection of essays published by the FRC in 2012 to mark the twentieth anniversary of the Cadbury Report—these can be found at https://www.frc.org.uk/getattachment/06870154-78a0-44f5-a1c5-48b42f860049/FRC-Essays_Comply-or-Explain.pdf. ➡

→ It is also useful to know the extent to which the Code is complied with, especially in an essay question involving the Code or its recommendations, and there are two excellent sources of data on compliance levels. First, the FRC itself publishes an annual Review of Corporate Governance Reporting. Second, an excellent and readable source of statistics can be found in the Corporate Governance Review that is conducted every year by Grant Thornton UK LLP.

6.2.2 The Wates Corporate Governance Principles

Given that many of the major corporate governance scandals have involved large companies, it is unsurprising that the UK Corporate Governance Code (and the UK's corporate governance system) has focused almost exclusively on large listed companies. However, following the BHS scandal (discussed in the example below), it was acknowledged that poor governance in unlisted companies can be just as damaging.

EXAMPLE

When Sir Philip Green purchased British Home Stores plc in 2000, one of the first things he did was to convert it to a private company (BHS Ltd). Over the years that followed, BHS paid out hundreds of millions in dividends, most of which went to companies controlled by Green's wife. This reduced the investment being made into BHS so that it became unable to compete and started to sustain serious losses. Green sold BHS in 2015 for £1, but it was sold to a company headed by Dominic Chappell, a man with a record of corporate failure. In April 2016, BHS entered administration with debts of £1.3 billion and a pension fund deficit of £571 million. The company later went into liquidation, with the loss of 11,000 jobs.

A parliamentary inquiry into the company's collapse noted that BHS's competitors were subject to the **UK Corporate Governance Code**, but BHS was not as it was a private company. The inquiry concluded that 'weaknesses in corporate governance contributed substantially to the ultimate demise of BHS'. Chappell was later disqualified for ten years for wrongfully diverting BHS funds to other companies he controlled, and ordered to pay £9.5 million into BHS's pension schemes. Green voluntarily contributed £363 million into the pension schemes.

The BHS scandal led to increased calls to improve governance safeguards in private companies. Accordingly, the government invited the FRC and other bodies to develop a voluntary set of corporate governance principles for large private companies. In January 2018, an industry group was set up by the government to draw up these principles, which resulted in the publication in December 2018 of the **Wates Corporate Governance Principles for Large Private Companies**. The Wates Principles consist of six Principles, with each Principle being accompanied by more detailed guidance on how the Principle could be applied. The six Principles are set out in Table 6.1.

6.2.2.1 Apply and explain

The **Wates Principles** operate on an 'apply and explain' basis as follows:

- Companies adopting the Principles are expected to apply them fully. They should apply each Principle and explain how they have addressed the Principle in their governance practices.

- The guidance that accompanies each Principle does not need to be reported on.

Table 6.1 The Wates Corporate Governance Principles for Large Private Companies

Principle One: Purpose	An effective board promotes the purpose of a company, and ensures that its values, strategy, and culture align with that purpose
Principle Two: Composition	Effective board composition requires an effective chair and a balance of skills, backgrounds, experience, and knowledge, with individual directors having sufficient capacity to make a valuable contribution. The size of a board should be guided by the scale and complexity of the company
Principle Three: Responsibilities	A board should have a clear understanding of its accountability and terms of reference. Its policies and procedures should support effective decision-making and independent challenge
Principle Four: Opportunity and risk	A board should promote the long-term success of the company by identifying opportunities to create and preserve value, and establishing oversight for the identification and mitigation of risks
Principle Five: Remuneration	A board should promote executive remuneration structures aligned to the sustainable long-term success of a company, taking into account pay and conditions elsewhere in the company
Principle Six: Stakeholders	A board has a responsibility to oversee meaningful engagement with material stakeholders, including the workforce, and have regard to that discussion when taking decisions. The board has a responsibility to foster good stakeholder relationships based on the company's purpose

The **Wates Principles** themselves do not state to which type of companies they apply. Instead, **Sch 7, Pt 8 of the Large and Medium-Sized Companies and Groups (Accounts and Reports) Regulations 2008** applies to any company that is not subject to **r 7.2** of the **Disclosure Guidance and Transparency Rules** and (i) has more than 2,000 employees, and/or (ii) has a turnover of more than £200 million and a balance sheet total of more than £2 billion. Such companies will be required to include in their directors' report a 'statement of corporate governance arrangements' that states:

- which corporate governance code, if any, the company applied in that financial year;
- how the company applied the code; and
- if the company departed from the code, its reasons for doing so.

The **Wates Principles** (along with the **UK Corporate Governance Code**) would be a code against which companies could report in their statement of corporate governance arrangements.

LOOKING FOR EXTRA MARKS?

Just like the UK Corporate Governance Code, you will want to be aware of how many companies have adopted the Wates Principles and how effectively they have reported on their compliance with the Principles. The first review of the Wates Principles was published in February 2022, namely FRC, 'The Wates Corporate Governance Principles for Large Private Companies: The Extent, Coverage and Quality of Corporate Governance Reporting' (FRC 2022).

6.3 Corporate governance issues

Here, several other key corporate governance issues will be discussed, namely:

1. the role of institutional investors,
2. the laws and principles relating to directors' remuneration, and
3. the role and effectiveness of non-executive directors.

6.3.1 Institutional investors

Often, we will transfer money to others so that they can look after it for us, or return it to us should certain events occur. We open bank accounts and trust banks to look after the money we place in those accounts. We pay money into pension funds so that, upon retirement, we will have a regular source of income. We pay premiums to insurance companies so that, if certain unfortunate events occur, we will be compensated for the losses caused by those events. When we transfer money to banks, pension funds, and insurance companies, they do not lock the money away until it can be returned to us. They use our money to make themselves a profit, with the purchasing of shares being a common method of obtaining (or trying to obtain) a profit. As they have access to significant funds, they can invest extremely heavily in the share market. The increasing share ownership of banks, pension funds, insurance companies, and unit trusts (or institutional investors as they have come to be known) has radically transformed the UK corporate governance landscape.

In 1963, 54 per cent of UK shares were in the hands of individual private investors, with 29 per cent of shares in the hands of institutional investors. Table 6.2 demonstrates how radically UK share ownership has changed since 1963.

The trend is obvious. Ownership by individuals has decreased significantly. In the 1990s, share ownership by institutional investors increased dramatically (especially domestic institutional investors). Today, domestic institutional investor share ownership has decreased notably,

Table 6.2 UK share ownership, 1963, 1990, and 2020

IDENTITY OF INVESTOR	% OF SHARES HELD IN 1963	% OF SHARES HELD IN 1990	% OF SHARES HELD IN 2020
Individuals	54	11.8	12
Insurance companies	10	20.4	2.5
Pension funds	6.4	31.7	1.8
Banks	1.3	0.7	3.1
Unit trusts	1.3	6.1	7.4
Overseas investors (largely overseas institutional investors)	7	11.8	56.3

but overseas share ownership (which consists largely of overseas institutional investors) has increased notably. The result is that most shares in quoted companies are controlled by institutional investors. The question to ask is what significance this has in relation to promoting good corporate governance. To answer this question, it is vital that you understand the relationship between the ownership and the control of a company.

6.3.1.1 The separation of ownership and control

In 1932, two American academics named Adolf Berle and Gardiner Means published a book entitled *The Modern Corporation and Private Property*. The text argued that modern corporations had become so large and their members so numerous that the members of such a company had become unwilling, or unable, to exercise any meaningful form of control over its directors. The company's controllers (the directors) had become separated from their owners (the members) and could therefore escape owner control. The result was that the directors were able to engage in activity that benefited themselves, often at the expense of the company and/or the members. Clearly, for Berle and Means, the separation of ownership and control was a significant problem, but it has since become a defining characteristic of large companies in the UK and the USA.

Many academics argued that the growth of institutional investment could halt or even reverse the separation of ownership and control. Many of the corporate governance codes seen in Figure 6.1 have emphasized how important the governance role of institutional investors is and, with the publication of the **UK Stewardship Code** (discussed later in this chapter at 6.3.1.3), there now exists a code devoted solely to encouraging institutional investor engagement. With most of the UK's shares in quoted companies in the hands of institutions, it might once again be possible for the members to intervene in corporate governance affairs and actively participate in the governance of companies. The owners could once again exercise a measure of control, with several American academics predicting that a new era of corporate accountability was on the horizon. This new era of accountability has yet to arrive, however, and institutional investors have generally not been able to live up to the bold promises made on their behalf.

6.3.1.2 The effectiveness of institutional investors

Before we discuss why institutional investors have not been as effective as many hoped, it is worth noting that the level of institutional investor activism may be higher than is apparent because institutional investors tend to engage in 'behind-the-scenes' negotiation. The reason for this is that, if a large institutional investor were to publicly display dissatisfaction with the way that a company is run, other members could panic which could trigger a 'race to the exit'. Certainly, experience has demonstrated that, in many cases, if a dispute between the company and its institutional investor becomes public, then everyone ultimately loses as the company's share price usually slumps. However, even taking into account the institutions' reputation for behind-the-scenes activism, there is still a widespread belief that institutional investors have not yet had the impact that many believed they would. The question is why.

Although over half of UK shares are in the hands of institutional investors, a single institutional investor will, in order to diversify their risk, typically not hold more than 5 per cent of shares in a single company. Accordingly, a single institutional investor will normally need to try and form a coalition with other investors. However, forming and maintaining a coalition of institutional investors can be a difficult task for several reasons:

- Shareholder activism involves expense in terms of time, effort, and cost. As the benefits of shareholder activism usually go to all the members (not just the active ones), it follows that passive members have no real incentive to expend resources in aiding the active members. This is known as the 'free rider' problem as the passive members can free-ride off the active members' efforts. This reduces the members' incentive to voluntarily coop-erate, thereby making it harder to form a coalition of the necessary size.

- Institutional investors can only carry out their functions effectively if they have adequate information on the companies in which they hold shares. Acquiring such information can be costly. For smaller members, the costs of acquiring such information will usually out-weigh the benefits. Larger members, such as institutional investors, may be able to bear the cost of acquiring information, but they will also need to disseminate that information to the other members. The combined costs of acquiring and disseminating the informa-tion may outweigh the benefits that would be gained should their efforts succeed.

A further problem is that, as Table 6.2 indicates, domestic institutional investment has declined notably, and overseas institutional investors are now the single largest group of shareholders in UK quoted companies. The problem is that geographical and logistical reasons will likely impact upon the ability of overseas investors to engage with the UK companies in which they hold shares. As a result, engagement from overseas investors is typically low.

However, despite the fact that institutional investors' activism has not resulted in a new era of accountability and shareholder control, they have still undoubtedly had an impact upon the UK's corporate governance system. In recent years, it has become clear that institutional inves-tors have started to take their governance role more seriously, but this has tended to occur in relation to specific areas, notably directors' remuneration.

 LOOKING FOR EXTRA MARKS?

The last ten years have witnessed a number of instances where remuneration reports have been rejected or have faced significant levels of shareholder opposition (e.g. RBS, AstraZenica, Aviva, Barclays, BP, Royal Mail, Tesco, Morrison Supermarkets). Indeed, some have branded this an example of a 'shareholder spring'. However, such claims are usually overstated and rejections of remuneration reports are notable due to their rarity. Even at the height of the 'shareholder spring' in 2012, the average voting level in fa-vour of a company's remuneration report was over 90 per cent and has remained so since.

There is still much scope for improvement. There are many who have argued that the 2007–8 financial crisis was caused, in part, by the failure of institutional investors to effectively moni-tor banks in which they held shares. The 2009 Walker Review backed this up to an extent by stating that institutional investors were 'slow to act' when concerns arose. Accordingly, the

Review recommended that a code be created that would encourage institutional investors to better engage with their role as stewards of the company.

6.3.1.3 The UK Stewardship Code

In order to encourage greater institutional investor engagement, in July 2010, the FRC published the **UK Stewardship Code**, which, according to Baroness Hogg, the then FRC Chair, was designed to 'be a catalyst for better engagement between shareholders and companies and create a stronger link between governance and the investment process'. The Code was updated in 2012 and 2019, with the 2019 Code being referred to as the **UK Stewardship Code 2020** (as it applies to reporting years beginning on or after 1 January 2020). The Code consists of twelve Principles for asset managers and asset owners (e.g. insurance companies, pension funds), and six Principles for service providers (e.g. investment consultants, proxy advisors).

Relevant persons and organizations may choose to sign up to the Code. The Code operates on an 'apply and explain' basis, under which signatories are expected to explain how they have applied the Code's Principles. Each Principle is followed by details on what information should be reported, and this information should be contained in an annual Stewardship Report. An exception to the apply and explain principle applies to FCA-regulated firms that manage investments on behalf of professional clients. Such firms must explain their commitment to the Code or, where they do not commit to the Code, they must explain their alternative investment strategy (i.e. comply or explain).

LOOKING FOR EXTRA MARKS?

The **UK Stewardship Code** was the first of its kind in the world (although other countries have followed the UK's lead and created Stewardship Codes of their own). As such, it is an extremely important development and you should be prepared to discuss how effective (or ineffective) the Code has been in improving shareholder engagement. Also be prepared to discuss how the 2020 Code differs from its predecessors and whether the 2020 reforms have been effective. The consultation documents that led to the publication of the 2020 Code and their responses will provide you with a significant amount of information on the weaknesses in the 2012 Code and how the 2020 Code sought to address these weaknesses. As to whether it has done so effectively, the FRC published a research study in 2022 that indicated a number of positive changes had come about due to the Code (FRC, 'The Influence of the UK Stewardship Code 2020 on Practice and Reporting' (FRC 2022)). In addition, the FRC publishes annual Reviews of Stewardship Reporting, which look at the number of signatories to the Code and how effective their reporting and implementation of the Stewardship Code has been.

6.3.2 Directors' remuneration

Generally, a director is an office-holder and not an employee (although a director with a service contract will also be an employee). A consequence of this is that directors are not, by default, entitled to be remunerated for acting as director (*Hutton v West Cork Railway Co (1883)*). However, this rule is usually excluded, either by providing for the payment of remuneration in the director's service contract or by including a provision in the company's articles providing the directors with the right to be remunerated for their services. Not only do the model articles provide the directors with a right to be remunerated, but they also provide that the directors themselves should determine the amount of remuneration they are to be paid. In the 1990s, concern over the levels of remuneration that directors were awarding themselves led to directors' remuneration becoming a controversial corporate governance issue. Recently, the remuneration awarded to the executive directors of banks and to prominent CEOs has once again placed the remuneration debate firmly in the public eye.

LOOKING FOR EXTRA MARKS?

If you are looking for detailed, but accessible, information on excessive director remuneration, then a wealth of up-to-date information can be obtained by visiting the website of the High Pay Centre at https://www.highpaycentre.org, or by following it on Twitter at @HighPayCentre.

It is now universally acknowledged that directors' remuneration, and the mechanisms that determine it, are two of the most important factors that shape and direct the board's behaviour. The importance of remuneration as a governance mechanism (and the extent to which it is indicative of income inequality in general) is also evidenced by the increasing amount of statutory regulation in relation to directors' pay. However, the most important mechanism in relation to remuneration is probably the remuneration committee.

6.3.2.1 Remuneration committees

The model articles allow the directors to determine their own pay, meaning that their level of remuneration is, as a matter of law, largely dependent upon their own self-discipline. Concern that directors would award themselves excessive remuneration packages led the Cadbury Committee to conclude that the determination of remuneration should be taken from the executive directors and given to another body, namely a remuneration committee. **Principle Q of the UK Corporate Governance Code** states that:

> A formal and transparent procedure for developing policy on executive remuneration and for determining director and senior management remuneration should be established. No director should be involved in deciding their own remuneration outcome.

Provisions 32 and 33 of the UK Corporate Governance Code then go on to state that the board should establish a remuneration committee consisting of at least three (or two in the case of smaller companies) independent non-executive directors (NEDs), which should have delegated responsibility for determining the remuneration of the executive directors, the chair, and senior management (the **Guidance to Principle Five of the Wates Corporate Governance Principles** contains a similar recommendation). The remuneration of the NEDs should be determined in accordance with the company's articles or by the board (**Provision 34**).

LOOKING FOR EXTRA MARKS?

Despite the fact that virtually all larger companies have established a remuneration committee, there is widespread dissatisfaction amongst academics with the effectiveness of remuneration committees for several reasons:

- Research suggests that companies with a remuneration committee actually pay their directors more than companies without such a committee.

- To ensure independence, the committee should consist entirely of NEDs, but, as is discussed later, at 6.3.3.2, the independence of many NEDs has been doubted.

- It is common for the committee to engage compensation consultants to help determine the levels of remuneration. These consultants may work for the remuneration committee, but are usually hired and/or paid by the executives. For more on the independence of remuneration consultants, see High Pay Centre, 'Are Remuneration Consultants Independent?' (2015), available from https://highpaycentre.org/wp-content/uploads/2020/08/remuneration_consultants_-_FINAL.pdf.

- Many of the excessive remuneration packages that have caused public criticism in recent years were determined by a remuneration committee.

6.3.2.2 Disclosure

Although the UK system of corporate governance is largely voluntary, directors' remuneration is one area where substantial statutory regulation does exist, especially in relation to the disclosure of directors' remuneration. The lack of compliance with the recommendations of the Greenbury Report led to the passing of the **Directors' Remuneration Report Regulations 2002**, the provisions of which have now been placed into **Pt 15 of the CA 2006** and accompanying subordinate legislation. These provisions require companies to disclose in their annual accounts significant amounts of information relating to directors' remuneration. Additionally, the directors of quoted or traded companies must prepare a directors' remuneration report which must contain extensive details regarding the directors' remuneration (**CA 2006, s 420**). Every member is entitled to a copy of the report.

 LOOKING FOR EXTRA MARKS?

The aim behind these provisions is to inform the company's members and other interested parties and there is no doubt that the disclosure requirements are extensive. However, whilst the legislation states what the directors must disclose, it did not, until recently, state how the information should be disclosed, leading to companies disclosing masses of technical information that only served to confuse members. Fortunately, **Sch 8 of the Large and Medium-Sized Companies and Groups (Accounts and Reports) Regulations 2008** was amended in 2013 to require quoted companies to provide in the remuneration report a standardized table that sets out a single total figure of remuneration for each director. This should allow for better comparison of remuneration between directors and across companies.

Granting the members access to details concerning the directors' remuneration would be of little value if they could not then use that information to hold the directors to account. Accordingly, **s 439 of the CA 2006** provides the company's members with the opportunity to approve the non-policy section of the remuneration report. It should be noted that a failure to obtain member approval will not invalidate the report—the members' role under **s 439** in relation to the non-policy part of the report is advisory only (as is discussed later, the members' vote is binding in relation to the policy section of the report). Even though the members' role in relation to the non-policy part of the report is advisory only, a rejection of a company's remuneration report will be extremely humiliating and, in most cases, the company will take corrective action.

REVISION TIP

Back up your discussion with practical examples. An excellent example that demonstrates the consequences of the members refusing to approve the remuneration report (the first time such a rejection had occurred) happened in 2003 when the remuneration report of GlaxoSmithKline plc was rejected by its members. Following the defeat, GlaxoSmithKline reduced drastically the **golden parachute** of its CEO, as well as halving the length of his service contract, and removed two key members from its remuneration committee.

If you are looking for examples of companies that had their remuneration report/policy rejected, then an excellent source is the public register maintained by the Investment Association (https://www.theia.org/public-register). This provides a searchable database of all resolutions tabled by FTSE All-Share companies, so you can easily locate resolutions rejecting remuneration reports/policies (and any other resolution).

Not all companies acted as Glaxo did, and some companies took no action at all, leading a government consultation document to state that 'historical voting records, feedback from shareholders and anecdotal evidence suggest that not all companies are responding adequately to shareholder concerns' ('Shareholder Pay: Shareholder Voting Rights Consultation' (BIS, 2012)). The government therefore decided to strengthen the members' say on pay, which led to a new **s 439A** being introduced into the **CA 2006**, which provides that a quoted company must table an ordinary resolution at the accounts meeting (usually the AGM) to decide whether to approve the remuneration policy section of the remuneration report. This resolution need not take place every year, but must take place at least every three years. The key feature of this resolution is that it is binding and a quoted company cannot make a remuneration payment to a director unless it is consistent with the remuneration policy or it has been approved by a resolution of the members (**CA 2006, s 226B(1)**). Any payments that contravene this will be of no effect and will be held by the recipient on trust for the company (**CA 2006, s 226E(1)**). The following example demonstrates the weaknesses of the advisory vote and how the presence of the binding vote can have a stronger effect on director pay.

EXAMPLE

The remuneration report and policy of BP plc were approved at its 2014 AGM. In 2015, as a result of the Deepwater Horizon incident and falling oil prices, BP posted its largest ever operating loss (£4.5 billion) and announced it was axing 7,000 jobs. Despite this, the company awarded its CEO, Bob Dudley, a 20 per cent pay increase, taking his pay up to £14 million. Institutional investors were angered by this and, at the 2016 AGM, 59.29 per cent of shareholders voted to reject the company's remuneration report. However, this vote was advisory only and no action was taken (indeed, Dudley had already received the money).

Conscious that the remuneration policy would be subject to a binding vote in 2017, BP's chairman ordered a review of its remuneration policy and entered into talks with major shareholders. The result was that Dudley's pay for 2017 was cut by 40 per cent to £9.3 million, the bonus scheme was amended to make it more difficult to earn bonuses, and the size of bonus payments was reduced. As a result of these changes, both the remuneration report and the remuneration policy were approved by over 97 per cent of shareholders at the 2017 AGM.

The introduction of the binding vote has had little overall effect and it is still very rare for a company's remuneration report or policy to be rejected. Since 2017, only twenty-four companies in the FTSE All-Share have had their remuneration reports rejected, and only two companies have had their remuneration policies rejected.

LOOKING FOR EXTRA MARKS?

Successive governments are perpetually coming up with reforms to try and deal with the issue of excessive directors' pay, and you should stay up to date with these reforms and be prepared to comment on them. The **Companies (Miscellaneous Reporting) Regulations 2018** contain several modest reforms relating to directors' pay, of which the most notable is the requirement that quoted companies with more than 250 employees must report annually on the ratio of CEO pay to average worker pay. Arguably, more useful reforms have come independently from other bodies. For example, the Investment Association has created a public register of FTSE companies that have received significant levels of shareholder opposition (defined as over 20 per cent) to proposed resolutions.

6.3.3 Non-executive directors

Over the last twenty to thirty years, the UK corporate governance system has come to place great emphasis on the importance of NEDs, with the Higgs Report branding them as the 'custodians of the governance process'. Indeed, the **UK Corporate Governance Code** places such importance on their role that **Provision 11** states that at least half the board, excluding the chair, should consist of NEDs whom the board considers to be independent.

6.3.3.1 What is a NED?

The **CA 2006** does not define what a NED is—in fact, it never uses the phrase 'non-executive director' and does not distinguish between executive directors and NEDs (see **CA 2006, s 250** discussed at 4.1). There is no doubt, however, that the NEDs do differ substantially from their executive counterparts, as Table 6.3 demonstrates.

Table 6.3 Executive and non-executive directors

	EXECUTIVE DIRECTORS	NON-EXECUTIVE DIRECTORS
Role	Engage in the day-to-day management of the company	Involved in management, but should also monitor the executives
Employment status	Usually appointed under an employment contract, so will be employees	Usually appointed via a letter of appointment and are therefore not employees
Full-time or part-time	Usually full-time	Part-time (usually around 1–2 days per month)
Remuneration	NEDs are paid much less than executive directors	

Perhaps the most noteworthy difference is in relation to their role. Whereas the executives' key role is the management of the company, the NEDs' role is to be involved in management and to monitor the executive directors. **Principle H of the UK Corporate Governance Code** states that NEDs should 'provide constructive challenge, strategic guidance, offer specialist advice and hold management to account'.

LOOKING FOR EXTRA MARKS?

The role of NEDs envisaged by the **UK Corporate Governance Code** has been criticized. It has been argued that the NEDs' two roles (i.e. management and monitoring of management) do not sit easily with one another and that the monitoring function of NEDs will have the effect of segregating them from the executives, thereby creating a split board. Some have argued that this will impose an implicit two-tier board philosophy upon a unitary board structure.

6.3.3.2 Independence

NEDs cannot effectively monitor management, nor can they bring a neutral viewpoint to developing policy, if they are not independent of the executives. **Provision 10 of the UK Corporate Governance Code** states that the annual report should identify which directors the board considers to be independent—the Code also provides a list of relationships or circumstances that are likely to, or could, impair a director's independence (e.g. the director is a significant shareholder or former employee of the company). The aim of **Provision 10** is to ensure that the NEDs are genuinely independent, and not merely independent in name.

REVISION TIP

Students often misunderstand **Provision 10** and state incorrectly that a director who falls within the list of specified relationships or circumstances will not be independent. **Provision 10** is not this absolute and merely provides that if such a director is identified as independent then the board should explain why in the annual report (which means that it is the directors who determine whether a NED is independent or not). Interestingly, **Provision 15** of the proposed 2018 Code provided that if any of the relationships or circumstances apply, then the NED should not be considered independent, but this did not make it into the final 2018 Code. Given the importance of NEDs being independent, do you think that the proposed **Provision 15** would have been more effective than the finalized **Provision 10**?

Unfortunately, there exists general concern over the independence and effectiveness of NEDs for several reasons:

- As NEDs work part-time, they are unlikely to have sufficient time to become fully conversant with the company's business. Accordingly, they will likely rely on the executives to draw their attention to what is important and the executives may be tempted to be selective in passing information onto the NEDs.

- Many NEDs are executives themselves for other companies. They may socialize with the executives they are tasked with monitoring and, as a result, it has been argued that many NEDs share the executives' ideologies and are likely to pull their punches for fear of encouraging their own NEDs to monitor critically.

- The appointment of NEDs is a cause for concern. Although the appointment of directors of listed companies is meant to be led by a nomination committee consisting of a majority of independent NEDs, the Higgs Report noted that the nomination committee is often the 'least developed of the board's committees' and this remains the case (as noted in Grant Thornton's 2019 Corporate Governance Review). There is also a widespread belief that the CEO of the company will often play a significant behind-the-scenes role in selecting the nominees, thereby diminishing the committee's independence.

REVISION TIP

In an essay question concerning the effectiveness of NEDs, it is crucial that you discuss the importance of independence, the extent to which NEDs are actually independent in practice, and how a lack of independence can affect a NED's ability to perform effectively.

KEY DEBATES

Topic	Corporate governance
Author/Academic	Financial Reporting Council
Viewpoint	Discusses the extent to which companies comply with, and effectively report on, the UK Corporate Governance Code.
Source	'Review of Corporate Governance Reporting' (FRC 2022)

Topic	Non-executive directors
Author/Academic	Charanjit Singh, Wangwei Lin, and Zhen Ye
Viewpoint	Discusses the evolving role, responsibilities, and liabilities of non-executive directors.
Source	'Reimagining the role, duties and liabilities of non-executive directors in 2020; 15 years of the Companies Act 2006 and the pathway to the UK Corporate Governance Code 2018, Parts 1 and 2' (2021) 32 ICCLR 20 and 89

Topic	Institutional investors
Author/Academic	Bobby V Reddy
Viewpoint	Discusses the effectiveness of the updates made to the UK Stewardship Code 2020.
Source	'The Emperor's New Code? Time to Re-evaluate the Nature of Stewardship Engagement Under the UK's Stewardship Code' (2021) 84 MLR 842

EXAM QUESTIONS

Essay question

'The effectiveness of the corporate governance recommendations contained in the UK Corporate Governance Code is heavily dependent upon the ability of the non-executive directors. Unfortunately, non-executive directors are subject to numerous limitations that render them a largely ineffective corporate governance mechanism.'

Discuss the validity of this statement.

See the Outline answers section in the endmatter for help with this question.

Problem question

Skyweb plc is a large company specializing in software research. Its board consists of ten directors, six of whom hold executive office, with each director requiring reappointment every four years. The company's shares have had a premium listing on the London Stock Exchange for the last two years.

The company decides to expand its board by appointing two new directors, one of whom will be a non-executive director. The board's nomination committee, which consists of three non-executives and two executives (one of whom is the company's Chairman), nominates several candidates to be put to the general meeting. Unfortunately, one member of the nomination committee did not contribute to the committee's work, as he was recently appointed for the first time to the office of director and had not yet received any training on his roles and responsibilities.

The company has made a handsome profit. Accordingly, the executives believe that all the directors of the board should receive a 25 per cent pay rise. The pay increase is agreed upon at a meeting of the entire board. The remuneration of all the directors consists solely of a base salary and the directors' service contracts are two years in length.

Several large institutional investors have expressed concern over the competence of the company's auditor. Accordingly, it is decided that Skyweb will appoint a new auditor. John, the CEO and Chairman, has a friend who has a reputation for being a very competent and thorough auditor. Accordingly, John convinces the board that his friend should be nominated. The appointment is confirmed by the company at the AGM. The newly appointed auditor also provides additional non-audit services to the company as and when required.

Adam is considering purchasing a substantial number of shares in Skyweb. However, he is concerned about the company's commitment to good corporate governance practices and, based on these events, he asks for your advice regarding any examples of poor corporate governance practices that the company might have engaged in.

 Online resources

For an outline answer to this problem question, as well as multiple-choice questions and further reading, please visit the online resources.

Capital and capital maintenance

7

- The two principal types of capital that companies acquire are share capital (capital obtained by selling shares) and debt capital (capital borrowed from others).

- A new allotment of shares must usually first be offered to existing shareholders.

- Companies are prohibited from allotting shares for less than their nominal value.

- Companies can issue different classes of shares with different class rights and the law regulates the ability to vary such class rights.

- Public companies are subject to minimum capital requirements when commencing business, whereas private companies are not.

- A reduction of share capital is only valid if the strict procedures relating to a reduction of capital found in the Companies Act 2006 are complied with.

- Companies are generally prohibited from purchasing their own shares, but the 2006 Act does provide exceptions to this prohibition.

- Private companies are permitted to provide financial assistance to acquire their own shares. Public companies are generally prohibited from providing such assistance, but there are exceptions.

- Companies can only pay a dividend out of 'profits available for the purpose'.

- The two principal types of charge are fixed charges and floating charges and, in order to be enforceable, charges need to be registered in accordance with the Companies Act 2006.

CHAPTER OVERVIEW

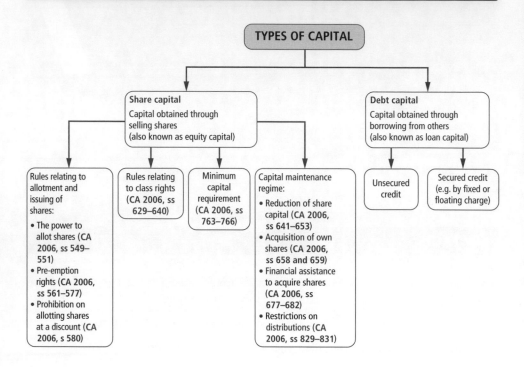

7.1 Shares and share capital

Section 540(1) of the CA 2006 defines a 'share' as a 'share in the company's share capital', but this definition fails to fully articulate the true nature of a share. A share is an item of property (**CA 2006, s 541**). Being intangible, a share has no physical existence, but instead confers a number of rights and liabilities upon its holder, including providing evidence of the existence of a contract between the shareholder and the company (this contract is discussed at 3.2). It is important to note that share ownership does not give the shareholder a proprietary right over the assets of the company (*Borland's Trustee v Steel Bros & Co Ltd* [1901]), as the assets belong to the corporate entity.

7.1.1 Classifications of share capital

The capital that the company acquires through the selling of shares is known as '**share capital**' or 'equity capital'. The law relating to share capital is terminology heavy, and an exposition of the terminology that you will encounter will be of use.

7.1.1.1 Nominal value

All shares in a limited company with a share capital are required to have a fixed '**nominal value**' and failure to attach a nominal value to an allotment of shares will render that allotment void (**CA 2006, s 542(2)**). The nominal value is a notional value of a share's worth, but in reality it may bear no resemblance to a share's actual value. The nominal value of a share represents the minimum price for which the share can be allotted and, as is discussed at 1.4.2, it also helps in determining the liability of a shareholder in the event of the company being liquidated. It is common for shares to be allotted for more than their nominal value, and the excess (i.e. the difference between the nominal value and the purchase price) is known as the '**share premium**'.

7.1.1.2 Authorized share capital

Under the **CA 1985**, companies were required to state in their memoranda the total nominal value of shares that could be allotted by the company and this value represented the company's authorized share capital. Accordingly, a company with an authorized share capital of £1 million could not allot shares with a combined nominal value of more than £1 million. For example, it could allot a million shares with a nominal value of £1, or 500,000 shares with a nominal value of £2, and so on.

LOOKING FOR EXTRA MARKS?

Essays often require you to critically evaluate law reforms and there is little doubt that the requirement to state the authorized share capital was rather pointless, for two reasons. First, many companies would simply choose an arbitrary and inflated figure, confident that it would never be reached. Second, even if that figure was reached, the company could increase the authorized share capital by simply passing an ordinary resolution.

Companies incorporated under the **CA 2006** do not need to state an authorized share capital and are therefore not limited in terms of the number of shares they can issue (unless they choose to include an authorized share capital clause in their articles). However, companies incorporated under prior Companies Acts may still have their authorized share capital stated in their memoranda and, as regards such companies, their ability to allot shares will be limited to the amount stated (although the statement can be removed).

7.1.1.3 Allotted, issued, and unissued share capital

The total nominal value of shares that actually has been allotted is known as the '**allotted share capital**'. So, for example, a company that has allotted 3 million shares that have a nominal value of £5 each would have an allotted share capital of £15 million. Once allotted shares have been registered to a member in the register of members, those shares are said to be issued, with the '**issued share capital**' representing the total nominal value of shares that have been issued (**CA 2006, s 546(1)(a)**). 'Unissued' share capital represents the difference between the authorized share capital and the issued share capital (i.e. the nominal value of shares that could still be issued). Obviously, companies that have no authorized share capital limitation will not have an unissued share capital.

7.1.1.4 Paid-up, called-up, and uncalled share capital

Companies may require full payment of shares upon allotment (as is the case in most private companies), or may permit part-payment on allotment with the remainder due at a later date. The combined total of the nominal share capital that has actually been paid is known as the '**paid-up share capital**'.

EXAMPLE (FICTIONAL)

FakeCo plc has allotted a million shares in total with a nominal value of £1 each (accordingly, its allotted share capital is £1 million). The company allows allottees to pay 50 pence per share upon allotment and the remainder at a later date to be specified by the company. All of the million shares are allotted and purchased, and every shareholder pays 50 pence per share only. FakeCo's paid-up share capital is therefore £500,000 (1 million shares × 50 pence).

If shares are partly paid for on allotment, the company can call for the remainder (or part of the remainder) to be paid, or the company might have required payment in instalments and an instalment has become due. The paid-up share capital plus the amount called for or the instalment due is known as the '**called-up share capital**'.

EXAMPLE (FICTIONAL)

Following on from the previous FakeCo example, the company calls for 25 pence per share on all unpaid shares to be paid. This will result in a total of £250,000 (1 million shares × 25 pence) becoming due. Accordingly, the called-up share capital will be £750,000 (i.e. £500,000 (paid-up share capital) + £250,000 (the amount that has been called upon)). Note that the amount called for forms part of the called-up share capital irrespective of whether it is actually paid or not.

The difference between a company's issued share capital and its called-up share capital is known as the **'uncalled share capital'** (i.e. the amount remaining to be called upon by the company).

7.1.2 The allotment and issuing of shares

There are two principal methods by which a person can become a shareholder in a company:

1. by obtaining new shares from the company, or

2. as shares are freely transferable items of property (subject to any limitations found in the articles), he can become a shareholder by obtaining shares (through sale, gift, bequest, etc.) from an existing shareholder.

Exam questions in this area usually relate to the company's ability to allot and issue shares and so this section of the chapter will focus on the first method. It is worth noting that, whilst the terms 'allotment' and 'issue' tend to be used interchangeably, there is a distinction, namely:

- Shares are allotted 'when a person acquires the unconditional right to be included in the company's register of members in respect of the shares' **(CA 2006, s 558)**.

- Shares are issued when the person's name is actually entered into the register of members (*National Westminster Bank v IRC* **[1995]**). From this, it follows that the issuing of shares takes place after they have been allotted.

7.1.2.1 The power to allot shares

The **CA 2006** lays down strict procedures regarding the allotment of shares and any director who knowingly permits or authorizes an unlawful allotment will commit an either way offence, although the allotment itself will remain valid **(CA 2006, s 549(4)–(6))**. The rules regarding the issuing of shares and the authorization required are set out in Table 7.1.

REVISION TIP

As is discussed at 4.4.2.1, many cases concerning the **s 171(b)** duty on directors to exercise their powers for the purpose for which they are conferred relate to the directors' power to allot shares. Accordingly, you will need to be aware of the link between directors' duties and the power to allot shares, as a problem question may combine the two topics. If a problem question involves the directors issuing shares, **s 171(b)** may be relevant.

Table 7.1 The power to allot shares

TYPE OF COMPANY	POWER TO ISSUE SHARES	PROVISIONS IN THE ARTICLES
Private company with only one class of share that wishes to allot shares of the same class	**Section 550 of the CA 2006** provides that the directors may allot shares of the same class, except to the extent that they are prohibited from doing so by the company's articles.	A provision in the articles empowering the directors to issue shares is not required, but the articles may limit the directors' power to allot shares (the model articles contain no such limitation).
Any other type of company, namely: • a private company with multiple classes of share; • a private company with only one class of share that wishes to allot a different class of share; • a public company	**Section 551 of the CA 2006** provides that the directors will only have the power to allot shares if: (a) they are authorized to do so by the company's articles; or (b) the members pass a resolution authorizing the directors to allot shares.	A provision in the articles is required, unless the members have authorized the allotment. The model articles contain no such authorization, but do provide that, subject to the articles, the company may issue shares of a different class with such rights or restrictions as may be determined by ordinary resolution.

7.1.2.2 Pre-emption rights

An inevitable consequence of an allotment of shares is that the shareholdings of existing shareholders (and consequently, their voting power and the return on their investment) will be diluted. The allotment may even cause control of the company to be transferred to a new person. To prevent these consequences occurring without shareholder consent, existing shareholders are given a right of **pre-emption**, meaning that any new allotment of shares must first be offered to the existing shareholders and must allow them to maintain their existing holdings (**CA 2006, s 561(1)**).

EXAMPLE (FICTIONAL)

FakeCo Ltd has issued 1,000 shares, divided between Jayne (100 shares), Ian (300 shares), and Katja (600 shares). The company decides to issue another 5,000 shares. In order to comply with the three shareholders' pre-emption rights, FakeCo will need to offer:
- 500 shares to Jayne, to maintain her 10 per cent holding;
- 1,500 shares to Ian, to maintain his 30 per cent holding;
- 3,000 shares to Katja, to maintain her 60 per cent holding.

If an allotment is made that contravenes the pre-emption rights of existing shareholders, then the allotment will remain valid, but the company and every officer who knowingly authorized the allotment will be liable to compensate the shareholders who would have benefited from the pre-emptive offer.

You should also remember that, in certain circumstances, the shareholders' pre-emption rights can be limited (e.g. where the shares allotted are **bonus shares**) or even completely excluded (e.g. where a private company has a provision in its articles excluding pre-emption rights). For best practice guidance on disapplying pre-emption rights, see the Pre-Emption Group's Statement of Principles, available from https://www.frc.org.uk/investors/pre-emption-group.

REVISION TIP

Problem questions involving a company that allots shares to an outside party against the wishes of existing shareholders are reasonably common. Be prepared to discuss whether or not the pre-emption rights of the existing shareholders have been breached. Essay questions might focus on the effectiveness and rationale of the pre-emption rules. For an analysis of the law relating to pre-emption rights and a discussion of why such rights are needed, see Paul Myners, 'Pre-Emption Rights: Final Report' (DTI 2005).

7.1.2.3 Prohibition on allotting shares at a discount

Section 580 of the CA 2006 provides that shares cannot be allotted at a discount (i.e. for less than their nominal value). Any contract that purports to allot shares at a discount is void and, if shares actually are allotted at a discount, the allottee is liable to pay the company an amount equal to the discount including interest. The company and every officer in default also commit an either-way offence.

However, the effectiveness of the prohibition, at least in relation to private companies, is weakened by the fact that shares do not have to be paid for in cash. **Section 582(1) of the CA 2006** provides that shares can be paid for in 'money or money's worth', and it is reasonably common for shares to be paid for in goods, in property, by providing a service, or by transferring an existing business to the company in return for shares (as Mr Salomon did). By overvaluing the non-cash consideration, private companies can effectively issue shares at a discount. This problem would be lessened if the courts were regularly willing to monitor the value of non-cash consideration, but the courts have stated that 'so long as the company honestly regards the consideration given as fairly representing the nominal value of the shares in cash, its estimate ought not to be critically examined' (***Ooregum Gold Mining Co of India Ltd v Roper* [1892]**). The result of this is that the courts will only review the adequacy of non-cash consideration where it is clearly colourable or illusory (***Re Wragg Ltd* [1897]**). Accordingly, private companies can easily avoid the prohibition should they choose to do so.

REVISION TIP

In an exam question requiring you to evaluate the effectiveness of the rules relating to the allotment of shares, the ineffectiveness of the law to prevent private companies from issuing shares at a discount is a notable weakness you should discuss.

Regarding public companies, the rules are more stringent in three ways. First, public companies cannot accept payment for shares in the form of services (**CA 2006, s 585(1)**). Second, if a public company allots shares for non-cash consideration, then that consideration must be independently valued by a person eligible for appointment as the company's auditor (**CA 2006, ss 593 and 1150**). This person must confirm that the value of the non-cash consideration is at least equal to the amount paid up on the shares. Third, a public company must not allot shares as fully or partly paid up for non-cash consideration if the consideration is or includes an undertaking which is to be performed more than five years after the date of the allotment (**CA 2006, s 587(1)**).

7.1.3 Classes of share

Most companies will only have one class of share and, in such companies, all the shareholders will have the same rights. However, providing that the articles so authorize (the model articles provide that companies may issue shares of a different class with such rights as may be determined by ordinary resolution), a company is free to issue different classes of share that confer different rights upon the holder. Examples of share classes include:

- **Ordinary shares**: If a company only has one class of shares, then they will be ordinary shares. Unless the articles provide otherwise, ordinary shareholders will typically have (i) the right to vote at general meetings, (ii) the right to a dividend once validly declared, and (iii) the right to surplus capital once the creditors have been paid in the event of a company's winding up. A company may have multiple classes of ordinary shares (e.g. ordinary shares with voting rights and non-voting ordinary shares).

- **Preference shares**: The precise rights granted to preference shareholders will depend upon the articles or terms of the share issue, but preference shares normally provide the holder with preferential claims on any surplus assets on winding up and/or entitle the holder to a predetermined fixed percentage dividend before anything is payable to the ordinary shareholders.

- **Deferred shares**: Deferred shares (or 'founders' shares') typically provide that their holders are not entitled to a dividend or surplus assets upon liquidation unless the ordinary shareholders have first been paid. Deferred shares were once common, but are rare today.

- **Redeemable shares**: Redeemable shares (discussed at 7.2.2.1) offer their holder temporary membership and can be bought back by the company, usually upon the company or holder's insistence.

7.1.3.1 Variation of class rights

The rights attached to differing classes of shares are known as '**class rights**' and shareholders of one class might attempt to change or remove the class rights of shareholders of another class (especially if the class rights confer a benefit upon the latter class of shareholders). The **CA 2006** provides that a variation of class rights will only be effective if strict formalities are complied with. It is therefore important to know what constitutes a 'variation'. One might assume that any alteration of a class right would constitute a variation, but this is not the case. The courts distinguish between an alteration that affects a class right (which may amount to a variation) and an alteration that merely affects the enjoyment of a class right (which will not amount to a variation) (*White v Bristol Aeroplane Co Ltd* [1953]). As the following case demonstrates, this has resulted in the courts taking a restrictive approach as to what constitutes a variation.

Re Mackenzie and Co Ltd [1916] 2 Ch 450 (Ch)

Facts: The company issued preference shares with a nominal value of £20 each. These shares entitled their owners to a 4 per cent dividend on the amount paid up and, as the shares were fully paid up, this equated to 80 pence per share. The articles were amended to reduce the nominal value of the preference shares to £12, thereby reducing the dividend to 48 pence per share.

Held: The alteration of the articles did not constitute a variation of a class right, as the right remained the same (i.e. 4 per cent of the amount paid up). Accordingly, the alteration had not affected the class right—it had simply affected the enjoyment of that right by rendering it less valuable. Providing that the right itself remains the same, the fact that an alteration renders the right less valuable (or even worthless), will prevent the alteration from amounting to a variation.

LOOKING FOR EXTRA MARKS?

Think about how shareholders can protect themselves. The courts' reluctance to hold that an alteration amounts to a variation must be regarded as a reduction of the protection afforded to shareholders who have had their class rights rendered less valuable. Powerful shareholders may be able to protect their class rights by inserting a provision into the articles that specifies what alterations to class rights will require a class meeting (see e.g. *Re Northern Engineering Industries plc* [1994]).

Sections 630 and **631 of the CA 2006** provide that class rights can only be varied in one of two ways:

1. if the company's articles contain a clause stating how class rights are to be varied, then a variation will be valid if it complies with that clause; or

2. if the company's articles do not contain a class rights variation clause, then a variation will be valid if it is (i) approved in writing by the holders of three-quarters in nominal value of the issued shares of the class in question, or (ii) approved by the passing of a special resolution at a meeting of holders of that class of share.

When voting on a variation to a class right, the shareholders must exercise their vote for the dominant purpose of benefiting the class as a whole (*British America Nickel Corp Ltd v MJ O'Brien Ltd* [1927]).

7.1.4 Minimum capital requirement

Private companies with a share capital are not subject to a minimum share capital requirement and can accordingly be set up by issuing a single 1 pence share to a single person. Conversely, a public company cannot conduct business until it has been issued with a trading certificate and the registrar of companies will not issue such a certificate unless he is satisfied that the nominal value of the company's allotted share capital is not less than £50,000 (**CA 2006, s 763(1)(a)**).

This minimum capital requirement aims to ensure that there is always a minimum level of capital available in order to satisfy the company's debts. However, in reality, it is universally acknowledged that the minimum capital requirement does little to aid creditors, for three reasons:

1. The figure of £50,000 is simply too low to offer creditors any real protection and has been described as 'miniscule compared to the debts of most public companies' (Louise Gullifer and Jennifer Payne, *Corporate Finance Law: Principles and Policy* (Hart Publishing, 2011) 127).

2. The shares do not even need to be fully paid up—only one-quarter of the nominal value and the whole of the premium need be paid up at the time of allotment (**CA 2006, s 586(1)**) and shares issued at the time of incorporation must be paid for in cash. The result is that a newly formed public company may have only £12,500 in cash when it starts business (with the right to call on the shareholders for at least a further £37,500).

3. The authorized minimum is measured at the time the company commences trading, but little account is taken of the fact that it may be reduced once trading commences. If the level of capital does fall below half the company's called-up capital, then a general meeting must be called to discuss what steps should be taken (**CA 2006, s 656(1)**), but by the time the assets reach this level, it is likely that some form of insolvency procedure will be in place, thereby rendering the general meeting useless. Even if this is not the case, the Act does not require that the meeting take any action.

 REVISION TIP

Whilst the **CA 2006** might contain several useful reforms in relation to share capital, it has done nothing to improve the effectiveness of the minimum capital requirement. Be aware of the weaknesses in the law that the 2006 Act has failed, or been unable, to remedy.

7.2 Capital maintenance

Having obtained share capital through the selling of shares, the law requires that the company 'maintain' that capital by not distributing it in unauthorized ways. The rationale behind this requirement is one of creditor protection—it is to the company's capital that the creditors look for payment and the less capital the company has, the greater the risk will be that the company will default and the creditors will not be paid. The creditors will expect capital to rise and fall in the course of trading, but will not expect the company to return capital to the shareholders (***Trevor v Whitworth* (1887)**). Accordingly, through a series of rules known collectively as the '**capital maintenance regime**', the law prohibits capital from being returned to the shareholders. Each rule will now be discussed.

REVISION TIP

The capital maintenance regime is an important topic and an exam question may require you to apply the rules to a set of facts (in the case of a problem question) or to discuss the effectiveness of the various rules or a single rule (in the case of an essay question). Alternatively, an essay question may focus on the effectiveness of the capital maintenance reforms contained in the **CA 2006**. Do they provide the creditors with adequate protection?

7.2.1 Alteration of share capital

A company may decide to alter the structure of its share capital, with **s 617** providing seven examples of share capital alteration, including:

- a company may increase its share capital by allotting new shares,
- a company may subdivide shares into shares of a smaller nominal value (e.g. converting 100 £10 shares into 200 £5 shares), or
- a company may consolidate its share capital by merging existing shares into shares of a higher nominal value (e.g. converting 100 £1 shares into 10 £10 shares).

These forms of share capital alteration do not adversely affect the level of share capital and so creditor interests are not jeopardized. However, a reduction of share capital may adversely affect the creditors' interests and so such reductions are heavily regulated. A reduction of capital will be unlawful unless the procedures found in **ss 641–653 of the CA 2006** are complied with. These sections provide companies with two methods to reduce share capital, namely (i) special resolution and court confirmation, and (ii) special resolution supported by a solvency statement.

LOOKING FOR EXTRA MARKS?

Be aware of how the law has changed in this area. The **CA 1985** stated that companies could only reduce capital if their articles so permitted, a special resolution was obtained, and the reduction was approved by the courts. Obtaining court approval proved to be unduly burdensome for many smaller companies (not to mention increasing the courts' caseload), so the 2006 Act provides private companies with a method of reducing capital that does not require court approval. This is an undoubted benefit for smaller companies, although the lack of court approval may arguably result in less scrutiny of the reduction.

7.2.1.1 Special resolution and court confirmation

The first method of effecting a reduction of capital is available to all types of company and provides that a reduction will be valid where the company authorizes the reduction by passing a special resolution and the company then applies to the court for an order confirming the reduction (**CA 2006, ss 641(1)(b) and 645**). If a public company wishes to reduce its share capital below the authorized minimum discussed earlier (£50,000), then the registrar of companies will not register the reduction unless the company first re-registers as private, or unless the court so directs (**CA 2006, s 650(2)**).

Court confirmation provides a significant measure of creditor protection as the courts' principal concern will be the protection of the company's creditors. This is backed up by **s 646**, which provides certain creditors with the right to object to the reduction. The interests of shareholders are also taken into account and the court will aim to determine whether the reduction would be fair and equitable between different classes of shareholders and between shareholders of the same class (*Scottish Insurance Corporation Ltd v Wilsons & Clyde Coal Ltd* **[1949]**). In practice, it is extremely rare for the court to not confirm a reduction, because the reduction is usually designed in such a way as to elicit the shareholders' and creditors' support.

7.2.1.2 Special resolution supported by solvency statement

The second method of effecting a reduction is available to private companies only and does not require court approval. A private company can effect a reduction of capital by passing a special resolution authorizing the reduction, supported by a statement of solvency from the directors (**CA 2006, ss 641(1)(a) and 642**). This statement must be made no more than fifteen days before the resolution is passed and states that the directors have formed the opinion that:

- there is no ground on which the company could then be found to be unable to pay its debts, and
- the company will be able to pay its debts as they fall due during the year immediately following the date of the statement. If the company is to be wound up within twelve months of the statement being made, the directors must be of the opinion that the company will be able to pay its debts in full within twelve months of the winding up commencing.

If the directors make this statement without reasonable grounds for the opinions expressed within it, every director who is in default commits an either way offence, although the reduction will remain valid.

7.2.2 The acquisition of own shares

The common law absolutely prohibited companies from purchasing their own existing shares as this would involve returning capital to the shareholders (*Trevor v Whitworth* **(1887)**) and would therefore reduce the funds available to pay the creditors. **Section 658 of the CA 2006** maintains a strict approach by providing that a limited company cannot acquire its own shares, except in accordance with the procedures laid down in the **CA 2006**. If these procedures are not followed, the purported acquisition of shares is void, and the company and every officer of the company in default will commit an either way offence. A company can acquire its own shares in one of two ways.

7.2.2.1 Redeemable shares

A company can acquire shares that it has issued as **redeemable shares** (**CA 2006, s 684**). Redeemable shares offer temporary membership of a company and tend to provide that the shares can be redeemed (i.e. bought back) by the company, usually upon the insistence of the company or the shareholder, or after a stated period has passed. To ensure that capital is not reduced, the company must pay for the shares out of its distributable profits or out of a fresh issue of shares (**CA 2006, s 687(2)**), although a specific method does exist whereby private companies can redeem shares out of capital.

7.2.2.2 Purchase by a company of its own shares

Redeemable shares are useful, but they do suffer from a notable flaw. Only redeemable shares can be redeemed, so they must be issued as redeemable shares, which requires a measure of foresight on behalf of the directors. What companies wanted was the power to acquire any shares (including redeemable shares) and this is often referred to as a 'share buyback'. Such a power exists under **s 690 of the CA 2006**. Several safeguards exist, including:

- only limited companies may acquire their own shares;
- the shares acquired must be fully paid up and, when purchasing the shares, the company must pay for the shares upon purchase;
- purchase of the shares must be made from distributable profits, or out of a fresh issue of shares (although there is a specific method whereby private companies can purchase their own shares out of capital).

Additional safeguards are provided depending whether the purchase is to take place on a recognized investment exchange. Basically, where the purchase is to take place on such an exchange, the additional safeguards imposed by the Act are less extensive as investment exchanges have their own safeguards in place.

7.2.3 Financial assistance to acquire shares

Since the **Companies Act 1928**, companies have been generally prohibited from providing financial assistance to another to purchase their shares on the ground that it would allow a company to manipulate its share price by providing assistance to others to purchase its shares. Exceptions did exist, but they were narrow and strictly regulated. The problem was that this prohibition served to prevent innocent and commercially beneficial transactions, especially ones involving private companies. Accordingly, as regards private companies, the prohibition is now much narrower and only applies in specified circumstances:

1. Where a person is acquiring, or proposing to acquire, shares in a public company, then that company or a subsidiary of that company is prohibited from giving financial assistance directly or indirectly for the purpose of the acquisition before or at the same time as the acquisition took place (**s 678(1)**). **Section 678(3)** contains an identical prohibition for when the shares have already been acquired and paid for, but the financial assistance is provided after the acquisition took place.

2. Where a person is acquiring, or proposing to acquire, shares in a private company, it is not lawful for a public company that is a subsidiary of that private company to give financial assistance directly or indirectly for the purpose of the acquisition before or at the same

time as the acquisition took place (**s 679(1)**). **Section 679(3)** contains an identical prohibition for when the shares have already been acquired and paid for, but the financial assistance is provided after the acquisition took place.

From this, it can be seen that the prohibition now largely applies to public companies only, and has been largely abolished as regards private companies. Contravention of the prohibition constitutes an either way offence (**s 680(1)**) and an agreement to provide unlawful financial assistance will be generally unenforceable (***Heald v O'Connor* [1971]**). The recipient of the assistance will also be required to account for the sum received if they knew of the impropriety of the transaction (***Belmont Finance Corp v Williams Furniture Ltd (No 2)* [1980]**).

LOOKING FOR EXTRA MARKS?

A convincing justification for the prohibition on financial assistance has never been fully articulated by the courts. Arden LJ in ***Chaston v SWP Group plc* [2002]** stated that the prohibition existed to prevent the resources of a target company being used to assist a purchaser as this can, in turn, prejudice the interests of the creditors of the target or its members. However, this justification is not generally accepted by academics, especially since the abolition of the prohibition in relation to private companies. For a discussion of possible justifications and their weaknesses, see Eilis Ferran, 'Corporate Transactions and Financial Assistance: Shifting Policy Perceptions but Static Law' (2004) 63 CLJ 225.

It should be noted that there are several instances where the prohibition will not apply, such as where the assistance is given in good faith and the principal purpose of the assistance is not to reduce or discharge any liability incurred by a person for the purpose of the acquisition of shares (**ss 678(4) and 679(4)**).

LOOKING FOR EXTRA MARKS?

Whilst the removal of the prohibition in relation to private companies is a welcome reform and is a notable example of how the 2006 Act aims to simplify the law and reduce regulation in relation to private companies, the retention of the general prohibition for public companies is still problematic. Companies are regularly forced to seek legal advice to ensure that perfectly innocent transactions do not fall foul of the prohibition and the Company Law Review Steering Group estimated that companies spend around £20 million per year on legal advice in this area. The prohibition for public companies was retained because it was required by the **Second EC Company Law Directive**, so the possibility does exist for it to be modified or abolished now the UK is no longer bound by EU law.

7.2.4 Distributions

As discussed at 4.4.2.2, directors are under a duty to promote the success of the company for the benefit of its members (**CA 2006, s 172**). The pro-member nature of such a duty indicates that the principal purpose of most commercial companies is to make a profit. Members will expect a share of the company's profits to be distributed to them, usually in the form of a **dividend**. Dividends are simply the distribution, usually in cash, of profits to the members, usually at a fixed amount per share. Accordingly, the more shares a member owns, the greater the dividend he will receive.

REVISION TIP

It is often incorrectly stated by students that members have the right to a dividend, but this is not usually the case. Until a dividend is declared or a company is wound up, companies are not under a legal obligation to distribute profits to their members (***Burland v Earle*** [1902]). However, a failure to pay a dividend can, in certain cases, amount to unfairly prejudicial conduct (discussed at 8.4) or can exceptionally justify the winding up of a company on just and equitable grounds (discussed at 8.5).

A final dividend can only be paid if it is properly declared and authorized and the process of declaration and authorization is a matter for the company's articles (the articles normally provide that interim dividends can be paid by the directors without member approval). The normal three-stage procedure (and the procedure found in the model articles) is shown in Figure 7.1.

7.2.4.1 Restrictions on distributions

In accordance with the general principle that capital should not be returned to the shareholders, **s 830(1) of the CA 2006** provides that companies cannot pay a dividend out of capital—instead a 'company may only make a distribution out of profits available for the purpose', with

Figure 7.1 The procedure for distributing profits by way of a final dividend

STAGE 1: RECOMMENDATION
The directors will recommend an amount of the company's profits to be distributed to the members by way of dividend.

STAGE 2: DECLARATION
The company will 'declare' the dividend by passing an ordinary resolution. This resolution cannot be passed until the directors have made their recommendation and the members cannot declare an amount that is greater than that recommended by the directors (although they can substitute a smaller amount). Once the dividend is declared it becomes a debt of the company owed to the members.

STAGE 3: PAYMENT
The directors pay out the dividend in accordance with the rights of the members (e.g. taking into account differing class rights).

such profits being defined as the company's 'accumulated, realised profits … less its accumulated, realised losses' (**CA 2006, s 830(2)**). You need to understand the importance of the words 'accumulated' and 'realised':

- The word 'accumulated' is included to require companies to include previous years' losses when determining the profits available for the purpose. The aim of this is to prevent a situation whereby a company has several years' poor performance and sustains significant losses, but then has a profitable year and pays out a dividend, even though that profitable year has not replaced the losses suffered in previous years.

- The word 'realised' is included to prevent companies from paying out a dividend based on estimated profits. Companies used to be able to pay out a dividend based on estimated profits, but if that level of profit were not reached, the shortfall would have to be paid out of capital. Companies are now required to determine profits based on gains and losses that are realized, and what is realized is to be determined using generally accepted accounting principles, with the **Financial Reporting Standard 18** providing that profits are realized only when realized in the form of cash or other assets, the cash realization of which can be assessed with reasonable certainty.

When determining whether or not a distribution is lawful, the courts will focus on the purpose and substance of the transaction, as opposed to its form (e.g. a distribution described as a dividend, but paid out of capital, would be found unlawful, despite the label attached to it). Although the courts favour an objective approach, they will look at all the facts, which can include the state of mind of the persons orchestrating the transaction (***Progress Property Co Ltd v Moorgarth Group Ltd*** [2010]).

7.2.4.2 Consequences of an unlawful distribution

The **CA 2006** provides only for one consequence following an unlawful distribution, namely that any member who, at the time of the distribution, knew or had reasonable grounds to believe that the distribution was unlawful, is required to repay it, or part of it, to the company (**CA 2006, s 847(1) and (2)**). Under the common law, the directors who authorized the distribution are liable to repay the money to the company if they knew or ought to have known that the distribution was unlawful (***Re National Funds Assurance Co (No 2)*** (1878)). This is a severe deterrent, as was seen in the case of ***Bairstow v Queens Moat Houses plc*** [2001] where the directors were ordered to repay just under £79 million. However, it should be noted that liability is fault-based, so if the directors were unaware of the facts rendering the dividend unlawful, they would not be liable if they took reasonable care to secure the preparation of accounts which showed that a lawful dividend could be paid (***Burnden Holdings (UK) Ltd v Fielding*** [2019]).

If an unlawful distribution is made based on erroneous accounts, the company's auditor, if negligent in failing to detect the error, will be liable to repay the company the amount of the unlawful distribution (***Leeds Estate Building and Investment Co v Shepherd*** (1887)).

Whilst this rule is clearly designed to protect the company's creditors, it should be noted that a company's creditors do not have legal standing to restrain an unlawful distribution

(*Mills v Northern Railway of Buenos Ayres Co* (1870)), although they can petition the court to have the company wound up.

LOOKING FOR EXTRA MARKS?

Stay up-to-date with developments in this area. In 2021, the government published a white paper that proposed a series of reforms relating to dividend distributions, and many of these were accepted by the government in its response document (BEIS, 'Restoring Trust in Audit and Corporate Governance: Government Response to the Consultation on Strengthening the UK's Audit, Corporate Reporting and Corporate Governance Systems' (BEIS 2022)). Notable reforms include:

- requiring certain companies to disclose their distributable reserves;
- giving ARGA formal responsibility for issuing guidance on when profits and losses will be realized;
- requiring companies to provide a narrative explanation to their approach to paying dividends and how this has been applied in the reporting year; and
- requiring directors to make a statement confirming the legality of proposed dividends and any dividends paid in the year.

7.3 Debt capital

It may be the case that a company can acquire all the capital it needs through trading or the selling of shares. However, in many companies, this will not be the case and the company will need to obtain additional capital by borrowing it from others. Such capital is known as '**debt capital**' (or 'loan capital') and it can be obtained in several ways, including making use of an overdraft facility, obtaining a loan from a bank, or issuing debt securities.

Whilst not a legal requirement, a prudent lender may insist on having some form of claim upon the assets of the company, so that if the company defaults on the loan, the lender can seize the relevant assets and sell them in order to satisfy the debt owed. Where the loan agreement provides the lender with a claim over the company's assets, the loan is said to be 'secured'. A further benefit of taking security is that, in the event of the company being liquidated, secured creditors have the right to be paid before the unsecured creditors (the distribution of a company's assets upon liquidation is discussed at 9.2.5). Given that insolvent companies will have limited assets, this is an extremely important advantage. There are several forms of security, but the most common (and the one that tends to appear in company law exams most often) is the '**charge**'.

7.3.1 Charges

The **CA 2006** provides that the word 'charge' includes a mortgage so, in this text, the word 'charge' will refer to any form of security where possession of property is not transferred. A charge usually entitles the chargeholder to appropriate the charged assets if the debtor defaults upon the loan. The creditor who obtained the charge is called the **'chargee'** or 'chargeholder' and the borrower who granted the charge is known as the **'chargor'**. There are two principal types of charge you need to be aware of, namely the fixed charge and the floating charge.

REVISION TIP

Charges often arise in problem questions concerning insolvency law (discussed in Chapter 9), where a company that has entered some form of liquidation or rescue procedure will have granted a charge to a creditor. The outcome of the case and the advice you offer will depend heavily on the type of charge concerned, so it is important that you are aware of the differences between fixed and floating charges. Table 7.2 sets out the principal differences between the two types of charge.

7.3.1.1 Fixed charges

The simplest form of charge is the fixed charge, so called because it is usually taken over a fixed, identifiable asset of the company, such as a building, a vehicle, or a piece of machinery. Should the debtor company default on the loan, the creditor can look to the charged asset to satisfy the debt, usually by selling it and recovering the proceeds of sale. The most straightforward and common example of a fixed charge is a mortgage, whereby the debtor company will borrow capital from the creditor, and the loan will be secured on a fixed asset of the company (e.g. a building). Should the company default on the loan, the creditor can obtain possession of the mortgaged asset and sell it.

Table 7.2 The differences between a fixed charge and a floating charge

	FIXED CHARGE	FLOATING CHARGE
Subject matter of charge	Usually taken over a specific, identifiable asset or assets	Usually taken over a class of assets, or the entire undertaking
Effect on the charged asset(s)	The ability of the chargor to deal with the charged asset will usually be limited	The chargor will usually be free to deal with the charged assets
Better suited for which assets?	Better suited for assets that the company does not need to deal with or dispose of	Suitable for all types of assets
Priority	Ranks ahead of all other debts	Ranks behind debts secured by fixed charge, moratorium debts, liquidation expenses, and preferential debts
Assets available to liquidator	Assets subject to a fixed charge fall outside the liquidator's control	Assets subject to a floating charge are within the liquidator's control
Set aside by liquidator	A liquidator/administrator has no power to set aside a fixed charge	A liquidator/administrator has the power to invalidate certain floating charges

Unless the charge contract provides otherwise, a company can grant multiple fixed charges over a specific asset, with prior charges having priority over subsequent ones (unless the terms of the prior charges provide that subsequent charges can be made that take priority, which would be highly unlikely).

LOOKING FOR EXTRA MARKS?

Be aware of the advantages and disadvantages of using fixed charges. From the chargeholder's point of view, fixed charges are extremely useful as they provide the chargeholder with a range of remedies should the chargor default on the loan (e.g. the ability to seize and sell the charged asset). A fixed charge can also help ensure that the chargeholder ranks ahead of all other creditors in the event of the company being liquidated. The charge contract will usually limit the chargor's ability to deal with the charged asset (e.g. the chargor will usually not be allowed to dispose of assets covered by a fixed charge). This makes the fixed charge a powerful form of security, but it also makes it inflexible, insofar as the chargor may wish to deal with the charged asset, but find itself unable to do so due to the existence of the fixed charge.

7.3.1.2 Floating charges

As noted, fixed charges can be inflexible as they limit the chargor's ability to use the charged asset. Accordingly, certain assets that fluctuate or assets that need to be used (e.g. raw materials) are not appropriate subjects of a fixed charge. A more flexible form of charge was therefore required, leading to the creation of the floating charge.

REVISION TIP

Essay questions on floating charges typically focus on the advantages and disadvantages that floating charges have over fixed charges. Problem questions involving floating charges tend to arise as part of a problem question involving another legal topic. For example, problem questions concerning insolvency law may feature an insolvent company that has assets subject to a floating charge.

There is no statutory definition of what amounts to a floating charge, but Lord Macnaghten in *Governments Stock and Other Securities Co Ltd v Manila Railway Co Ltd* [1897] described it as:

> an equitable charge on the assets for the time being of a going concern. It attaches to the subject charged in the varying condition in which it happens to be from time to time. It is of the essence of such a charge that it remains dormant until the undertaking charged ceases to be a going concern, or until the person in whose favour the charge is created intervenes.

In *Re Yorkshire Woolcombers' Association Ltd* **[1903]**, Romer LJ identified three factors that may indicate a charge is a floating charge (although he acknowledged that a charge may not have these and still be floating):

1. the charge will be taken over a class of assets (e.g. machinery, raw materials, or even the entire undertaking), as opposed to a specific asset;

2. the class of assets charged is normally constantly changing (e.g. raw materials will be used and replenished); and

3. floating charges leave the company free to use and deal with those assets.

The third factor is what provides the floating charge with its flexibility. A floating charge 'floats' over the charged assets and while it continues to float, the company is free to use and dispose of those assets. The company can even grant charges on the assets over which the charge floats, which may (depending on the terms of the floating charge) rank ahead of the floating charge (*Wheatley v Silkstone and Haigh Moor Coal Co* **(1885)**). However, the company cannot create a subsequent floating charge over the exact same class of assets as a prior floating charge and have the subsequent charge rank ahead of the prior charge, unless the terms of the prior charge allow for this (*Re Benjamin Cope & Sons Ltd* **[1914]**). The company can, however, create subsequent floating charges over part of the assets charged by a prior floating charge (*Re Automatic Bottle Makers Ltd* **[1926]**) and the general rule is that later charges rank behind earlier ones (although the terms of the first charge may provide otherwise).

Upon the occurrence of certain events, the charge will cease to float and will become affixed to the charged assets, whereupon the company's ability to deal with the charged assets will be limited (this process is known as '**crystallization**'). Certain events will always cause a charge to crystallize, including:

- the company going into liquidation,
- the business of the company ceasing,
- a receiver being appointed, or
- an event occurring that the charge instrument provides will automatically cause the charge to crystallize (this is known as an 'automatic crystallization clause').

➕ LOOKING FOR EXTRA MARKS?

Floating charges clearly have advantages over fixed charges, but floating charges also suffer from notable disadvantages that you should be aware of, including:

- Upon winding up, floating charges rank behind debts secured by fixed charge, liquidation expenses, and preferential debts.
- A floating charge attaches only to the class of assets charged. Accordingly, if the charged assets have been dissipated, or are subject to a retention of title clause, there will be no assets for the charge to fix upon. ➡

- **Section 245 of the Insolvency Act 1986** (discussed at 9.2.4.4) provides that, in certain cases, a floating charge can be avoided upon the company's liquidation.

7.3.1.3 Determining the class of charge

There are significant differences between fixed and floating charges, with each form of charge having its own advantages and disadvantages. Identifying whether a particular charge is fixed or floating is not always straightforward and a chargeholder may use this ambiguity to his advantage (e.g. by creating a charge with the characteristics of a floating charge, but later arguing that it is in fact a fixed charge in order to gain priority upon liquidation). Accordingly, the approach the courts use in determining whether a charge is fixed or floating is of crucial importance and a substantial body of case law has developed in this area.

In *Agnew v Commissioner for Inland Revenue* **[2001]** (also known as *Re Brumark*) the Privy Council stated that the process for determining the classification of a charge is twofold:

1. The court will look at the charge instrument to determine the rights and obligations that the parties intended to grant each other—it is not the task of the court to determine what type of charge the parties intended to create.

2. The courts will use these rights and obligations to determine, as a matter of law, whether the charge was fixed or floating.

As the courts are not concerned per se with the type of charge that the parties intended to create, it follows that the courts will not regard the parties' own classification of the charge as conclusive (*Street v Mountford* **[1985]**) and will contradict the parties' classification if the rights and obligations imposed by the charge are not consistent with the label that the parties have attached to it (see e.g. *Russell Cooke Trust Co Ltd v Elliott* **[2007]** where the High Court held that a charge that was described in the charge instrument as a floating charge was in fact a fixed charge). In the following case, the House of Lords held that, in determining the class of charge as a matter of law, the courts should be led by 'the commercial nature and substance of the arrangement'.

Re Spectrum Plus Ltd [2005] UKHL 41

Facts: Spectrum Plus Ltd ('Spectrum') obtained an overdraft facility from a bank, with the bank taking what was purported to be a fixed charge over Spectrum's **book debts** as security. The charge required that Spectrum could not sell, charge, or assign the book debts without the bank's consent, and that the proceeds of the book debts were to be paid into the bank account that Spectrum held with the bank. Spectrum was, however, free to draw upon the account, providing that the overdraft facility was not exceeded. Spectrum entered liquidation and, in order to determine the priority of its creditors, the court had to determine whether the charge was fixed or floating.

Held: The House held that the charge was a floating charge. Lord Scott stated that the key feature of a floating charge was that it grants the chargor (Spectrum) the right to use the charged asset, including removing it from the scope of the charge. As Spectrum could draw from the bank account, the rights granted to it indicated strongly that the charge was a floating charge.

Re Spectrum Plus Ltd is a seminal case. For a lucid analysis of the decision of the House in this case, see Richard Nolan, 'A Spectrum of Opinion' (2005) 64 CLJ 554.

7.3.1.4 Registration

For obvious reasons, prior to providing a company with capital, a potential creditor will want to know of any charges over the company's assets. Accordingly, successive Companies Acts have long provided for a system of registration of charges. It should be noted that the law in this area has changed significantly following **Pt 25, Ch A1 of the CA 2006**, which came into force in April 2013. Prior to that date, the law relating to registration was deemed to be overly complex and the new rules simplify notably the registration system.

Prior to April 2013, the parties to a charge were required to register it and a limited company was under a legal obligation to maintain, at its registered office, a register of charges. Failure to comply with these rules constituted a criminal offence. The new system does not require mandatory registration of charges by the parties, nor does it require the company to maintain a register of charges. Instead, **s 859A of the CA 2006** provides that if any person interested in a charge registers at Companies House, within the period allowed for delivery, a statement of particulars relating to the charge, then the registrar of companies must register the charge. The company or any other party interested in the charge may register the charge, but the registration will only be effective if it is made within the 'period allowed for delivery', which is twenty-one days beginning on the date of the creation of the charge (**CA 2006, s 859A(4)**). Upon successful registration, the registrar will issue a certificate that will provide conclusive evidence that the statement of particulars was delivered to the registrar within the period allowed for delivery.

As noted, prior to April 2013, companies were under an obligation to maintain a register of charges. However, the failure to maintain a register did not affect the validity of the charge concerned and criminal prosecutions were rarely sought. Accordingly, the requirement to maintain a register has been abolished, but **ss 859P and 859Q** require companies to keep copies of any charge instrument capable of registration and to make such documents available for inspection. Under the **CA 1985**, only members and creditors were able to inspect the register of charges, but **s 859Q** provides any person with a right to inspect the charge instrument. Table 7.3 sets out the differences between the pre-2013 and the current system of registration.

LOOKING FOR EXTRA MARKS?

Be prepared to compare the two systems of registration. At first, it may be thought that the abolition of the requirement placed on the parties to register a charge would be a significant step. However, the consequences of non-registration are so severe that, in practice, it is likely to be the case that the vast majority of registrable charges will be registered. If the statement of particulars relating to the charge is not registered at Companies House within the twenty-one-day period (or such longer period as allowed by the courts), then the security afforded to the creditor by the charge will be void against a liquidator, administrator, or creditor of the company (**CA 2006, s 859H**).

Table 7.3 The registration of charges

	PRE-2013 SYSTEM	CURRENT SYSTEM
Charges capable of being registered?	Only those charges specified in statute	All charges, subject to limited exceptions
Company required to keep a register of charges?	Yes	No, but may do so if it wishes
Charge must be registered with Companies House?	Yes	No, but Companies House must register the charge if a person interested in the charge registers a statement of particulars
Criminal sanctions for failure to register?	Yes	No
Company required to keep copies of charge instruments?	Yes	Yes
Charge generally void if not registered?	Yes	Yes

KEY DEBATES

Topic	The capital maintenance regime
Author/Academic	John H Armour
Viewpoint	Discusses the effectiveness of the capital maintenance rules from an economic viewpoint and argues that certain restrictions imposed are haphazard and are not justified. Although this article was written prior to the passing of the **CA 2006**, many of the arguments raised are still extremely relevant.
Source	'Share Capital and Creditor Protection: Efficient Rules for a Modern Company Law' (2000) 63 MLR 355

Topic	Prohibition on providing financial assistance to acquire shares
Author/Academic	Eilis Ferran
Viewpoint	Discusses several cases concerning the prohibition on providing financial assistance to acquire shares. Argues that justifications for the prohibition are unsatisfactory and provides recommendations regarding how the prohibition should be limited.
Source	'Corporate Transactions and Financial Assistance: Shifting Policy Perceptions but Static Law' (2004) 63 CLJ 225

Topic	Debt capital and creditor protection
Author/Academic	Eilis Ferran
Viewpoint	Despite its age, this article still provides an excellent discussion of the role and advantages of debt capital and examines the extent to which company law should protect a company's creditors.
Source	'Creditors' Interests and "Core" Company Law' (1999) 20 Co Law 314

 EXAM QUESTIONS

Essay question

'Whilst the Companies Act 2006 has undoubtedly improved the overall effectiveness of the rules relating to share capital and capital maintenance, it has failed to remedy a number of significant pre-2006 weaknesses in the law.'

Discuss the validity of this statement.

See the Outline answers section in the endmatter for help with this question.

Problem question

Milo Ltd was incorporated in November 2017 and has issued 5,000 shares, all with a nominal value of £1 each. The company's two directors, Ceri and Ross, each own 1,000 shares. Theo, a local businessman, owns 2,000 shares and the remaining 1,000 shares are owned by a number of local investors.

Since it was incorporated, the company has run at a loss and has never made a profit. Theo believes that this is due to Ceri and Ross's poor management of the company. He also believes that, with new management, the company could be extremely profitable. He therefore starts buying from the local investors the shares that they hold in Milo Ltd with a view to voting Ceri and Ross out of office.

Ceri and Ross discover Theo's plan. Accordingly, they cause the company to issue 3,000 new shares and offer to sell them to their friend, Gabrielle. However, Gabrielle cannot afford to buy these shares, but she does offer to sell her car to Milo Ltd as part-payment for the shares. The car is only worth £1,500 but Ceri and Ross accept the car as part-payment providing that Gabrielle uses the voting rights attached to her shares to defeat any resolution that aims to remove Ceri and Ross from office. The remaining payment comes in the form of £500, which Gabrielle borrows from Milo Ltd.

Theo, realizing that his scheme to oust Ceri and Ross has failed, wishes to sell his shares, but he cannot find a buyer. Ceri tells Theo that Milo Ltd will purchase the shares. By now, Theo has 2,500 shares, which he agrees to sell to Milo Ltd. The company purchases the shares and they are duly cancelled. Having rid themselves of the troublesome Theo, Ceri and Ross recommend that a dividend be paid at a rate of 10 pence per share. Gabrielle agrees and between them, the dividend is declared and paid out.

Discuss the validity of Ceri and Ross's actions.

 Online resources

For an outline answer to this problem question, as well as multiple-choice questions and further reading, please visit the online resources.

8 Members' remedies

KEY FACTS

- The rule in *Foss v Harbottle* provides, *inter alia*, that, generally, a member cannot commence proceedings to redress a wrong done to the company.

- In certain circumstances, the Companies Act 2006 allows members to commence proceedings for wrongs sustained by the company, via a derivative claim.

- A member can petition the court for a remedy where his interests have been unfairly prejudiced. The usual remedy is for that member's shares to be bought at a reasonable price.

- A member can petition the court for an order winding up a company and the court can grant such an order if it thinks it just and equitable to do so.

- The court will not order a winding up where an alternative remedy exists and the claimant is acting unreasonably in not seeking that alternative remedy.

CHAPTER OVERVIEW

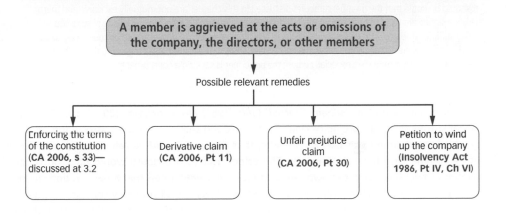

Introduction

The previous chapters discussed several methods by which the law protects the members of a company. However, problems arise where the company or the members are wronged by the acts or omissions of the directors or majority shareholders. In such cases, the persons who cause the harm are also the persons who have standing to obtain redress. Without the law's aid, members, especially minority shareholders, who sustain loss due to the actions of the directors or majority shareholders would be left without a remedy. Accordingly, statute provides members with three principal remedies, namely:

1. the derivative claim under **Pt 11 of the CA 2006,**

2. the unfair prejudice remedy under **Pt 30 of the CA 2006,** and

3. the petition for winding up the company under **Pt IV, Ch VI of the Insolvency Act 1986 (IA 1986).**

In addition, where the constitution of the company has been breached, a member may be able to enforce the provision that was breached or obtain a remedy for breach of contract. This has already been discussed (at 3.2) and so will not be discussed further here.

REVISION TIP

It should be noted that the member remedies discussed in this chapter are not mutually exclusive and there exists a significant overlap between all three. Indeed, it is common for problem questions to require you to discuss multiple remedies and to identify which remedy is more appropriate and/or would be more likely to succeed. Note, however, that in some cases, the courts have sought to lay down rules regarding the relationship between the various remedies, especially where the petitioner is seeking a court order to wind up the company.

It is worth noting that in *Fulham Football Club (1987) Ltd v Richards* [2011], the Court of Appeal stayed an unfair prejudice claim on the ground that the Football Association's Rules (by which the claimant was bound) provided that disputes should be referred to arbitration before commencing legal proceedings. The effect that such a clause would have on other member remedies is not yet known (although it is well established that an arbitration clause contained within the articles can form part of the **CA 2006, s 33** statutory contract (see 3.2)), but the general nature of the Court's discussion indicates that the *ratio* could indeed apply to the other remedies discussed in this chapter.

Before looking at the three statutory member remedies noted above, it is worth first discussing the relationship between personal actions and corporate actions.

8.1 Personal actions and corporate actions

An act or omission of a person may cause loss to both the company and, in turn, to its members. This might grant the company the right to bring an action against the wrongdoer. In addition, the members might also have a personal right to bring an action against the wrongdoer for the loss they have suffered. In such a case, the general rule is that both actions can proceed (*Pender v Lushington* (1877)). However, there is a major exception to this which can prevent a member's claim from proceeding, namely the reflective loss principle.

8.2 The 'reflective loss' principle

Imagine that the directors of a company engage in negligent conduct that causes the company financial loss and, as a result, the company does not make sufficient profits to issue a dividend and the company's share price decreases. Usually, both the company and the members could sue the directors for their respective losses, but the members will be prevented from doing so where the reflective loss principle applies. This principle basically states that, where the loss sustained by the members is reflective of the loss sustained by the company, then the members will not be permitted to recover those losses that are reflective of the loss that could be recovered by the company. In the example above, the members' loss is reflective of the loss sustained by the company and so the company will be the proper claimant (which, as we will see, is the first principle of the rule in *Foss v Harbottle*) and its claim will generally trump that of the members, as the following case demonstrates.

Prudential Assurance Co Ltd v Newman Industries Ltd (No 2) [1982] Ch 204 (CA)

Facts: Bartlett and Laughton were directors of two companies, namely Newman Industries Ltd ('Newman') and Thomas Poole & Gladstone China Ltd ('TPG'). TPG was experiencing financial difficulties and so Bartlett and Laughton devised a scheme to sell TPG's assets to Newman. Bartlett and Laughton provided misleading information resulting in Newman paying £445,000 more for the assets than it need have paid. Shareholder approval for the sale was obtained, again based on misleading information provided by Bartlett and Laughton. Upon discovering the deception, Prudential, which held shares in Newman, commenced proceedings against Bartlett, Laughton, and TPG via three different claims:

(i) a derivative action on behalf of Newman for the losses sustained by Newman,

(ii) a personal action against the defendants for the losses Prudential sustained, and

(iii) a representative action on behalf of all the other members of Newman.

At first instance, it was held that the defendants had indeed perpetrated a fraud and that the derivative and personal claims could be joined in one action. Bartlett and Laughton appealed.

Held: The Court of Appeal stated that the personal claim brought by Prudential was 'misconceived' and that a member cannot:

> recover damages merely because the company in which he is interested has suffered damage. He cannot recover a sum equal to the diminution in the market value of his shares, or equal to the likely diminution in dividend, because such a 'loss' is merely a reflection of the loss suffered by the company. The shareholder does not suffer any personal loss. His only 'loss' is through the company, in the diminution in the value of the net assets of the company . . . . The plaintiff's shares are merely a right of participation in the company on the terms of the articles of association. The shares themselves, his right of participation, are not directly affected by the wrongdoing.

Whether Prudential had the right to bring a derivative action did not form a ground of appeal and so the Court did not rule on this.

The reflective loss principle applies to any situation where the company and members have a cause of action (it need not be the same cause of action) deriving from the same facts against the same wrongdoer. The principle was heavily criticized at first (see e.g. LS Sealy, 'A Setback for Minority Shareholders' (1982) 41 CLJ 247), but it is now well established. However, in the years following *Prudential*, the courts expanded the scope of the reflective loss principle until it started to resemble 'some ghastly legal Japanese knotweed' (Andrew Tettenborn, 'Creditors and Reflective Loss—A Bar Too Far? (2019) 135 LQR 182, 183). In the following leading case, the Supreme Court stated that this expansion had 'unwelcome and unjustifiable effects on the law' and so it sought to clarify the purpose and scope of the principle.

Sevilleja v Marex Financial Ltd [2020] UKSC 21

Facts: Two companies controlled by Mr Sevilleja were ordered by the High Court to pay Marex Financial Ltd over $7 million. A confidential draft of the Court's judgment was given to the parties prior to it being formally handed down, at which point Sevilleja transferred $9.5 million from the companies' bank accounts to other accounts under his personal control. The result was that the two companies could not pay the amount ordered by the Court. Sevilleja then placed the two companies into liquidation. ➡

➡ Marex sued Sevilleja for the amount owed under the High Court judgment, but Sevilleja argued that the claim was barred due to the reflective loss principle. At first instance and in the Court of Appeal, the courts agreed and Marex's claim failed. Marex appealed.

Held: The Supreme Court allowed the appeal. Lord Reed PSC, who gave the leading judgment, defined the reflective loss principle as follows:

> a diminution in the value of a shareholding or in distributions to shareholders, which is merely the result of the loss suffered by the company in consequence of a wrong done to it by the defendant, is not in the eyes of the law damage which is separate and distinct from the damage suffered by the company, and therefore not recoverable.

From this, it follows that previous cases that based the reflective loss principle on the prevention of double recovery were incorrect, as the shareholders' loss is not distinct from the company and therefore they suffer no loss at all. As a result, a number of prior cases that had expanded the scope of the reflective loss principle on this basis were overruled, and the principle was limited to 'claims by shareholders that, as a result of actionable loss suffered by their company, the value of their shares or distributions they receive as shareholders has been diminished.' As a result, the reflective loss principle did not apply to Marex's claim as it was not a shareholder—it was a creditor. Marex was therefore allowed to pursue its claim against Sevilleja.

Whilst the Supreme Court may have been unanimous in its decision, it was not unanimous regarding the scope of the principle. Notably, Lord Sales JSC questioned whether the principle should be recognized at all. To date, all post-*Sevilleja* cases involving reflective loss have followed the narrow approach set out by Lord Reed PSC and have refused to expand the scope of the principle (see e.g. ***Broadcasting Investment Group Ltd v Smith*** [2020], where the Court refused to expand the principle to cover claims brought by an individual who was not a shareholder of the company, but was connected to the company by a chain of shareholdings). However, some inconsistencies still remain. For example, in ***Nectrus Ltd v UCP plc*** [2021], the Court stated that the reflective loss principle did not apply to claims made by ex-shareholders, but the Privy Council in ***Primeo Fund v Bank of Bermuda (Cayman) Ltd*** [2021] stated that *Nectrus* was 'wrongly decided' and the rule had to apply to ex-shareholders or it could be avoided simply by the shareholder selling their shares. However, permission to appeal in the case of *Nectrus* has been granted, with the Court of Appeal basing this, in part, on it being likely that the appellant would succeed in its reflective loss arguments in light of *Primeo*.

A useful summary of the law relating to the reflective loss principle was set out in para 30 of ***Burnford v Automobile Association Developments Ltd*** [2022].

8.3 The derivative claim

If *A* sustains loss due to the actions of *B*, then generally only *A* can sue *B* to obtain redress. A third party could not sue *B* on *A*'s behalf. As companies have separate personality, this principle applies equally in the corporate context. If a company sustains loss due to the actions of another, then generally only the company can sue to obtain redress. However, where the company sustains loss due to the actions of its directors, problems arise in that the powers of the company are usually delegated to the directors and this would include the authority to determine whether or not the company will commence litigation. Clearly, in such a case, the directors will not likely cause the company to initiate litigation against themselves. The question that therefore arises is can the members commence litigation on the company's behalf? Due to three principles known collectively as 'the rule in *Foss v Harbottle*', the answer is generally no.

8.3.1 The rule in *Foss v Harbottle*

The rule in *Foss v Harbottle* is a cardinal principle of company law. In the case of *Foss v Harbottle* (1843), the court established three principles:

1. The 'proper claimant' principle, which provides that only the company, and not the members, can commence proceedings for wrongs committed against it. This principle is a corollary of a company's corporate personality.

2. The 'internal management' principle, which provides that where a company is acting within its powers, the courts will not interfere in matters of internal management, unless the company itself commences proceedings. This principle is a corollary of the courts' long-established reluctance to become involved in the internal affairs of businesses.

3. The 'irregularity' principle, which provides that where some procedural irregularity is committed, an aggrieved member cannot commence proceedings where the irregularity is one that can be ratified by a simple majority of the members. This principle is a corollary of the principle of majority rule.

 REVISION TIP

Remember that the irregularity principle applies both to rights vested in the company and to rights vested personally in the members. Accordingly, even where the right to commence proceedings is vested personally in a member, the member will be unable to commence proceedings if the members can ratify the irregularity by passing an ordinary resolution.

8.3.1.1 Common law derivative actions

The rule in *Foss v Harbottle*, however, is not absolute. If it were, wrongs committed by the directors would rarely be subject to litigation. Accordingly, the courts crafted four so-called exceptions to the rule (so-called because, as we shall see, only one was actually an exception), whereby members could commence an action on the company's behalf. Such actions were known as 'derivative actions' because the member was bringing an action based on rights derived from the company. This derivation is reinforced by the fact that, if the action succeeded, the remedy was granted to the company. With the creation of the statutory derivative claim, the derivative action has been largely abolished, but knowledge of the common law exceptions will be of aid should an essay question require you to compare the common law derivative action to the statutory derivative claim. Four such exceptions existed, with the first three being simple and straightforward, namely:

1. Where the act complained of was illegal (*Taylor v National Union of Mineworkers (Derbyshire Area)* [1985]) or *ultra vires* (*Simpson v Westminster Palace Hotel Co* (1860)), a member could commence a derivative action.

2. Where the act infringed the personal rights of a member (e.g. the improper rejection of a member's votes), a derivative action could be brought.

3. Where the act complained of could only be done or sanctioned by the passing of a special resolution, a derivative action could be brought (*Edwards v Halliwell* [1950]).

The fourth exception was more complex and perhaps the most important, and occurred where those persons who controlled the company had committed some sort of fraud on the minority. 'Fraud' included actual fraud (e.g. breach of the **Theft Act 1968** or the **Fraud Act 2006**) and equitable fraud (e.g. conduct tainted by impropriety). Negligence, even gross negligence, would not suffice (*Pavlides v Jensen* [1956]), but where the negligence benefited those who controlled the company, this would suffice as the negligence would be tainted by impropriety (*Daniels v Daniels* [1978]). The courts would not allow a claim based on fraud on the minority to succeed if it would not serve the interests of justice (e.g. where the independent members had indicated that they did not wish the claim to proceed (*Smith v Croft (No 2)* [1988])).

LOOKING FOR EXTRA MARKS?

If an essay question requires you to discuss the old common law exceptions to *Foss*, it is worth noting that fraud on the minority is the only true exception to the rule in *Foss*. A true exception to *Foss* is one whereby a member enforces a right belonging to the company. In the cases of illegal/*ultra vires* acts, personal rights, or acts requiring a special resolution, the right is actually vested personally in the member and so they are not true exceptions to *Foss*.

8.3.2 The statutory derivative claim

Whilst the Law Commission agreed with the underlying approach of the rule in *Foss v Harbottle*, it was of the opinion that the rules relating to derivative actions had become 'complicated and unwieldy'.

REVISION TIP

An essay question may require you to discuss the deficiencies of the rule in *Foss v Harbottle* and the rules relating to derivative actions, so ensure that you can critically analyse the rule and its exceptions. For a clear discussion of the rule, see Law Commission, *Shareholder Remedies* (Law Com CP No 142, 1996) and Law Commission, *Shareholder Remedies* (Law Com Report No 246, 1997). Both can be obtained from https://www.lawcom.gov.uk.

The Law Commission therefore recommended that a statutory derivative claim be introduced and this claim can now be found in **Pt 11 of the CA 2006**.

 REVISION TIP

Part 11 of the CA 2006 does not abolish the rule in *Foss v Harbottle*—the rule itself retains much of its force. However, the common law derivative action has been largely abolished and replaced by the statutory derivative claim. There are two instances where the common law rules will continue to apply, namely:

- in relation to the 'multiple derivative action' (i.e. where a member of a parent company sues on behalf of a subsidiary), then the common law derivative action will still apply (*Re Fort Gilkicker Ltd* [2013]); or

- where the company in question is not registered under the **CA 2006** (e.g. an overseas company), then the common law derivative action will apply (*Novatrust Ltd v Kea Investments Ltd* [2014]).

Accordingly, in a problem question, make sure you apply the correct rules. Regarding essay questions, be prepared to discuss how the statutory derivative claim differs from the common law derivative action (as set out in Table 8.1) and whether the derivative claim provides a more effective source of member protection.

Table 8.1 The differences between the derivative action and the derivative claim

	COMMON LAW DERIVATIVE ACTION	STATUTORY DERIVATIVE CLAIM
Status	The common law derivative action no longer applies, except in relation to 'multiple derivative actions' and claims involving foreign companies	A derivative claim can only be brought under the **CA 2006**
Source of law	Case law spanning over 150 years	**CA 2006, Pt 11**
Grounds for claim	• Illegal/*ultra vires* acts • Acts which infringe personal rights of a member • Acts requiring a special majority • Acts which are a fraud on the minority	• Negligence • Default • Breach of duty • Breach of trust
Covers acts/omissions committed by	Director(s) or member(s)	Director(s) only (including former directors and shadow directors)
Claim can be brought by	A member only	A member, or a person who is not a member, but to whom shares have been transferred/transmitted by operation of law
Claim can be brought against	A director of the company	A director of the company or another person (or both)
Claim for negligence	Claim could only be brought if a director benefited personally	Claim can be brought, irrespective of whether or not a director benefited personally

8.3.2.1 Scope

Section 260(2) of the CA 2006 provides that a derivative claim can only be brought under **Pt 11** of the Act, or in pursuance of a court order under **s 994** (**s 994** is discussed later in this chapter at 8.4). **Section 260(3)** provides that a derivative claim can only arise from an actual or proposed act or omission involving:

- *Negligence*—negligence could not found a common law derivative action, unless the wrongdoer gained a benefit from the negligent act. This limitation has not been preserved by the **CA 2006**, leading many directors to fear an increase in the number of derivative claims (as is discussed later, this increase in claims has not occurred).

- *Default*—'**default**' is a general term used in many pieces of legislation that refers to a failure to perform a legally obligated act (e.g. to appear in court when required).

- *Breach of duty*—a derivative claim can accordingly be founded on a breach of the general duties (discussed at 4.4.2), as well as any other breach of duty.

- *Breach of trust.*

It will be noted that the scope of the statutory derivative claim differs substantially from the scope of the common law derivative action. In many respects, the scope of the derivative claim is wider, especially in relation to negligence and breach of duty.

REVISION TIP

If an essay requires you to discuss the differences between the common law derivative action and the statutory derivative claim, it is vital that you discuss the differences in scope of the two remedies. Ensure you are aware of how the scope of the statutory derivative claim is wider and narrower than that of the common law derivative action (Table 8.1 sets out the differences in their scope).

The persons against whom a derivative claim can be brought have also been amended. Under the common law, a derivative action could only be brought against a director. A derivative claim, however, may be brought against a director or another person (or both) (**CA 2006, s 260(3)**). In one respect, however, the derivative claim is narrower, namely that the act or omission must be made by a director. Under the common law, the actions of members could found a derivative action, but this is no longer the case.

REVISION TIP

In problem questions, the identity of the wrongdoer will aid you in determining which remedy is relevant. Where a member has engaged in the wrongful act or omission, then the appropriate remedy to discuss will likely (but not always) be the unfair prejudice remedy (discussed later in this chapter at 8.4). Where the wrongdoer is a director, then the unfair prejudice remedy or derivative claim may be relevant. Note that, although a derivative claim must be based on an act or omission of a director, the derivative claim itself need not be brought against the director (e.g. a claim could alternatively or also be brought against a member who was involved in the director's wrongful act or omission).

There is little doubt that, overall, the scope of the statutory derivative claim is broader than that of the common law derivative action. However, an important limitation on the use of derivative claims is the requirement to obtain permission to continue the claim.

8.3.2.2 Permission from the court

Section 261(1) of the CA 2006 provides that a member who brings a derivative claim must apply to the court for permission to continue it, with **ss 261–264** establishing a three-stage process for determining whether permission should be granted. Under the first stage, the member must establish that he has a *prima facie* case. If the member cannot establish a *prima facie* case for permission, the court must dismiss the claim and can make any consequential order that it considers appropriate. If the member can establish a *prima facie* case, a hearing will be convened and the company will be directed to provide evidence. The purpose of this procedure is clearly to screen out unmeritorious or weak claims before the defendant becomes involved and, based on the cases to date, it is clear that establishing a *prima facie* case is not an overly difficult hurdle to overcome (this is borne out by the fact that virtually all derivative applicants have, since the **CA 2006** was introduced, successfully established a *prima facie* case).

LOOKING FOR EXTRA MARKS?

In a number of cases to date, the defendant has conceded that, or decided not to contest that, a *prima facie* case existed. Given that it appears to be relatively easy to establish a *prima facie* case and a derivative claimant would be unlikely to commence a claim if it did not have such a case, it has been contended that the *prima facie* test does not serve a useful function and should therefore be abolished (it is worth noting that this stage was not part of the Law Commission's recommendation, but was added to the Act at a late stage in the House of Lords). Abolishing the *prima facie* stage could also reduce costs and encourage applicants to bring claims. Do you agree? For more, see David Gibbs, 'Has the Statutory Derivative Claim Fulfilled its Objectives? A Prima Facie Case and the Mandatory Bar: Part 1' (2011) 32 Co Law 41.

If the member establishes that he has a *prima facie* case, then the court will move onto the second stage, under which the court will apply **s 263(2)** to the claim. **Section 263(2)** provides that the court *must* refuse permission if it is satisfied that any one of the following conditions applies:

- where a person acting in accordance with **s 172 of the CA 2006** (duty to promote the success of the company for the benefit of its members—discussed at 4.4.2.2) would not seek to continue the claim. This reinforces the fact that a derivative claim must be for the benefit of the company. Refusal of permission on this ground is likely to be rare, especially following the case of *Iesini v Westrip Holdings Ltd* **[2009]** where the court held that permission would only be refused on this ground if no director acting in accordance with **s 172** would seek to continue the claim;

- where the cause of action arises from an act or omission that is yet to occur, that the act or omission has been authorized by the company; or

- where the cause of action arises from an act or omission that has already occurred, that the act or omission was authorized by the company before it occurred, or has been ratified by the company since it occurred (ratification is discussed at 4.4.4).

If the conditions found in **s 263(2)** do not apply, then the court will move onto the third stage. Here the court will finally decide whether to grant permission, but in doing so, it must take into account the factors set out in **s 263(3) and (4)**. Figure 8.1 sets out the three-stage procedure for granting permission.

Many directors were concerned that the increased scope of the statutory derivative claim would result in a significant increase in the number of derivative proceedings than was the case under the common law. Clearly this has not occurred and cases to date involving the requirement for court permission indicate that the courts are reluctant to allow statutory derivative claims to proceed (the case of *Kiani v Cooper* [2010], heard in January 2010, was the first case under the **CA 2006** where the court permitted the claim to continue), and permission to continue has been refused in most cases. One factor specified in **s 263(3)** that the court must take into account is the importance that a person acting in accordance with **s 172** would attach to continuing the claim. Several cases

Figure 8.1 The process for determining whether permission is granted

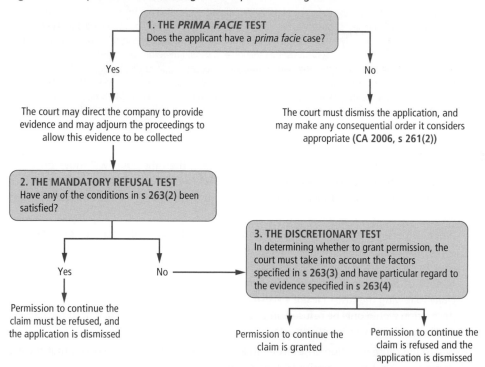

(including *Mission Capital* discussed below) have focused on this factor and indicate that the views of a hypothetical director will often be a determining factor, as will the availability of a personal claim.

Mission Capital plc v Sinclair [2008] EWHC 1339 (Ch)

Facts: Emma and Ronald Sinclair were directors of Mission Capital plc ('MC'). Their service contracts provided that their employment could be immediately terminated if they engaged in unacceptable conduct. MC terminated their employment on the grounds that they failed to submit financial information and failed to meet financial forecasts. The Sinclairs disputed this. MC obtained an injunction that excluded the Sinclairs from its premises. The Sinclairs, *inter alia*, brought a derivative claim and sought permission to continue it.

Held: Permission to continue the claim was denied. Although the court believed that the Sinclairs were acting in good faith, it held that a notional director acting in accordance with **s 172** would not seek to continue the claim, as the damage suffered by MC was 'speculative'. Further, the court held that the Sinclairs were not seeking anything that could not be recovered via a personal claim under **s 994 of the CA 2006** (discussed later in this chapter at 8.4).

 REVISION TIP

The need for permission from the court is a developing area of law that will have a significant impact upon the effectiveness of the derivative claim. In problem questions, students frequently forget to discuss the requirement for court permission. Ask yourself whether or not the facts of the problem provide any reasons why the court might refuse to grant permission. This is especially important if you are advising a potential derivative claimant. It is worth remembering that most derivative claims brought to date under the 2006 Act have failed because the court refused to grant permission to continue with the claim. An excellent summary of the relevant law can be found in *Saatchi v Gajjar* **[2019]**, paras 23–38. For an excellent discussion of the permission procedure, see Andrew Keay and Joan Loughrey, 'Derivative Proceedings in a Brave New World for Company Management and Shareholders' [2010] JBL 151.

8.4 Unfairly prejudicial conduct

Part 30 of the CA 2006 consists of a mere six sections, yet it contains what is perhaps the most important member remedy. **Section 994** allows a member to petition the court for a remedy on the ground:

(a) that the company's affairs are being, or have been conducted in a manner that is unfairly prejudicial to the interests of members generally or of some part of its members (including at least that one member); or

(b) that an actual or proposed act or omission of the company is or would be so prejudicial.

Section 994 re-enacts almost identically **s 459 of the CA 1985**, so pre-2006 case law will still be highly relevant. **Section 459** was regarded as an extremely useful remedy, largely because of the courts' willingness to interpret it in a liberal manner. Key to the effectiveness of the remedy is how the courts interpret the phrases 'unfairly prejudicial' and 'interests of members'.

REVISION TIP

These two phrases also help to establish the structure you should use when answering problem questions involving s 994, namely (i) is the conduct complained of unfairly prejudicial, and, if so (ii) is it unfairly prejudicial to the interests of the members? You may find it easier to first establish whether or not the facts of the problem concern interests that are recognized by s 994 and, if so, then go on to discuss whether or not those interests have been unfairly prejudiced.

8.4.1 What are the 'interests of members'?

The conduct complained of must unfairly prejudice the 'interests of members', so the scope of the members' interests must be discussed. A member's interests are wider than their rights and so a member's interests can be unfairly prejudiced even if their rights have not been (see e.g. *Re Sam Weller & Sons Ltd* [1990]).

Historically, the courts would only grant a remedy where the petitioner was bringing the claim in his capacity as a member (i.e. his membership interests were unfairly prejudiced). Thus, where an employee of a company, who was also a member of the company, was dismissed by the company, the court refused to grant a remedy on the ground that the member had brought his claim in his capacity as an employee and not in his capacity as a member (*Re John Reid & Sons (Strucsteel) Ltd* [2003]). Where the conduct complained of has nothing to do with the petitioner's interests as a member, then a remedy under s 994 will not be granted.

However, there is little doubt that the member *qua* member requirement has been interpreted broadly and has been extended to cover interests that are sufficiently close to the petitioner's interests as a member. In a series of cases, the courts have stated that, in certain companies known as quasi-partnerships (discussed at the end of this chapter at 8.5.2), the right to be involved in management may be regarded as a membership right. In the following case, the Privy Council held that loaning capital to a company is an interest that can be recognized under s 994 of the CA 2006.

Gamlestaden Fastigheter AB v Baltic Partners Ltd [2007] UKPC 26

Facts: Baltic Partners Ltd ('Baltic') was set up to operate a joint venture entered into by Gamlestaden Fastigheter AB ('Gamlestaden') and a man named Karlsten. To finance the venture, Gamlestaden made substantial loans to, and purchased a substantial number of shares in, Baltic. However, shortly thereafter, Gamlestaden alleged that Karlsten and Baltic's directors had improperly removed funds from Baltic. Gamlestaden contended that this constituted unfairly prejudicial conduct and that Baltic's directors should account to Baltic for the withdrawals made. At the time of the hearing, Baltic had become insolvent, and so its directors argued that the payment of compensation to Baltic would benefit Gamlestaden in its capacity as a creditor of Baltic, and so the claim should be dismissed.

Held: The court rejected Baltic's directors' arguments and found for Gamlestaden. Lord Scott stated that, in such cases, a claimant should not be precluded from a remedy simply because the remedy would benefit it as a creditor and not as a member.

LOOKING FOR EXTRA MARKS?

This case clearly demonstrates how far the courts will relax the member *qua* member requirement in order to achieve a just and equitable result. Further, as Gamlestaden was apparently seeking to enforce a right that belonged to Baltic, one would assume that the rule in *Foss v Harbottle* would prevent the claim. This clearly demonstrates that a principal reason for the creation of the unfair prejudice remedy was to outflank the rule in *Foss v Harbottle* where fairness requires. For a discussion of this case, see Tony Singla, 'Unfair Prejudice in the Privy Council' (2007) 123 LQR 542.

8.4.1.1 Equitable considerations

Section 994 focuses on the members' interests as opposed to their rights. The members' rights are found in the company's constitution, but the courts have repeatedly stated that their interests can be wider than their rights (*Re Sam Weller & Sons Ltd* [1990]). In particular, in certain companies, the members may agree that the company should be run in a certain manner, but this agreement may never be formalized or inserted into the constitution. In such companies, the courts will not permit the constitution to be relied upon if such reliance unfairly prejudices the interests of the members by defeating the 'legitimate expectations' (since rephrased as 'equitable considerations') that such agreements give rise to. In *O'Neill v Phillips* [1999], Lord Hoffmann stated that:

> A member of a company will not ordinarily be entitled to complain of unfairness unless there has been some breach of the terms on which he agreed that the affairs of the company should be conducted. But . . . there will be cases in which equitable considerations make it unfair for those conducting the affairs of the company to rely upon their strict legal powers.

The approach established in this statement is demonstrated well by the facts of *O'Neill v Phillips*.

O'Neill v Phillips [1999] 1 WLR 1092 (HL)

Facts: Phillips was director of Pectal Ltd and owned all 100 of its shares. He gave twenty-five shares to O'Neill and appointed him as a director. Phillips also retired from the board, leaving O'Neill as the *de facto* managing director. Pectal's profits were initially split 75:25 in favour of Phillips, but this was later amended to provide for an equal share. Pectal experienced financial difficulties and Phillips returned to oversee management. He also claimed to once again be entitled to 75 per cent of Pectal's profits. O'Neill left the company and commenced an unfair prejudice claim.

Held: The House held that Phillips had not promised that O'Neill would always receive 50 per cent of the profits and, at most, had promised that O'Neill would receive 50 per cent of the profits only while he acted as *de facto* managing director. Phillips had not breached Pectal's constitution, nor was there anything giving rise to the equitable considerations of which Lord Hoffmann spoke. Accordingly, O'Neill's action failed.

LOOKING FOR EXTRA MARKS?

O'Neill v Phillips is a seminal case and was the only case involving unfair prejudice to ever reach the House of Lords. For a discussion of the case, see Dan D Prentice and Jennifer Payne, 'Section 459 of the Companies Act 1985: The House of Lords' View' (1999) 115 LQR 587.

What *O'Neill* establishes is that, in the majority of cases, the members' rights and interests will be the same and will be set out in the company's constitution (especially in the case of listed companies). In other cases, however, notably those involving quasi-partnership companies (discussed at the end of this chapter at 8.5.2), equitable considerations will arise which can widen the members' interests beyond those rights found in the constitution. The category of equitable considerations is open-ended, but exclusion from management is a good example and is the issue that arises in most **s 994** cases. In most companies, the members will not expect to be involved in management and so exclusion from management will not constitute unfairly prejudicial conduct. Conversely, in quasi-partnership companies, the members will usually expect to be involved in management, but such an expectation will usually derive from an informal agreement as opposed to the company's constitution. In such companies, exclusion from management will likely amount to unfairly prejudicial conduct.

8.4.2 When is conduct 'unfairly prejudicial'?

If the interest affected is one that is recognized by **s 994**, the next step is to discuss whether or not the company's affairs have been run in a way so as to unfairly prejudice that interest. Note that **s 994** only applies where *the company's affairs* have been conducted in an unfairly prejudicial manner. Accordingly, a **s 994** petition will fail if it is brought against a person acting in his private capacity (e.g. a director or employee acting in relation to his own affairs, as occurred in *Re Legal Costs Negotiators Ltd* [1999]).

The courts take an objective approach when determining whether or not the conduct complained of is unfairly prejudicial. Accordingly, there is no requirement for the petitioner to 'come with clean hands', but unmeritorious conduct on behalf of the petitioner might lead the court to hold that the conduct is not unfair, or that the remedy granted should be reduced (*Re London School of Electronics Ltd* [1986]).

In *Re Saul D Harrison and Sons plc* [1994], Neill LJ stated that the conduct complained of 'must be both prejudicial . . . and also unfairly so: conduct may be unfair without being prejudicial or prejudicial without being unfair, and it is not sufficient if the conduct only satisfies one of these tests'.

REVISION TIP

It is important to understand that unfair and prejudice are two separate requirements, and that you understand how they differ. For example, in *Grace v Biagioli* [2005], the petitioner was a member and director of a company. He was removed from office because he was attempting to set up a rival company. The court held that the conduct complained of (i.e. removing him) was prejudicial but, given the obvious conflict of interest that his actions had created, it was not unfair. For an example of a case where the conduct complained of was unfair, but not prejudicial, see *Rock (Nominees) Ltd v RCO (Holdings) plc* [2004].

The courts have repeatedly stated that the words 'unfairly prejudicial' are general words and are not to be given a narrow technical meaning. The courts have also not sought to establish a general standard or test to determine whether or not conduct is unfairly prejudicial. As Lord Hoffmann stated in *O'Neill v Phillips* [1999], the rationale behind this is to 'free the court from technical considerations of legal right and to confer a wide power to do what appeared just and equitable'. He did, however, go on to say that what is fair would depend upon the context of the case, adding that '[c]onduct which is perfectly fair between competing businessmen may not be fair between members of a family'. Accordingly, the individual facts of the case are all important.

Examples of conduct that the courts have held capable of being unfairly prejudicial include:

- non-payment of dividends (*Re a Company (No 00370 of 1987)* [1988]) or payment of low dividends (*Re Sam Weller & Sons Ltd* [1990]);
- exclusion from the management of a quasi-partnership company (*Re Ghyll Beck Driving Range Ltd* [1993]);
- serious mismanagement (*Re Macro (Ipswich) Ltd* [1994]). Note that the mismanagement must be serious—normal mismanagement will not usually constitute unfairly prejudicial conduct (*Re Elgindata Ltd (No 1)* [1991]);
- abuse of a controlling position (e.g. where the directors sell company assets at an undervalue to another company they control (*Re Little Olympian Each Ways Ltd (No 3)* [1995]));
- breach of directors' duties, statutory rights, or the constitution;
- criminal conduct (*Bermuda Cablevision Ltd v Colica Trust Co Ltd* [1998]);
- preventing the members from obtaining the best price for their shares (*Re a Company (No 008699 of 1985)* [1986]);
- the payment of excessive remuneration to the directors (*Re Cumana Ltd* [1986]); and
- the improper transfer of assets (*Re London School of Electronics Ltd* [1986]).

8.4.3 Remedies

Where a **s 994** petition is successful, the court has considerable remedial flexibility in that it can make 'such order as it thinks fit for giving relief in respect of the matters complained of' (**CA 2006, s 996(1)**). **Section 996(2)** provides a non-exhaustive list of examples of orders that the court could make, including:

- an order regulating the conduct of the company's affairs in the future (e.g. depriving a director of certain powers (*Re HR Harmer Ltd* [1959]));

- an order requiring the company to refrain from doing an act, or to perform an act that it has failed to perform;

- an order requiring the company not to make any changes to its articles without the court's permission; or

- an order requiring the petitioner's shares to be purchased by the company or by another member.

In practice, the final remedy (known as a share purchase order) is by far the most common remedy, under which the courts will usually order that the majority shareholders purchase the petitioner's shares. Debate exists as to whether winding up a company is an available remedy under **s 996**—nothing in **s 996** indicates winding up is not available, but the Law Commission opined that winding up is not available, citing *Re Full Cup International Trading Ltd* [1995] as authority.

A **s 994** petition is not subject to a limitation period but, as the granting of relief under **s 994** is discretionary, the court may refuse to grant a remedy where a significant period of time has elapsed between the conduct complained of and the petition being brought (see e.g. *Re Grandactual Ltd* [2005] where a nine-year delay was enough to persuade the court to refuse a remedy).

LOOKING FOR EXTRA MARKS?

The lack of a limitation period has been criticized on the ground that it encourages counsel to trawl through the company's history and adduce excessive amounts of evidence. As a result, **s 994** claims have gained a reputation for being overly lengthy and expensive. In an essay discussing **s 994**, these weaknesses should be noted and backed up with authority. In *Re Elgindata Ltd (No 1)* [1991], the dispute concerned shares worth £24,600, yet the legal costs of the case exceeded £320,000. The case of *Re Freudiana Music Co Ltd* [1995] took over 165 days of court time, with the successful respondent awarded costs of £2 million.

8.5 The petition for winding up

Perhaps the most extreme remedy available to an aggrieved member is to petition the court for an order winding up the company. It is generally believed that such a remedy is not available under **s 996** (*Re Full Cup International Trading Ltd* [1995]), but it is available under **s 122(1) of the Insolvency Act 1986**, which lists seven circumstances in which a winding up may be ordered. For our purposes, the two principal circumstances are:

1. A company can be wound up where the company passes a special resolution resolving that the company should be wound up (**IA 1986, s 122(1)(a)**). However, this remedy will be of little use to a minority shareholder.

2. The key provision is found in **s 122(1)(g)**, which allows the court to wind up a company where it is of the opinion that it is just and equitable to do so. A single member can petition the court under **s 122(1)(g)**, so it is potentially an extremely significant remedy.

REVISION TIP

A member may have multiple potential remedies. Problem questions may require you to discuss the unfair prejudice remedy and the petition for winding up, so you should ensure you are aware of the relationship between the two remedies. Historically, it was common for members to seek a remedy under both **s 994 of the CA 2006** and **s 122(1)(g) of the IA 1986** in order to place undue pressure upon the defendant. Given this concern, a Practice Direction was issued stating that petitioners should not apply under **s 994 and s 122(1)(g)**, unless a winding up is genuinely preferred. **Section 125(2) of the IA 1986** provides that the court will not order a winding up where an alternative remedy is available and the petitioner is acting unreasonably in seeking winding up. This indicates that the remedies are complementary, but winding up will only rarely be ordered.

8.5.1 When will a court order a winding up?

The words 'just and equitable' are broad terms and the courts have not sought to exhaustively define when a winding up will be ordered. Despite this, certain instances can be identified where courts are more likely to order a winding up:

- where the company is fraudulently promoted (*Re London and County Coal Co* (1866)) or is set up for a fraudulent purpose (*Re Walter Jacob Ltd* [1989]);

- where the company is deadlocked, which will occur (i) where an inability of the members to cooperate in the management of the company leads to the inability of the company to function at a board or shareholder level, or (ii) where there is an irretrievable breakdown in trust and confidence between the participating members of a quasi-partnership company (*Chu v Lau* [2020]).

- where the company's objects clause indicates that it has been formed for a specific purpose (this is known as the company's '**substratum**'), and it becomes impossible to fulfil this purpose (*Re German Date Coffee Co* (1882)). With the introduction of default unrestricted objects, cases involving loss of substratum will lessen significantly over time. More guidance on this was provided in *Re Klimvest plc* [2022] when a listed company was, for the first time, wound up due to a loss of substratum;

- where the petitioner can demonstrate there is a 'justifiable lack of confidence in the management of the company's affairs' (*Loch v John Blackwood Ltd* [1924]). Examples include a failure to submit accounts or hold general meetings when required (*Loch v*

John Blackwood Ltd [1924]), stealing money from the company (*Re Worldhams Park Golf Course Ltd* [1988]), or controlling the company in an oppressive manner (*Re HR Harmer Ltd* [1959]). Note that mere negligence or inefficiency will not suffice (*Re Five Minute Car Wash Service Ltd* [1966]).

8.5.2 Quasi-partnerships

Section 122(1)(g) of the IA 1986 (along with other member remedies) acquires an increased importance where the company in question is a 'quasi-partnership'. What constitutes a quasi-partnership and the importance of **s 122(1)(g)** to such companies was the subject of the following case.

Ebrahimi v Westbourne Galleries Ltd [1973] AC 360 (HL)

Facts: In 1945, Ebrahimi and Nazar formed a partnership. In 1958, they incorporated the business and became the company's directors. Shortly thereafter, George (Nazar's son) also became a director. Between them, Nazar and George held the majority of the company's shares. In 1969, a dispute arose and Nazar and George used their shares to vote Ebrahimi out of office. Ebrahimi petitioned the court for a winding-up order.

Held: In many companies, the rights of the members will be exhaustively stated in the company's constitution. However, quasi-partnerships will conduct business based on legitimate expectations and agreements made between the members and, in such companies, effect should be given to these expectations and agreement. Although the requirements that make a quasi-partnership cannot be exhaustively stated, typically quasi-partnerships will display all, or some, of the following characteristics:

* the company will be formed based on mutual trust and confidence,
* there will be an agreement that some, or all, of the members will be involved in management, and/or
* the shares will not be freely marketable, meaning that an aggrieved shareholder may be locked into the company.

The company in *Ebrahimi* was clearly a quasi-partnership and was formed on the basis that the shareholders would be involved in management. As this understanding was breached, the House ordered the company to be wound up.

The majority of cases involving **s 122(1)(g)** involve members of quasi-partnerships who have been excluded from management.

LOOKING FOR EXTRA MARKS?

For a discussion of the importance of **s 122(1)(g)** in relation to quasi-partnerships, see MR Chesterman, 'The "Just and Equitable" Winding Up of Small Private Companies' (1973) 36 MLR 129.

CASE	FACTS	PRINCIPLE
Ebrahimi v Westbourne Galleries Ltd [1973] AC 360 (HL)	The three sole members of a quasi-partnership company were also its directors. Two of them used their votes to remove the third from the board.	In quasi-partnerships, the members will usually expect to be involved in management. Where this expectation is breached, the court may order the company to be wound up.
Foss v Harbottle (1843) 2 Hare 461	The directors had misapplied company property, thereby causing the company loss. Two members commenced proceedings to make the directors account for the misapplied property.	The loss was sustained by the company and so only the company could sue for redress. The members cannot commence proceedings for loss sustained by a company—the company is the proper claimant.
Gamlestaden Fastigheter AB v Baltic Partners Ltd [2007] UKPC 26	The directors of a company had improperly removed funds from the company. The company became insolvent. The claimant (a member and creditor of the company) argued that the directors' conduct was unfairly prejudicial.	In such cases, the claimant should not be denied a remedy, even though the remedy will benefit him principally as a creditor, and not as a member.
Grace v Biagioli [2005] EWCA Civ 1222	A director was removed from office because he was attempting to set up a rival company.	The conduct complained of was prejudicial but, given the obvious conflict of interest that the director's actions had created, it was not unfair.
Mission Capital plc v Sinclair [2008] EWHC 1339 (Ch)	The defendant directors' employment was terminated. The defendants sought permission to continue a derivative claim.	Permission will likely be refused where a notional director would not seek to continue the claim, or where the derivative claimant has a personal claim.
O'Neill v Phillips [1999] 1 WLR 1092 (HL)	The defendant retired from the board and the claimant acted as *de facto* managing director. The defendant also increased the claimant's share of the profits. The defendant later reassumed control of the company and reduced the claimant's share of the profits.	In quasi-partnership companies, the courts will apply equitable considerations to give effect to informal agreements between the parties. However, in this case, the agreement was not to last indefinitely, but only so long as the claimant remained managing director.
Prudential Assurance Co Ltd v Newman Industries Ltd (No 2) [1982] Ch 204 (CA)	The directors had engaged in a transaction at an undervalue and had misled the members. The members brought a personal action.	Where the loss sustained by the members is reflective of the company's loss, then the company is the proper claimant and the members will not be permitted to recover the reflective loss.
Re Ghyll Beck Driving Range Ltd [1993] BCLC 1126 (Ch)	The claimant and three others were members and directors of a quasi-partnership company. Following an argument, the claimant was excluded from management by the others.	Where a member legitimately expects to be involved in management (as in a quasi-partnership company), then his exclusion from management can amount to unfairly prejudicial conduct.

CASE	FACTS	PRINCIPLE
Re John Reid & Sons (Strucsteel) Ltd [2003] EWHC 2329 (Ch)	An employee of the company, who was also a member, was dismissed. He alleged that his dismissal was unfairly prejudicial.	His claim was dismissed as he was bringing his claim in his capacity as an employee and not in his capacity as a member.
Re Macro (Ipswich) Ltd [1994] BCC 781 (Ch)	The directors of a company had engaged in significant and serious acts of mismanagement.	Whilst mismanagement will not normally amount to unfairly prejudicial conduct, mismanagement that is sufficiently serious can amount to unfairly prejudicial conduct.
Sevilleja v Marex Financial Ltd [2020] UKSC 21	Sevilleja transferred money away from companies he controlled to avoid a court judgment requiring those companies to pay a debt.	The reflective loss principle is limited to claims by shareholders that, as a result of actionable loss suffered by their company, the value of their shares or distributions they receive as shareholders has been diminished.

KEY DEBATES

Topic	The derivative claim
Author/Academic	Andrew Keay and Joan Loughrey
Viewpoint	Discusses in detail the statutory derivative claim, focusing especially on the criteria the court must consider when deciding whether to permit the claim to continue.
Source	'Something Old, Something New, Something Borrowed: An Analysis of the New Derivative Action Under the Companies Act 2006' (2008) 124 LQR 469

Topic	The unfair prejudice remedy and the derivative claim
Author/Academic	Jennifer Payne
Viewpoint	Discusses the relationship between the unfair prejudice remedy and the derivative claim and argues that the two remedies should be merged.
Source	'Section 459–461 Companies Act 1985 in Flux: The Future of Shareholder Protection' (2005) 64 CLJ 647

Topic	The reflective loss principle
Author/Academic	Jonathan Hardman
Viewpoint	Discusses the case of *Sevilleja* and the reflective loss principle
Source	'*Sevilleja v Marex Financial Ltd*: Reflective Loss and the Autonomy of Company Law' (2022) 85 MLR 232

EXAM QUESTIONS

Essay question

'The statutory derivative claim provides a much more useful remedy than the common law derivative action.'

Discuss the validity of this statement.

See the Outline answers section in the endmatter for help with this question.

Problem question

Helen, Tom, and Joseph have, for ten years, run a small but successful partnership. In 2020, they decide to incorporate the business and a new company (JME Ltd) is created and the business is transferred to the new company. Helen, Tom, and Joseph become directors and each take 300 shares in the company. A further 200 shares are issued and allotted to Dave, a local businessman. The articles of JME Ltd provide that (i) no director can be removed without his or her prior consent, (ii) each director is to receive a salary of £150,000 per year, and (iii) any shareholder who wishes to sell his shares must first offer them to the directors.

After incorporation the company was successful but no dividends were paid as all the profits were ploughed back into the company, the directors drawing only their salaries of £150,000 each year.

In 2023, Joseph had an argument with Tom and Helen over matters of business policy. After this argument, Tom and Helen made all the business decisions in advance and outvoted Joseph at all the directors' meetings. Joseph initially complained but has now lost interest and ceased attending meetings.

Recently, Tom and Helen have voted to remove Joseph as a director at a general meeting and also have voted to distribute the profits by increasing the directors' salaries to £300,000 per annum.

Discuss whether or not JME Ltd has been run in a manner that is unfairly prejudicial or whether any conduct has taken place that would justify winding up the company.

 Online resources

For an outline answer to this problem question, as well as multiple-choice questions and further reading, please visit the online resources.

9 Corporate rescue and liquidation

KEY FACTS

- The Insolvency Act 1986 aims to establish a rescue culture by creating mechanisms designed to help companies that are experiencing financial difficulties.

- The most pro-rescue mechanism is administration, the principal aim of which is to rescue the company as a going concern.

- A company and its creditors can enter into a legally binding arrangement known as a company voluntary arrangement.

- The Corporate Insolvency and Governance Act 2020 introduced two new recue procedures, namely the restructuring plan and the moratorium.

- The process whereby a company's assets are collected and distributed to persons entitled to them, prior to the company being dissolved, is known as liquidation (or winding up).

- There are two types of liquidation, namely a compulsory winding up and a voluntary winding up. There are two types of voluntary winding up, namely a members' voluntary winding up and a creditors' voluntary winding up.

- A liquidator is given substantial powers in relation to collecting assets of the company, increasing the pool of assets available for distribution, and invalidating or obtaining redress for certain transactions and agreements.

- Upon liquidation, the liquidator of a company must distribute its assets to entitled persons in a specified order.

CHAPTER OVERVIEW

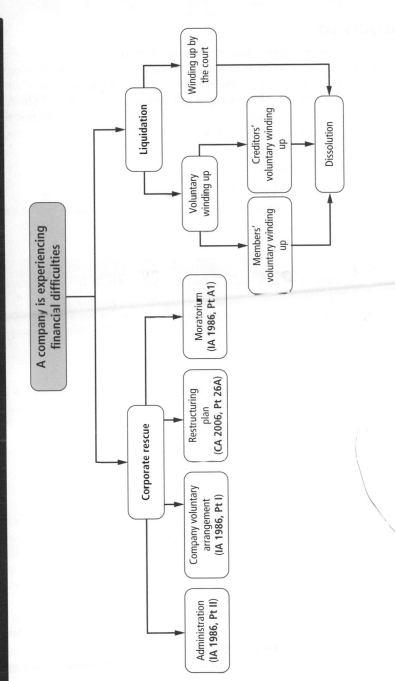

Introduction

This final chapter discusses the various procedures available to companies that are experiencing financial difficulties that are so severe that the company's survival is in jeopardy. A company need not utilize any of these procedures and may simply try to trade its way out of difficulty, but in many cases such a strategy will not succeed and the company will need the law's aid in order to survive. Conversely, the company might decide, or be forced to conclude, that there is no prospect of avoiding **insolvency** and may begin the process to end its existence. This chapter discusses the various procedures that:

- aim to help struggling companies,
- help creditors recover monies owed, and
- commence the process of ending the company's existence and provide for the distribution of its remaining assets.

 REVISION TIP

Not all company law courses discuss the various insolvency procedures. If your course does not discuss insolvency law, then much of this chapter may not be relevant. Note, however, that some areas of insolvency law (e.g. the provisions relating to wrongful trading) are relevant to other areas of company law that your course may cover.

It should also be noted that a lot of the detailed technical rules relating to insolvency law can be found in a piece of subordinate legislation called the Insolvency Rules. Ensure you are using the correct and up-to-date rules, namely the **Insolvency (England and Wales) Rules 2016 (IR 2016)**.

9.1 Corporate rescue

The failure of a company and its subsequent liquidation can have a substantial adverse effect on a significant number of persons. The company's employees will lose their jobs. The company's creditors are unlikely to recover in full, if at all, the debt owed to them. The shares of the company will become worthless, thereby causing the members to lose the value of their investment. The company's suppliers and retailers will likely suffer. If the company is large enough, its liquidation may even adversely affect the local or even national economy in which it is based (see e.g. the collapse of Lehman Brothers Holdings Inc, which had worldwide consequences).

Given these consequences, one would assume that the law would be keen to help struggling companies, but prior to the **Insolvency Acts of 1985 and 1986**, the law offered little aid and struggling companies had to fend for themselves. The Cork Report of 1982 strongly favoured establishing a 'rescue culture' under which legal mechanisms would be created that aided financially struggling companies.

LOOKING FOR EXTRA MARKS?

A possible essay question might require you to discuss whether the law should aid struggling companies or whether they should simply be left to die. For a discussion of the merits of a rescue culture, see Muir Hunter, 'The Nature and Functions of a Rescue Culture' [1999] JBL 491 and Vanessa Finch, *Corporate Insolvency Law: Perspectives and Principles* (2nd edn, CUP 2009) ch 6.

Legislation provides for several mechanisms that aim to rescue struggling companies, to bring them back to profitability or to achieve a more advantageous winding up. Originally the key rescue mechanisms were administration and the company voluntary arrangement. **The Corporate Insolvency and Governance Act 2020 (CIGA 2020)** has since added two more, namely the restructuring plan and the moratorium. For a discussion of why these new procedures were introduced, see Insolvency Service, 'A Review of the Corporate Insolvency Framework' (Insolvency Service 2016) and BEIS, 'Insolvency and Corporate Governance: Government Response' (August 2018). All four mechanisms will be discussed.

9.1.1 Administration

The most pro-rescue procedure is almost the most popular rescue procedure, namely administration. Administration simply involves a person (known as the administrator) being appointed to 'manage the company's affairs, business and property' **(IA 1986, Sch B1, para 1(1))**. The last few decades have been notable for the number of high-street companies entering administration (e.g. HMV, Blockbuster, Comet, JJB Sports, Toys R Us, Mothercare, House of Fraser), with many retail companies turning to administration to try and survive during the COVID-19 lockdown (e.g. Laura Ashley, Debenhams, Oasis, Warehouse, Peacocks).

LOOKING FOR EXTRA MARKS?

Be aware of the advantages that administration can have over liquidation, including:

- administration is usually cheaper than liquidation;
- administration may allow the business of the company to continue or be sold as a going concern, rather than as a 'fire sale' on liquidation, under which the assets are sold off for whatever price the liquidator can obtain; and
- the creditors may have better prospects of being paid than they would if the company was liquidated.

The pro-rescue nature of administration is evident in the hierarchy of objectives (known as 'the purpose of administration') that an administrator is appointed to achieve, as set out by **Sch B1, para 3 of the IA 1986**, illustrated by Figure 9.1.

Figure 9.1 The purpose of administration

```
┌─────────────────────────────────────────────────────────────────────┐
│           OBJECTIVE I—RESCUE THE COMPANY AS A GOING CONCERN           │
│  The administrator should perform his function with this objective    │
│  solely in mind. However, if this objective is not reasonably         │
│  practicable, or if objective II would achieve a better result for    │
│  the company's creditors as a whole, then the administrator should    │
│  move on to objective II.                                             │
└─────────────────────────────────────────────────────────────────────┘
                                    │
                                    ▼
┌─────────────────────────────────────────────────────────────────────┐
│   OBJECTIVE II—ACHIEVE A BETTER RESULT FOR THE COMPANY'S CREDITORS    │
│   AS A WHOLE THAN WOULD BE LIKELY IF THE COMPANY WERE WOUND UP         │
│   If it is not reasonably practicable to achieve objective I or II,   │
│   only then should the administrator aim to fulfil objective III.     │
└─────────────────────────────────────────────────────────────────────┘
                                    │
                                    ▼
┌─────────────────────────────────────────────────────────────────────┐
│  OBJECTIVE III—REALIZE PROPERTY IN ORDER TO MAKE A DISTRIBUTION TO    │
│  ONE OR MORE SECURED OR PREFERENTIAL CREDITORS                        │
└─────────────────────────────────────────────────────────────────────┘
```

This seemingly strict hierarchy of objectives is not so strict in practice, as much is based on the professional judgement of the administrator (e.g. whether objectives II or III are pursued depends in part on what the administrator 'thinks' is reasonably practicable). This allows the administrator to quite easily depart from objective I which is rarely pursued in practice (although it should remain the first objective considered). The most common outcome of administration is the business of the company is sold to a third party and the company itself is then liquidated and dissolved (this outcome would fall within objective II). This demonstrates that administrators distinguish between rescuing the business of the company and rescuing the company itself (a distinction that the **IA 1986** itself does not make).

A company enters administration when an administrator is appointed and leaves administration when the administrator's appointment is ended. The appointment of an administrator can occur in one of three ways:

1. the court can appoint an administrator by making an administration order;

2. a qualifying floating chargeholder can appoint an administrator; or

3. an administrator can be appointed by the company or its directors.

The administrator will manage the company's business, property and affairs, with **Sch 1 of the IA 1986** providing administrators with substantial powers to achieve the purpose of administration.

✛ LOOKING FOR EXTRA MARKS?

There is controversy regarding some of the administrator's powers, notably the administrator's ability to sell the company's property. This allows the administrator to sell all the company's business and property via a 'pre-pack administration' without consulting the company's creditors. This is especially ➔

→ controversial where the assets are sold to the company's directors or members. For a discussion of the controversy and how the law has sought to remedy it, see Lee Roach, *Company Law* (2nd edn, OUP 2022) 680–684 and Eugenio Vaccari, 'English Pre-Packaged Corporate Rescue Procedures: Is There a Case for Propping Industry Self-Regulation and Industry-Led Measures Such as the Pre-Pack Pool?' (2020) 31 ICCLR 170.

To help the administrator achieve the purpose of administration, entering administration brings about several effects:

- existing winding up petitions will be dismissed (if the administrator was appointed by administration order) or suspended (if the administrator was appointed by a floating chargeholder **(IA 1986, Sch B1, para 40(1))**;

- the directors remain in office, but cannot exercise any managerial powers without the administrator's consent **(IA 1986, Sch B1, para 64(1))**;

- a moratorium will come into effect that provides that, unless permission is obtained from the court or the administrator, no creditor may enforce security over the company's property, repossess goods in the company's possession, or institute or continue any legal proceedings against the company **(IA 1986, Sch B1, para 43)**.

9.1.2 The company voluntary arrangement

The company voluntary arrangement (CVA) is an important rescue procedure found in **Pt I of the IA 1986** that basically allows the company to enter into a binding arrangement with its creditors (e.g. to reduce or restructure monies owed). A CVA involves a number of stages, as set out in Figure 9.2.

Unlike administration, a CVA does not provide for a statutory moratorium. A moratorium used to be provided for small companies, but this was rarely used and so was abolished when the free-standing moratorium (discussed at 9.1.4) was introduced.

LOOKING FOR EXTRA MARKS?

Be aware of how the use of CVAs has evolved. Due to the lack of a moratorium, CVAs were historically underused and were much less popular than administration. However, from the point of view of the directors, a CVA may be preferable as it will allow them to remain in control of the company. There are examples of companies that have chosen a CVA over administration for justifiable reasons (e.g. see the CVA entered into by Travelodge Hotels Ltd in 2012, which resulted in a more beneficial outcome than would have been the case had it been placed into administration).

More recently, CVAs have started to become more popular with high-street retail businesses, who have used them to reduce the rental payments they need to pay to their landlords (notable examples include Regis UK, Debenhams, New Look, and Caffè Nero). In all these cases, the →

➡ companies significantly reduced their rental payments by getting CVAs approved. In most cases, the landlords objected, but were outvoted, leading to accusations that CVAs are now being used to single out landlords.

Figure 9.2 The CVA process

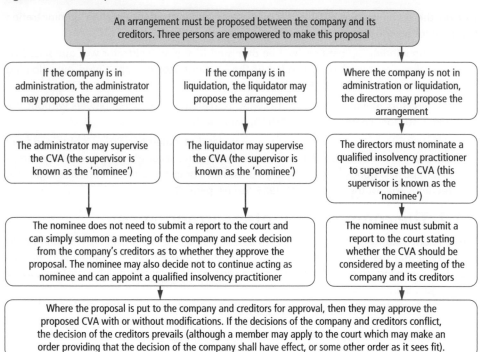

An arrangement must be proposed between the company and its creditors. Three persons are empowered to make this proposal

- If the company is in administration, the administrator may propose the arrangement
- If the company is in liquidation, the liquidator may propose the arrangement
- Where the company is not in administration or liquidation, the directors may propose the arrangement

- The administrator may supervise the CVA (the supervisor is known as the 'nominee')
- The liquidator may supervise the CVA (the supervisor is known as the 'nominee')
- The directors must nominate a qualified insolvency practitioner to supervise the CVA (this supervisor is known as the 'nominee')

The nominee does not need to submit a report to the court and can simply summon a meeting of the company and seek decision from the company's creditors as to whether they approve the proposal. The nominee may also decide not to continue acting as nominee and can appoint a qualified insolvency practitioner

The nominee must submit a report to the court stating whether the CVA should be considered by a meeting of the company and its creditors

Where the proposal is put to the company and creditors for approval, then they may approve the proposed CVA with or without modifications. If the decisions of the company and creditors conflict, the decision of the creditors prevails (although a member may apply to the court which may make an order providing that the decision of the company shall have effect, or some other order as it sees fit).

If the proposal is approved by both the company and its creditors, it takes effect and will become binding. It will be supervised by the nominee.

9.1.3 The restructuring plan

In 2016, the Insolvency Service noted that 'the CVA in its current form and scope is limited as a tool for company rescue' (Insolvency Service, 'A Review of the Corporate Insolvency Framework' (Insolvency Service 2016) para 9.2) and proposed the introduction of a 'restructuring plan' that was similar to the scheme of arrangement found under **Pt 26 of the CA 2006**. A scheme of arrangement is simply a compromise or arrangement between a company and (i) its creditors or any class of them, or (ii) its members, or any class of them. This restructuring plan was introduced by the **CIGA 2020** by inserting a new **Pt 26A** into the 2006 Act.

A restructuring plan is only available to companies that meet two conditions, namely Condition A and B:

A. the company has encountered, or is likely to encounter, financial difficulties that are affecting, or will or may affect, its ability to carry on business as a going concern (s 901A(2)); and

B. the purpose of the restructuring plan is to eliminate, reduce or prevent, or mitigate the effect of any of those financial difficulties (s 901A(3)(b)).

The three-stage procedure for implementing a restructuring plan is largely identical to implementing a scheme of arrangement, namely:

1. **The convening hearing**: An application is made to the court to summon meetings of the affected creditors (or any class of them) or members (or any class of them) (s 901C). If the plan only affects certain creditors/members, then the application must indicate this and separate meetings will be needed for each class of creditor/member affected. It is not always easy to determine what constitutes a 'class' of creditor/member and, if the application gets it wrong, the court will refuse to sanction the scheme at stage 3.

2. **The meetings**: The meetings will be summoned by the court to determine if the affected creditors/members approve the scheme. For each meeting, the plan will be approved only if a number representing 75 per cent in value of the creditors or class of creditors or members or class of members (as the case may be) vote in favour of the plan (s 901F(1)).

3. **The sanctions hearing**: If the plan is approved by the creditors/members, then an application can be made to the court to sanction the plan (s 901F(1)). A useful summary of the role of the court was set out by Sir Alistair Norris in *Re Amicus Finance plc* [2021]. If the court sanctions the plan, then it will come into effect and will bind those creditors/members who are parties to it, including those who voted against it.

The major difference between a scheme of arrangement and the restructuring plan relates to the courts' ability to sanction the scheme. Under a **Pt 26** scheme of arrangement, the court can only sanction the scheme if all the stage 2 meetings approve the scheme. However, the court can sanction a **Pt 26A** restructuring plan, even if a stage 2 meeting did not approve the plan. However, to exercise this so-called cross-class cram down two conditions must be satisfied:

1. the court must be satisfied that, if it did sanction the plan, none of the members of the dissenting class would be any worse off than they would be in the event of the relevant alternative (i.e. what would be most likely to occur if the plan were not sanctioned) (s 901G(3) and (4)); and

2. the plan must have been agreed by at least one of the stage 2 meetings (i.e. the court cannot sanction the plan if none of the stage 2 meetings approved the plan) (s 901G(5)).

REVISION TIP

The best way to understand the operation of the restructuring plan and the cross-class cram down is to look at practical examples of it in action. The first restructuring plan to be approved was that of

→ Virgin Atlantic (*Re Virgin Atlantic Airways Ltd* **[2020]**), but the cross-class cram down was not needed in that case. The first case where the cram down was used was *Re DeepOcean 1 UK Ltd* **[2021]**, which provides an excellent example of the cram-down conditions in action (for an account of this case, see Lee Roach, *Company Law* (2nd edn, OUP 2022) 648). Several companies have now had restructuring plans approved, including Virgin Active and Pizza Hut.

9.1.4 The moratorium

A moratorium is available to a company in administration, but placing a company in administration is a dramatic step that may not be warranted in some cases. Accordingly, in 2016, the Insolvency Service proposed that a free-standing moratorium should be introduced to provide a 'company in financial distress a breathing space in which to explore its rescue and restructuring options free from creditor action' (**Explanatory Notes to the CIGA 2020, para 4**). This was implemented by the **CIGA 2020** inserting a new **Pt A1 into the IA 1986**.

Almost any company can obtain a moratorium, either by filing specified documents with the court or applying to the court for a moratorium (the exact method depends on whether the company is UK-registered and whether it is subject to an outstanding winding-up petition). The moratorium, if granted, will be supervised by a monitor and will last for an initial period of 20 business days, after which it will end, unless it is terminated prior to this or extended (**IA 1986, s A9(1) and (2)**). The effects of the moratorium include:

- no insolvency proceedings may be brought against the company, subject to specified exceptions;
- no steps can be taken to enforce any security over the company's property, subject to specified exceptions;
- floating chargeholders cannot give notice of crystallization;
- the company cannot obtain credit of more than £500 unless it informs the lender that the moratorium is in force;
- the company can only grant security over its property if the monitor consents; and
- the company can only dispose of property in the ordinary course of business if the monitor consents or a court order is obtained

A moratorium will end once its initial period or extension period expires. A moratorium can also be terminated prior to this in several ways (e.g. if the company enters into administration or liquidation).

9.2 Liquidation

Liquidation is the final step before a company's dissolution and is the process whereby the assets of the company are collected and realized, its debts and liabilities paid, and the surplus distributed to persons so entitled. Liquidation can occur because a company could not trade its way out of financial difficulty, a rescue attempt did not work, or a solvent company may be liquidated for commercial reasons.

9.2.1 Types of liquidation

Liquidations come in two forms:

1. voluntary winding up, and
2. winding up by the court.

9.2.1.1 Voluntary winding up

Voluntary liquidations significantly outnumber compulsory liquidations (of the 23,393 liquidations that took place in the UK in 2022, 21,153 were voluntary). A company can be voluntarily wound up in one of two ways:

1. a members' voluntary winding up, or
2. a creditors' voluntary winding up.

In both cases, the winding up is commenced by the members passing a special resolution agreeing that the company is to be wound up voluntarily (**IA 1986, s 84(1)(b)**). The distinction between a members' and a creditors' voluntary winding up depends on whether a declaration of solvency is made. A declaration of solvency is a declaration by the majority of the directors which states that the directors have made a full enquiry into the company's affairs and have formed the opinion that the company will be able to pay its debts in full within a period, not exceeding twelve months from the commencement of the winding up, as may be specified in the declaration (**IA 1986, s 89(1)**).

Where such a declaration is made, the winding up will be a members' winding up and the creditors will likely be paid in full. Where no declaration is made, the winding up will be a creditors' winding up and the creditors may not be paid in full.

9.2.1.2 Winding up by the court

Winding up by the court (or 'compulsory winding up' as it is usually known) occurs where a person petitions the court for an order to wind up the company, and the court makes such an order. The court has no power to compulsorily wind up a company on its own initiative: a winding-up order can only be made following a petition from a specified person, with **s 124 of the IA 1986** providing that persons who can petition the court include:

- the company itself,
- the directors of the company,
- any creditor of the company,
- an administrator or official receiver, or
- a contributory of the company (this would include members of the company).

The court will only consider a petition from these persons on specific grounds, which can be found in **s 122(1) of the IA 1986** and include:

- where the company has, by special resolution, agreed that the company should be wound up;
- where the company is unable to pay its debts; and
- where the court is of the opinion that it is just and equitable that the company should be wound up (discussed at 8.5).

Most compulsory winding-up orders are made on the ground that the company is unable to pay its debts and, of orders sought under this ground, the vast majority of the petitions are brought by a creditor (usually the creditor whose debt the company has failed to repay).

9.2.2 The role and powers of a liquidator

Irrespective of the type of winding up, a liquidator will be appointed to oversee the company's liquidation. The liquidator occupies an extremely important position and his role is basically to gather in all the assets of the company, to pay off its debts and liabilities, and to distribute the remaining assets to persons entitled to them in the correct order.

REVISION TIP

Problem questions requiring you to advise or act as a liquidator in the carrying out of his functions are popular in exams (unless corporate insolvency is not taught as part of your Company Law module). Ensure that you are aware of the role of the liquidator and the powers given to him to aid him in carrying out his various functions.

To enable the liquidator to carry out his various functions, **Sch 4 of the IA 1986** grants liquidators an extremely wide array of powers, including:

- the ability to pay any creditors in full,
- the power to bring or defend legal proceedings on behalf of the company,
- the power to carry on the running of the business to achieve a more beneficial winding up, and
- the power to sell any of the company's property.

9.2.3 Malpractice before and during liquidation/ administration

Sections 212–219 (which apply to companies in liquidation) and **246ZA–ZC** (which apply to companies in administration) of the **IA 1986** empower the court to order certain persons who have engaged in specified forms of malpractice to make a contribution to the company's assets. This benefits the company's creditors by providing additional assets that can be used to pay off the company's debts and liabilities in the event of the company going into liquidation or administration.

9.2.3.1 Summary remedy

Section 212 of the IA 1986 applies where, during the course of a liquidation, it appears that an officer of the company, a liquidator, an administrative receiver, or other person involved in the promotion, formation, or management of the company has misapplied or retained, or become accountable for, any money or other property of the company, or has been guilty of any **misfeasance** or breach of any fiduciary or other duty in relation to the company. Misfeasance refers to the improper or unlawful performance of a lawful act.

> **REVISION TIP**
>
> It is important to understand that s 212 does not create a legal wrong, nor does it impose any new rights or obligations upon persons. It merely provides a procedural remedy that allows certain persons (notably a liquidator, creditor, or contributory) to commence a claim that would normally be vested in the company (e.g. it would allow a liquidator to bring a claim against a director for breach of a general duty, as occurred in *Re Glam and Tan Ltd* **[2022]**).

Where **s 212** has been breached, the court can order the defendant to contribute to the pool of assets for distribution by the liquidator, or to repay, restore, or account for any money or property that was misapplied or retained.

9.2.3.2 Fraudulent trading

Sections 213 (which applies to companies in liquidation) and **246ZA** (which applies to companies in administration) **of the IA 1986** provide that if, in the course of a winding up or administration of a company, it appears that any business of the company has been carried on with intent to defraud creditors of the company or creditors of any other person, or for any fraudulent purpose, then the court, on the application of the liquidator or administrator, may declare that any persons (not just the directors) who were knowingly parties to the carrying on of the business in such a way are liable to make such a contribution to the company's assets as the court thinks proper.

As liability can be imposed on anyone who is a knowing party, liability is not restricted to directors or persons who have a controlling or managerial function within the company (*Tradition Financial Services Ltd v Bilta (UK) Ltd* **[2023]**) Where a director has engaged in fraudulent trading, the court can also disqualify the director for up to fifteen years (**Company Directors Disqualification Act 1986, s 10**).

REVISION TIP

Fraudulent trading under **ss 213 and 246ZA** should not be confused with the criminal offence of fraudulent trading under **s 993 of the CA 2006**. **Sections 213 and 246ZA** only apply during winding up or administration respectively and impose civil liability only. **Section 993** can apply at any time and imposes criminal liability only. However, it is possible for one fraudulent transaction to breach several provisions and civil and criminal liability to be imposed.

9.2.3.3 Wrongful trading

As fraud must be proved beyond reasonable doubt and the liquidator must prove subjective knowledge of the fraud, successful fraudulent trading actions are rare. The Jenkins Committee (1962) and the Cork Committee (1982) therefore recommended that an alternative form of civil liability be introduced, which was implemented by **s 214 of the IA 1986**. **Sections 214** (which applies to companies in liquidation) and **246ZB** (which applies to companies in administration) allow the court to require directors to make a contribution to the assets of the company where they have engaged in 'wrongful trading', namely that, during the course of a winding up or administration, it appears that:

1. the company has gone into insolvent liquidation or insolvent administration; and
2. at some point before the commencement of the winding up of the company/company entering administration, that person knew, or ought to have concluded, that there was no reasonable prospect that the company would avoid going into insolvent liquidation or insolvent administration; and
3. that person was a director of the company at the time.

REVISION TIP

In problem questions, wrongful trading is often difficult to identify. Where the facts of a problem include (i) a recommendation (usually from an auditor) or opinion that the company should enter administration or that insolvency is unlikely to be avoided, or (ii) a director states that he believes the company should be placed into administration or wound up, or (iii) the company suffers financial losses (e.g. poor trading prospects, increasing overdraft, loss of key contracts, etc.), but continues to trade, this is providing a hint that you should discuss whether or not the directors have engaged in wrongful trading.

The first reported case concerning **s 214** provides a good example of the operation of the wrongful trading provisions in practice.

> **Re Produce Marketing Consortium Ltd [1989] BCLC 520 (Ch)**
>
> **Facts:** Produce Marketing Consortium Ltd ('PMC') was incorporated in 1964 and was involved in importing fruit. It was profitable until 1980 but, between 1980 and its liquidation in October 1987, its profitability and turnover decreased, it built up a large overdraft, and its liabilities exceeded its assets. By February 1987, one of PMC's two directors was of the opinion that insolvency was inevitable, but PMC continued to trade until October 1987, in order to dispose of fruit that had been in cold storage. PMC's liquidator sought a contribution from the two directors under **s 214**.
>
> **Held:** The two directors should have realized by July 1986 that liquidation was inevitable. Liquidation at this time would have saved PMC £75,000 and so the two directors were ordered to contribute this amount to PMC's assets.

On several occasions, the courts have stressed that trading whilst insolvent does not, in itself, constitute wrongful trading and the directors may properly conclude that continuing to trade whilst insolvent is the correct course of action (e.g. Chadwick J in *Secretary of State for Industry v Taylor* [1997]), as the following case demonstrates.

> **Re Hawkes Hill Publishing Co Ltd [2007] BCC 937 (Ch)**
>
> **Facts:** Hawkes Hill Publishing Co Ltd ('HHP') published a free magazine whose profitability was dependent upon revenue generated through advertising. HHP had exhausted all of its loan capital, experienced significant cash-flow problems, and was trading at a loss. The directors believed that there were investors willing to invest in HHP and extra revenue could be generated by raising the amount and the cost of advertising space, so HHP continued to trade. Their belief proved incorrect and, soon thereafter, HHP went into liquidation. The liquidator alleged that the directors had engaged in wrongful trading.
>
> **Held:** Wrongful trading does not occur simply because a company continues to trade at a time when the directors knew, or ought to have known, that the company was insolvent or could not pay its debts. Liability will only be imposed where a company continues to trade at a time when the directors knew, or ought to have known, that there was no reasonable prospect of avoiding insolvent liquidation or administration. Here, the directors did not know this—they reasonably believed that HHP could trade its way out of difficulty and return to solvency. Accordingly, the directors had not engaged in wrongful trading.

Finally, it should be noted that liability will not be imposed if, after the person realized that there was no reasonable prospect of avoiding insolvent liquidation or administration, he took every step that he ought to have taken to minimize the potential loss to the company's creditors (**IA 1986, ss 214(3) and 246ZB(3)**).

9.2.3.4 Restriction on re-use of company names

Sections 216 and 217 of the IA 1986 are primarily, though not exclusively, designed to combat what has become known as the 'Phoenix syndrome', which is demonstrated via the following example.

EXAMPLE (FICTIONAL)

FakeCo Ltd is insolvent and unable to pay its debts. The directors (who are also its members) decide to voluntarily wind up the company, leaving many of its creditors unpaid. A few days later, the directors set up a new company, FakeCorp Ltd. This new company acquires the assets of FakeCo Ltd (at a knock-down price) and engages in exactly the same business as FakeCo Ltd.

FakeCorp Ltd essentially continues business as normal, trading on the goodwill acquired by FakeCo Ltd, but it is no longer burdened by the debts of FakeCo Ltd. Conversely, the unpaid creditors of FakeCo Ltd will understandably feel aggrieved. To combat this, **s 216** regulates the re-use of company names. It applies to a person where a company (known as the 'liquidating company') has gone into insolvent liquidation and that person was a director or shadow director of that company at any time in the twelve-month period leading up to the date of liquidation (**IA 1986, s 216(1)**). Unless that person obtains the leave of the court, **s 216(3)** provides that he cannot, for a period of five years beginning on the date of the company's liquidation:

- be a director of any other company that is known by a prohibited name;
- in any way, whether directly or indirectly, be concerned or take part in the promotion, formation, or management of a company with a prohibited name; or
- in any way, whether directly or indirectly, be concerned or take part in the carrying on of a business carried on (otherwise by a company) under a prohibited name.

Under **s 216(2)**, a 'prohibited name' is:

(a) a name by which the liquidating company was known at any time in the twelve-month period prior to its liquidation, or

(b) a name which is so similar to a name falling within (a) as to suggest an association with that company (this would clearly apply to FakeCorp Ltd in the above example).

A person who contravenes **s 216** commits a criminal offence and can be made personally liable for the company's debts (**IA 1986, s 217**).

9.2.4 Adjustment of prior transactions

The directors of a company that is to be liquidated or placed into administration may enter into certain transactions or agreements, the effect of which is to prejudice the company's creditors (e.g. by selling off the company's assets prior to liquidation). Accordingly, **ss 238–246 of the IA 1986** empower the courts or specified persons to adjust or invalidate certain transactions, or to require a contribution to be paid to offset the effects of certain transactions.

9.2.4.1 Transactions at an undervalue

The directors of a struggling company may sell off the company's assets cheaply (usually to the directors themselves or other connected persons) in order to place them out of the control of a future liquidator or administrator. To combat this, **s 238 of the IA 1986** provides that where, at the relevant time, a company has gone into liquidation or administration, the liquidator or administrator may apply to the court for a remedy on the ground that the company has entered into a transaction at an undervalue. If the application is successful, the court will make such an order as it thinks fit for restoring the company to the position it would have been in had the company not entered into the transaction (**IA 1986, s 238(3)**).

Section 238 only applies where the transaction was entered into at the 'relevant time', with the relevant time being two years ending on the date of insolvency (**IA 1986, s 240(1)(a)**). However, the transaction will only fall within the relevant time if, at the time the transaction was made, the company was unable to pay its debts, or became unable to pay its debts due to the transaction (**IA 1986, s 240(2)**).

9.2.4.2 Preferences

Upon liquidation, the liquidator will pay off the company's creditors, with differing types of creditor ranking more highly than others, who will accordingly be paid first (this hierarchy is discussed later in this chapter at 9.2.6). A company may attempt to avoid this hierarchy by paying off certain low-ranking creditors prior to liquidation (especially if the creditor is connected to the company or directors), with the result that, upon liquidation, there may not be enough assets to pay the higher-ranking creditors. This is known as a 'preference', with s **239(4) of the IA 1986** stating that a company gives a preference to a person if:

- that person is a creditor, surety, or guarantor of the company; and
- the company does anything or suffers anything to be done which (in either case) has the effect of putting that person into a position which, in the event of the company going into insolvent liquidation, will be better than the position he would have been in if that thing had not been done.

Where the company has provided a person with a preference, a liquidator or administrator can apply to the court, which can make such an order as it thinks fit for restoring the company to the position in which it would have been had the company not given the preference (see e.g. *Carton-Kelly v Darty Holdings SAS* [2022], where the court ordered that £90 million preference be repaid to the company). However, this application can only be made if the preference was made at the 'relevant time'. What constitutes the relevant time will depend upon the identity of the person to whom the alleged preference was granted:

- If the company granted the alleged preference to someone connected with the company (e.g. directors, or wives, husbands, business partners, or employees of connected persons), then the relevant time is two years ending on the date of insolvency.
- In all other cases, the period is six months ending on the date of insolvency.

In addition, the preference will only fall within the relevant time if, at the time the preference was made, the company was unable to pay its debts, or became unable to pay its debts due to the preference (**s 240(2)**).

Finally, to find that a company has made a preference to a person, it must also be shown that the company desired to give that person a preference (**s 239(5)**). However, this desire to prefer will be presumed where the preference was given to a person connected with the company (**s 239(6)**).

9.2.4.3 Extortionate credit transactions

Section 244 of the IA 1986 allows a liquidator or administrator to petition the court for a remedy where, within a three-year period ending on the date of insolvency or the granting of the administration order, the company entered into an 'extortionate credit transaction'. Unless the contrary is proven, a credit transaction will be presumed to be extortionate if it requires grossly exorbitant payments to be made or if it grossly contravenes ordinary principles of fair dealing.

Where **s 244** has been breached, the court has extremely strong remedial powers, including the ability to completely set aside the transaction, or to vary the terms of the transaction.

It should be noted that, as part of its consultation on insolvency and corporate governance, the government has stated that it plans to examine and reform the law relating to extortionate credit transactions.

9.2.4.4 Avoidance of certain floating charges

The directors of a company may cause the company to grant them (or someone connected to them) a floating charge over the assets of the company, thereby prioritizing themselves over unsecured creditors in the event of the company's liquidation. To prevent this, **s 245 of the IA 1986** invalidates floating charges created within the relevant time prior to insolvency, with the relevant time being:

- two years where the charge was granted to a person connected with the company, or
- twelve months where the charge was granted to an unconnected person.

9.2.5 Distribution of assets

Once the liquidator has collected and realized the assets of the company, he will then need to use these assets to meet the company's debts and liabilities.

REVISION TIP

Where a problem question has you advising, or acting as, a liquidator, you will usually be required to discuss how the assets of the liquidated company should be distributed. Alternatively, you may be advising a creditor on his chances of recovering fully the amount loaned to the company. Either way, the rules relating to the distribution of assets upon liquidation are of crucial importance.

The distribution of assets is generally subject to the ***pari passu*** rule (*pari passu* means 'with equal step'), which means that if there are insufficient assets to pay off all the company's debts, each creditor will receive an equal percentage of the debt owed to them (not an equal amount). However, as we shall see, the *pari passu* rule is subject to numerous exceptions that result in a hierarchy of debts. These debts will be paid off one by one, meaning that once a group is paid in full, the remaining assets are used to pay the next group.

If there are insufficient assets to pay a group fully, each creditor amongst that group will receive the same percentage of their debt (i.e. the *pari passu* rule applies amongst members of each group, unless otherwise stated). Of course, lower ranking creditors will then go unpaid. Therefore, the higher the creditor ranks, the more likely the creditor will be paid in part or in full. The hierarchy of debts is discussed more below and is set out in Figure 9.3.

9.2.5.1 Debts secured by fixed charge

Assets subject to a fixed charge (discussed at 7.3.1.1) are outside the scope of the liquidator's control. Such a chargeholder can, upon the company's liquidation, simply take the charged assets, sell them, and use the proceeds to satisfy the debt owed to him. Accordingly, a fixed chargeholder does not need to rely upon the liquidator to obtain satisfaction of his debt and, therefore, debts secured by fixed charge effectively rank ahead of all other debts.

9.2.5.2 Moratorium debts etc

Where winding-up proceedings are commenced within a 12-week period following the end of a moratorium under **Pt A1 of the IA 1986**, then moratorium debts, pre-moratorium debts, and any fees or expenses of an official receiver will be the first debts paid off by the liquidator (**IA 1986, s 174A**).

9.2.5.3 Liquidation expenses

The next dets to be paid will be the liquidation expenses, which rank ahead of all other debts (**IA 1986, ss 115, 156, and 176ZA**), except those of fixed chargeholders (who need not rely on the liquidator to obtain satisfaction of the debt) and moratorium debts. **Rule 7.108(1) of the IR 2016** provides that '[a]ll fees, costs, charges and other expenses incurred in the course of the winding up are to be treated as expenses of the winding up'. **Rule 7.108(4)** then lists eighteen types of expenses that are classified as liquidation expenses. Liquidation expenses do not rank equally amongst themselves, with **Rule 7.108(4)** also setting out the order of priority in which the eighteen types of liquidation expenses must be paid.

9.2.5.4 Preferential debts

Statute classifies certain debts as preferential debts, meaning that they rank ahead of most other debts (except debts secured by fixed charge, moratorium debts, and liquidation expenses). The categories of preferential debts can be found in **Sch 6 of the IA 1986**, but it is worth noting that Crown debts (e.g. debts owed to HM Revenue & Customs) are, following the **Enterprise Act 2002**, no longer generally classified as preferential, with the Insolvency Service estimating that this will result in around £70 million per year being paid to other creditors. However, since December 2020, taxes paid by employees and customers of the company that are held by the company (e.g. VAT, income tax, employee NI contributions) are classed as preferential debts. Other preferential debts include:

- pension scheme contributions,
- remuneration owed to employees (but only sums up to £800 will rank as preferential—the remainder will rank as unsecured), and
- any amount owed by way of accrued holiday pay.

9.2 LIQUIDATION

Figure 9.3 The distribution of assets

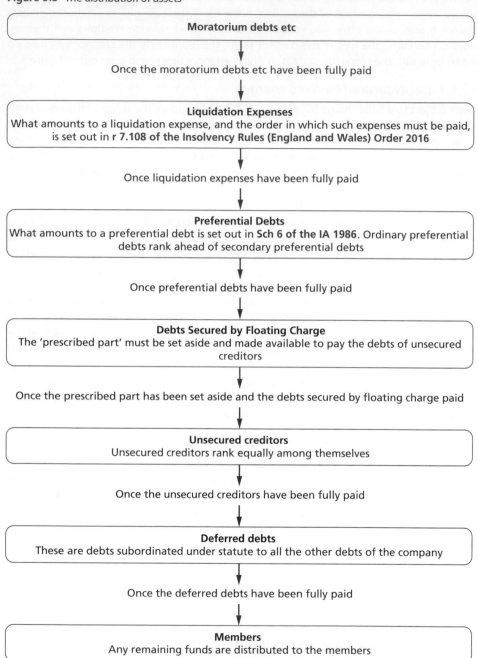

Moratorium debts etc

Once the moratorium debts etc have been fully paid

Liquidation Expenses
What amounts to a liquidation expense, and the order in which such expenses must be paid, is set out in **r 7.108 of the Insolvency Rules (England and Wales) Order 2016**

Once liquidation expenses have been fully paid

Preferential Debts
What amounts to a preferential debt is set out in **Sch 6 of the IA 1986**. Ordinary preferential debts rank ahead of secondary preferential debts

Once preferential debts have been fully paid

Debts Secured by Floating Charge
The 'prescribed part' must be set aside and made available to pay the debts of unsecured creditors

Once the prescribed part has been set aside and the debts secured by floating charge paid

Unsecured creditors
Unsecured creditors rank equally among themselves

Once the unsecured creditors have been fully paid

Deferred debts
These are debts subordinated under statute to all the other debts of the company

Once the deferred debts have been fully paid

Members
Any remaining funds are distributed to the members

Preferential debts are classed as either 'ordinary preferential debts' or 'secondary preferential debts' **(IA 1986, s 386(1A) and (1B))**. The significance of this is that secondary preferential debts are only paid once the ordinary preferential debts have been paid in full **(IA 1986, s 175(1B))**. Ordinary and secondary preferential debts rank equally amongst themselves.

9.2.5.5 Debts secured by floating charge

Debts secured by floating charge suffer from two notable weaknesses. First, such debts rank behind debts secured by fixed charge, moratorium debts, liquidation expenses, and preferential debts. Second, once the liquidator has determined the assets that would go to floating chargeholders, he must set aside a percentage of those assets (often known as the 'prescribed part') to pay off the unsecured creditors. The percentage is:

- 50 per cent of the first £10,000, and
- 20 per cent of the remainder, up to a limit of £800,000.

9.2.5.6 Unsecured debts

Any remaining funds (including the prescribed part if applicable) will then be distributed to the unsecured creditors. Unsecured creditors rank equally amongst themselves, so if there are insufficient funds left to fully pay all the unsecured creditors, they will be paid *pari passu*.

9.2.5.7 Deferred debts and the members

Certain debts are classified as 'deferred debts' (e.g. sums due to any member by way of dividend) and are subordinated to all other debts of the company. If there are any funds remaining once all the deferred debs have been paid, they belong to the company's members, with the articles determining how such funds are to be distributed.

 KEY CASES

CASE	FACTS	PRINCIPLE
Re Hawkes Hill Publishing Co Ltd [2007] BCC 937 (Ch)	A company continued to trade even though it was insolvent and the directors knew that the company could not pay its debts.	Trading whilst insolvent is not enough, in itself, to establish liability for wrongful trading. Liability will only be imposed if the directors also knew, or ought to have known, that there was no reasonable prospect of avoiding insolvent liquidation.

CASE	FACTS	PRINCIPLE
Re Produce Marketing Consortium Ltd [1989] BCLC 520 (Ch)	A company, which was profitable until 1980, became increasingly unprofitable until its liquidation in 1987. The directors continued to trade at a time when insolvency looked inevitable.	Prompt liquidation in July 1986, by which time the directors should have realized that insolvency was unavoidable, would have saved the company £75,000. The directors had therefore engaged in wrongful trading and were ordered to contribute £75,000 to the company's assets.

KEY DEBATES

Topic	The rescue culture
Author/Academic	Muir Hunter
Viewpoint	Discusses in depth what constitutes a rescue culture and whether such a culture is desirable or justified.
Source	'The Nature and Functions of a Rescue Culture' [1999] JBL 491

Topic	Wrongful trading
Author/Academic	Andrew Keay
Viewpoint	Discusses the arguments for and against **s 214** of the **IA 1986**, and considers whether companies and their creditors should be able to opt out of the wrongful trading provisions.
Source	'Wrongful Trading and the Liability of Company Directors: A Theoretical Perspective' (2005) 25 LS 431

Topic	Pre-pack administrations
Author/Academic	Teresa Graham
Viewpoint	Discusses the controversy surrounding pre-pack administrations. Looks in depth at the advantages and disadvantages of pre-packs and provides recommendations for reform.
Source	'Graham Review Into Pre-Pack Administration' (2014)

Q EXAM QUESTIONS

Essay question

To what extent has the UK adopted a rescue culture and should the law aid struggling companies?

See the Outline answers section in the endmatter for help with this question.

Problem question

In March 2019, Emily and Becky incorporated a company (Shoes in the City Ltd) that specialized in selling ladies' footwear. Emily and Becky were the company's only members and each owned 100 £1 shares. Emily and Becky were the company's only directors.

The company began to experience financial difficulties. In September 2022, the company's overdraft with the Black Horse Bank plc had reached its limit of £250,000. In return for increasing the overdraft limit to £300,000, the Black Horse Bank plc demanded security and took a floating charge over all the company's assets. The business continued to struggle and, in January 2023, Emily and Becky were informed by the company's auditor that insolvent liquidation was inevitable, although Emily and Becky disagreed and held out hope that the company's financial prospects would improve. Emily and Becky decided to try and trade their way out of their financial difficulties by having a sale. Unfortunately, the sale failed to increase business and in March 2023, Shoes in the City was wound up. By this time, the company's overdraft with Black Horse Bank amounted to £290,000.

Barry has been appointed liquidator and has discovered several disturbing facts: (i) in August 2022, Emily and Becky caused the company to repay an unsecured loan of £5,000, which Becky had made to the company some months before; (ii) in addition to the money owed to Black Horse Bank, the company owes £10,000 to the Inland Revenue, £30,000 to employees in wages, and £100,000 to unsecured creditors.

Barry estimates that the total remaining assets of Shoes in the City amount to £150,000. Barry's expenses in acting as liquidator amount to £3,000. Advise Barry.

Online resources

For an outline answer to this problem question, as well as multiple-choice questions and further reading, please visit the online resources.

Exam essentials

Identify the topic(s)

In any exam, one of the most crucial skills is the ability to correctly identify the legal topic(s) involved. Often, exam questions (especially problem questions) will not expressly identify the legal topic involved, so you will have to identify the topic and, if you misidentify the topic, you will lose the majority, if not all, of your marks. Identifying the correct topic(s) in company law problem questions can be a challenge because, as is discussed in the next section, company law topics can often impact upon one another. However, some exam problem questions may tell you to focus on a particular legal topic—in such a case, follow the instructions and do not be tempted to show off your knowledge of other areas of the law.

Be aware of how topics can overlap

Students often assume that each exam question will cover a single topic, but this is often not the case. Company law topics do not exist in isolation from each other and it is perfectly possible that an exam question (especially a problem question) could cover multiple topics. For example, a problem question involving a director who engages in acts that are outside the scope of the company's constitution might require you to discuss (i) the *ultra vires* rules, (ii) enforcing the statutory contract, (iii) whether or not the director had breached the duty found in s 171 of the CA 2006, and (iv) whether or not a derivative claim can be brought. You should be aware of how topics could overlap and, throughout this text, potential overlaps have been highlighted.

Legislative reforms

Much of the law in the CA 2006 differs from that found in the CA 1985 (where appropriate, this text has identified the key differences between the 1985 and 2006 Acts). Further, the 2006 Act has been substantially amended and added to since its enactment. Essay questions often require you to discuss reforms to the CA 2006, so it pays to be aware of how the 2006 Act differs from its 1985 predecessor, and how the 2006 Act has been amended since its enactment. Be prepared to discuss to what extent, if any, the 2006 Act has improved the law in key areas, or how the 2006 Act has (or has not) been improved by subsequent amendments. In particular, be aware of how the CA 2006 and the IA 1986 have been amended by subsequent legislation (e.g. the Enterprise and Regulatory Reform Act 2013, the Small Business, Enterprise and Employment Act 2015, the Corporate Insolvency and Governance Act 2020).

Avoid focusing exclusively on the CA 2006

Although the CA 2006 is central to our company law system, students tend to focus on it exclusively, and tend to ignore other rules and recommendations that are of significant importance. In particular, do not ignore:

- *The constitution of the company* The CA 2006 is silent in relation to many areas of corporate activity (especially concerning the internal activities of companies), preferring to leave such issues to be determined by the companies themselves via the company's constitution. The articles form the principal constitutional document and can, in some cases, modify or disapply provisions found in the **CA 2006**. In many problem questions, the content of the articles is not stated, and so it is safe to assume that the model articles are used. Accordingly, it is wise to have a sound knowledge of the provisions of the model articles and how such articles differ to prior model articles found under previous Companies Acts.

- *Corporate governance principles, reports, and codes* As regards certain areas of company law, the **CA 2006** is silent (e.g. non-executive directors, remuneration/nomination/audit committees). In such cases, the principles found in the relevant corporate governance principles, reports, and codes (notably the **UK Corporate Governance Code, the Wates Corporate Governance Principles**, and the **UK Stewardship Code 2020**) are of clear importance and usually go well beyond what is required by the law. Unfortunately, many students lack sufficient knowledge of the relevant reports and codes, which is a major mistake given the importance of such codes, especially to larger companies.

- *The Listing Regime* UK listed companies are required to adhere to a strict body of rules found in the FCA Handbook, of which the notable rules for our purposes are: (i) the **Listing Rules**, (ii) the **Disclosure Guidance and Transparency Rules**, and (iii) the **Prospectus Regulation Rules**.

- *EU law* EU law has had a significant impact upon the UK system of company law, as many provisions within the **CA 2006** were included, or have since been modified, in order to comply with EU legislation (usually the various EU company law directives). Certain provisions of the **CA 2006** may have been criticized but cannot currently be changed as they were included to satisfy our EU membership obligations. Be aware of the influence that EU law has had, and continues to have, on our system of company law. Although the UK has left the EU, it is likely that EU law will continue to influence UK law and will be of importance to UK companies that also operate within the EU or have EU-based subsidiaries.

Stay up to date with legal developments

Company law and corporate governance are constantly evolving topics (especially corporate governance) and it is vital that you remain up to date with legal developments. Be wary when relying on ageing sources and ensure that your textbooks are up to date (do not rely on old editions, and even new editions may be out of date in parts). Journal articles are excellent sources of academic criticism and authority, but always double check the information found in older articles to see if it is still correct.

Staying up to date with legal developments can be onerous. Fortunately, this book is accompanied by a Twitter account (@ UKCompanyLaw), which will do much of the work for you by providing updates of legal developments in relation to company law and corporate governance.

Outline answers

Further help for problem questions is available online at
www.oup.com/lawrevision/

CHAPTER 1

Essay question

Background

• In order to answer this question, you should discuss the historical background to the **Limited Liability Partnerships Act 2000 (LLPA 2000)**. Understanding why the Act was passed will enable you to discuss whether the Act was designed to provide a new business vehicle for small businesses.

• It is important that you state that the lobbying for LLP legislation came almost entirely from large professional firms, especially the largest accountancy firms. You will want to discuss why these firms believed that neither the ordinary partnership nor the company suited their needs.

• Before examining the LLP, you should discuss why the standard partnership and the registered company are not ideal business structures for small businesses, namely:

• Whilst the partnership is a flexible and private business structure, the liability of the partners for the firm's debts and liabilities is joint and unlimited.

• Companies are subject to a significant amount of regulation and formality, and it has historically been argued that company law legislation is not drafted with the needs of small businesses in mind.

The limited liability partnership

1. Discuss to what extent the LLP is a suitable business structure for small businesses generally. You may wish to state at the outset that there is little doubt that the LLP was not designed to meet the needs of small businesses in general, largely because the LLP is so similar to a registered company.

2. Like a company, the LLP will have corporate personality and the liability of its members will be limited. Accordingly, the LLP's members will not normally be liable for its debts. This certainly

remedies the principal weakness of an ordinary partnership.

3. However, **s 1(5) of the LLPA 2000** states that, unless the Act provides otherwise, LLPs will be governed by company law and not partnership law. Accordingly, LLPs will be regulated, for the most part, in the same manner as companies. Therefore, the formality, regulation, and loss of privacy and flexibility that can come from conducting business through a company will also apply to the LLP.

4. It is worth stating at this point that the **CA 2006** does appear to provide a more suitable regulatory regime for small businesses than the **CA 1985**, but compliance with the Act can still be costly, burdensome, and can result in a loss of privacy.

5. It is largely accepted that the LLP does not provide a suitable business structure for small businesses in general (as evidenced by the fact that fewer than 60,000 LLPs have been incorporated), but it is a business structure designed for those who lobbied for its creation, namely large professional firms (virtually all of whom have adopted LLP status).

6. The LLP does indeed have some of the best features of a company, but it also has virtually all the drawbacks and, arguably, it lacks some of the major advantages of an ordinary partnership.

CHAPTER 2

Essay question

• Normally, you would not be required to provide the facts of a case when writing an essay. However, where the essay requires you to discuss a single case, setting out the facts of the case is often useful. Accordingly, provide a brief overview of the relevant facts of Salomon and the arguments of the parties involved.

• In order to appreciate the true significance of Salomon, you will want to discuss the decisions of the three courts the case was heard in:

1. At first instance, Vaughan Williams J was not prepared to grant relief based on the liquidator's claims, but he did grant relief based on the concept that the company was an agent or nominee for Mr Salomon.

2. The Court of Appeal upheld the trial judge's decision, stating that the whole transaction was contrary to the true intent of the Companies Act, and that the company was a sham and an alias, agent, trustee, or nominee for Mr Salomon. Also, the Court of Appeal was in no doubt that when Parliament stipulated seven members, it meant seven genuine and active members.

3. The House of Lords unanimously reversed this decision. It held that the company was validly formed since the Act merely required seven members holding at least one share each. The Act said nothing about them being independent or that they should take an active role in the company.

Justifications

1. The decision of the House in *Salomon* can be applauded as well as criticized. The decision encourages individuals to set up businesses by making it less risky. This is certainly true. However, as a corollary, certain individuals will set up companies that are under-capitalized, content in the knowledge that, should the company fail, they will be protected by the company's separate personality. Accordingly, the ability to use corporate personality to shield oneself from liability may encourage the setting up of unstable businesses which will have a negative effect on the economy. This, ultimately, makes business more risky for everyone. Parliament has responded by attaching personal liability in certain circumstances.

2. Some argue that the market for shares relies on the ability to shield oneself from liability. Without it, shareholdings would be limited to a few wealthy investors who can monitor their shareholdings. Small investors would be deterred from investing by the prospect of unlimited personal liability. Further, shareholders often diversify their shareholdings across a large number of companies to minimize risk. If investors could not shield themselves from liability, diversification would increase the shareholders' risk, not decrease it.

The impact of *Salomon*

• The decision of the House of Lords in *Salomon* is often credited with establishing the concept of separate personality. This is not true—the concept of corporate personality was recognized long before 1897, and was a clearly intended consequence of the **Joint Stock Companies Act 1844**.

• What *Salomon* did was to demonstrate that the courts had not, until then, fully appreciated the consequences of separate legal personality. In upholding the separate personality of the company

even where the individual's control of the company was absolute, the House of Lords established that the corporate form could be used legitimately to shield an 'owner' of the business from liability. Some academics argue that this is essential in order to encourage companies to engage in risky, but potentially profitable, activities. Others argue that it encourages the setting up of unsuitable or ill-thought-out businesses.

• Two other consequences of the decision should also be noted:

1. *Salomon* implicitly recognized the validity of the one-man company (that is, a company run by one person with a number of dormant, nominee members) long before company law overtly allowed one-man companies to be created. The ability to create a one-man private company was only granted in 1992, and the ability to create a one-man public company was established by the **CA 2006**.

2. *Salomon* established that a relationship of agency or trusteeship will not be created simply because a person holds shares in a company (even if he owns all the shares).

CHAPTER 3

Essay question

• Begin by briefly defining the scope of a company's constitution. State that **s 33 of the CA 2006** provides that the constitution forms a contract between the members and the company, and between the members themselves. Accordingly, breach of the constitution will amount to breach of contract, providing the innocent party with a remedy.

The statutory contract

• The statutory contract created by **s 33** is indeed an unusual one. Provide examples of how the statutory contract differs from a standard contract, including:

1. The terms of the statutory contract can be altered against the wishes of one of the parties, even after the contract has been entered into.

2. The courts will not rectify the statutory contract, nor can it be defeated on the grounds of misrepresentation, undue influence, or duress.

3. Whereas all terms of a standard contract can form the basis of an action for breach of contract, only terms relating to membership rights will form part of the statutory contract.

Enforcing the statutory contract

- You will need to discuss how straightforward it is to enforce the statutory contract. The constitution forms a contract between the company and its members, so if the company breaches the constitution, a member can obtain a remedy. The case of *Pender v Lushington* (1877) provides a good example of this.

- However, the ability of the members to enforce the constitution is subject to an important limitation, namely that a member can only enforce the constitution if he is acting in his capacity as a member. Only provisions relating to membership rights will form part of the statutory contract. The case of *Beattie v E and F Beattie Ltd* [1938] provides a good example of this.

- This limitation can be criticized. If the company breaches a term of the constitution that does not relate to a membership right, then that term will not form part of the statutory contract and so cannot be enforced. In effect, the company would have been permitted to ignore a provision of the constitution, without having to amend it. In practice, in such cases, the member will almost certainly be able to commence proceedings under **s 994 of the CA 2006**, which demonstrates that the unfair prejudice remedy is likely to be a preferable remedy to enforcing the statutory contract.

- In the case of quasi-partnership companies, the dividing line between directors and members is often blurred. Accordingly, in such companies constitution provisions relating to the rights of directors will also form part of the statutory contract (*Rayfield v Hands* [1960]).

- Often, the members may breach the constitution, which may adversely affect other members. Accordingly, the statutory contract can also be enforced by a member against another member (as occurred in *Rayfield v Hands* [1960]), providing that the right breached is a membership right.

CHAPTER 4

Essay question

- Begin by pointing out that, prior to the **CA 2006**, directors' duties were found in a mass of case law and statute. As a result, the law was unclear and inaccessible and many directors had little knowledge of the duties they were subject to.

- Point out that codification was not meant to radically reform the law—this is made clear by **s 170 of the CA 2006**. Accordingly, it could be argued that codification has done little to improve the law. However, the fact that the codified duties are based on pre-2006 law does not mean that codification was an unnecessary step, for two reasons:

1. Placing the duties in statute has a number of notable advantages.

2. The duties under the **CA 2006** are different in several respects from their pre-2006 common law counterparts.

Advantages and disadvantages of codification

- You will then want to discuss the advantages and disadvantages of codification. Advantages include:

1. Improved accessibility—theoretically, anyone can look to the **CA 2006** and reasonably comprehend the duties owed.

2. Successful codification could result in the law becoming more predictable and will remove the judge's discretion to develop the law in subjective and unpredictable ways.

3. The duties could be expressed in broad and general language which could be applied to a wide range of situations. This would allow the law to adapt to emerging practices.

- However, codification suffers from some noteworthy disadvantages:

1. Codification may provide a clearer and more accessible statement of duties, but the duties have not been fully codified. The codified duties will need to be interpreted by the judges in marginal cases where the law is not clear. In such cases, recourse to the statute will not be enough and the relevant case law will need to be known. Accordingly, it could be argued that accessibility will only be slightly improved.

2. A corollary of this is that the codified law may not result in a notable increase in predictability. The codified duties cannot cover every situation and Parliament cannot be expected to foresee every situation that might occur. The judges will still need to fill in any gaps that arise.

3. It is not easy to amend codified law. Most areas of company law are dynamic and the law needs to be able to respond to new situations. To amend the statutory statement of duties, an Act of Parliament would need to be passed. Amending legislation can be a lengthy and complex

process, so codified law may be slow to adapt to changing circumstances.

Similarities and differences between the common law and statutory duties

• Students should also point out those areas where the law has remained the same and those areas where the codified duties differ. As a general rule, the duties found in the 2006 Act are the same as the common law duties, albeit with some slight alterations. **Section 178(1)** even provides that the remedies for breach of the general duties will remain the same as for breach of their common law counterparts (which does not aid accessibility at all).

• However, the 2006 Act has reformed the duties in some notable ways, with the obvious example being the duty contained in **s 172**, namely to promote the success of the company for the benefit of its members. You should discuss how the **s 172** duty differs from the previous 'bona fide in the interests of the company' duty. It has been argued by many that the common law duty was shareholder-focused, whereas the duty contained in **s 172** is more stakeholder-friendly. This is backed up by the list of relevant factors contained in **s 172(1)**, which includes the interests of employees, the community, and the environment, as well as the likely consequences of any decision in the long term. However, in keeping with the enlightened shareholder approach, directors must have regard to these factors, but they cannot be used to override the primary duty to promote the success of the company for the benefit of its members.

CHAPTER 5

Essay question

• Point out that, even though the general power to manage is vested in the directors, significant power is placed in the hands of the members.

• However, historically, there has been a perception that the rules and procedures by which general meetings are run operate in order to favour the views of the company's directors and prevent the members from effectively exercising their decision-making powers.

The calling of meetings

• The power to call meetings is a good example of how the procedures relating to general meetings can favour the directors. **Section 302 of the**

CA 2006 vests the power to call a general meeting in the directors. **Section 303** grants the members the power to require the directors to call a general meeting, but the Act does not make it easy for members to exercise this power.

• The directors will only be required to call a meeting if a sufficient percentage of the members require the meeting. In the case of companies with a share capital, the request must come from members representing at least 5 per cent of the company's paid-up share capital.

• This will not be an easy requirement to meet, especially in the case of large private companies and public companies where the members may be numerous and highly dispersed. Certainly for many individual members, this will likely prove an insurmountable obstacle.

Controlling the agenda and the circulation of information

• The directors normally draw up the notices of general meetings. This is an important power because, apart from any matters designated as ordinary business in the articles, only those matters of which notice has been given can be discussed at a meeting.

• Within the boundaries of their fiduciary duties, the directors can, at the company's expense, send out circulars explaining why the members should support their resolutions.

• The members have the power to require the company to circulate a statement of not more than 1,000 words in relation to a matter referred to in a proposed resolution, or any other business dealt with at the meeting (**CA 2006, s 314(1)**). However, this power only arises if a sufficient number of members require the statement to be circulated.

• If these requirements cannot be met, then the members will have to pay for the cost of sending the circulars themselves and this can be extremely expensive. Accordingly, this appears to be one area where the dice are still loaded in the management's favour. In practice, resolutions are nearly always proposed by the directors, not by the members.

General meetings in practice

• In order for general meetings to be an effective mechanism for shareholder democracy, two conditions must be satisfied:

1. the majority of the shares should be held by members who are not directors, and

2. all or most of the members should be willing to participate in general meetings.

- Unfortunately, only one or neither of these conditions are present in companies at either end of the size spectrum. As regards small owner-managed companies, the shares are held wholly or mainly by the directors. These companies are run informally without reference to company law for the main. Where the directors and members are the same people, formal general meetings serve little or no use.

- General meetings fail for a different reason in the case of large public companies. Here, there may be hundreds of thousands of members living all over the world. It is impracticable for more than a tiny minority of them to attend a general meeting and many members either do not attend or vote or allow the directors to act as their proxy, thereby increasing the voting power of the directors.

- Most commentators agree that general meetings are a key mechanism in ensuring that the directors are made accountable to the members. However, the limitations discussed are also generally accepted by commentators. It appears that there is an unspoken feeling that general meetings, as a form of governance accountability, are becoming increasingly moribund.

CHAPTER 6

Essay question

- Begin by pointing out that the **UK Corporate Governance Code** does indeed rely heavily on non-executive directors (NEDs) in two ways:

1. NEDs are tasked with monitoring the activities of the executive directors, as well as contributing to management.

2. The Code recommends that the audit committee, nomination committee, and remuneration committee consist primarily of NEDs.

- There is no doubt that NEDs are the governance mechanism that is currently in favour, with the Higgs Report describing them as 'custodians of the governance process'.

- You should provide a brief definition of a NED and explain how they differ from executive directors. You should also discuss the dual role of NEDs, namely to contribute to management policy and to monitor management.

Advantages of NEDs

- Discuss the advantages that NEDs have over other corporate governance mechanisms. Monitoring

at board level, theoretically, has several advantages over monitoring by the members:

1. NEDs should have better access to information than the members.

2. NEDs do not suffer from the collective action problems that affect members.

3. The NEDs have much more regular, and closer, contact with the executives than the majority of members.

Disadvantages of NEDS

- Despite the fact that NEDs have some notable strengths, many academics believe that they are outweighed by the weaknesses, including:

1. As NEDs work only part-time, they may be unable to become fully conversant with the company's business and so end up relying on the executives for information. The executives, for obvious reasons, might be selective in terms of what information they provide to the NEDs.

2. It is often argued that the NEDs' two roles (i.e. management and monitoring) do not sit easily with one another and could result in a segregated board.

3. NEDs can only be effective if they are truly independent of the executives. However, for several reasons, there is widespread doubt regarding their independence in practice. It is believed that many NEDs are selected on the basis that they will fit in with the executives' ideologies and that, even when NEDs are nominated by a nomination committee, the CEO will play a significant 'behind the scenes' role.

4. There is a general belief that NEDs lack the motivation to stringently monitor the executives.

- The result of these weaknesses is that, despite efforts (such as the Higgs Report) to improve the effectiveness of NEDs, there is a general feeling that NEDs do not in general provide significant improvements to corporate governance.

CHAPTER 7

Essay question

- This question requires you to discuss how the **CA 2006** has reformed the law relating to share capital and capital maintenance. It is important to remember that sometimes you will need to know not only what the law is, but also what it was, so that you can compare the two.

- You may want to begin by giving a brief overview of the rules relating to capital maintenance, noting in particular the aims behind these rules, notably to protect the company's creditors by preventing capital from being returned to the shareholders.

• Before going on to discuss the 2006 reforms, it is also worth pointing out that the pre-2006 law was widely regarded as being overly technical and complex, anachronistic, and ineffective.

• There is little doubt that the 2006 Act has introduced a number of reforms that have improved the law in this area and you should discuss the benefits of these reforms. Beneficial reforms would include:

1. The abolition of the concept of authorized share capital. As discussed at 7.1.1.2, the requirement was largely pointless and simply served to inconvenience companies.

2. Allowing private companies to reduce share capital without the need to obtain court approval. Prior to the 2006 Act, in order to reduce capital, all companies needed to obtain court approval. Court approval was a major burden for private companies, especially given that for many smaller companies, the capital maintenance rules are of little practical relevance.

3. Abolishing the prohibition on providing financial assistance for the purchase of shares in relation to private companies. The prohibition served to ban transactions that were innocuous and commercially beneficial.

• Despite this, however, there are still problems that the 2006 Act has failed to remedy. Such problems include:

1. The 2006 Act has done little to prevent companies allotting shares at a discount. As noted at 7.1.2.3, the rules contained in the **CA 1985** were somewhat lax in relation to private companies, and the **CA 2006** has done nothing to strengthen these rules.

2. As discussed at 7.1.4, the minimum capital requirements imposed on public companies are universally regarded as weak and the 2006 Act has not strengthened them in any way.

3. Although the prohibition on providing financial assistance has been abolished in relation to private companies, it remains for public companies. However, a convincing rationale for the prohibition has never been fully articulated by the courts and many believe that the prohibition should be abolished completely (which is possible

now the UK is no longer bound by the **Second EEC Company Law Directive**).

• The conclusion that will likely be drawn is that the statement is an accurate one. The 2006 Act has improved the law, but not in all respects, and several notable weaknesses remain.

CHAPTER 8

Essay question
The rule in *Foss v Harbottle*

• Briefly explain the three principles that form the Rule in *Foss v Harbottle* (hereinafter referred to as 'the Rule'). However, the Rule cannot be absolute. Were it so, wrongs committed by the directors or the majority shareholders would rarely be subject to litigation. Accordingly, in limited situations, the courts would allow members to bring actions on a company's behalf (the 'derivative action').

• While the existence of, and justifications behind, the Rule itself are not open to significant criticism, there is little doubt that the operation of the Rule and its exceptions came in for significant criticism. The Law Commission identified four major problems:

1. The Rule and its exceptions are a creation of case law, much of which was created many years ago.

2. A member who wished to bring an action to recover damages where the company suffered loss due to a breach of the directors' fiduciary duties would need to establish that the wrongdoers had control of the company. However, what constituted 'control' was not clear.

3. A member who wished to bring an action to recover damages where the company suffered loss due to the negligence of a director would need to show that the negligence conferred a benefit on the controlling shareholders (*Pavlides v Jensen* [1956]), or that the failure of the other directors to bring an action constituted a fraud on the minority.

4. A member who wished to bring a derivative action would need to establish standing by showing that he has a *prima facie* case. The potential exists for these standing hearings to become mini-trials which further increases the already high cost of litigation.

• Accordingly, the Law Commission, along with a number of respondents to the consultation paper and the Company Law Review Steering Group, recommended that a new derivative action be created. The result was the creation of the 'statutory derivative claim', the details of which can be found in **Pt 11 of the Companies Act 2006**.

The statutory derivative claim

• **Part 11** of the 2006 Act does not abolish the Rule in *Foss v Harbottle* and the Rule itself and its justifications retain much of their force. However, the common law derivative action has been largely abolished and, in most cases, a member can only bring an action on behalf of the company in accordance with the rules relating to the new statutory derivative claim.

• Discuss the operation of the statutory derivative claim, focusing in particular on the differences that exist between the common law derivative action and the statutory derivative claim. Notable differences include:

1. The rules relating to the derivative action can be found in a mass of common law, which adversely affected the accessibility and clarity of derivative actions. Having a statutory derivative claim will better alert members, directors, and other interested parties to the existence of the remedy. The disadvantage of placing the remedy in statute is that alteration of the remedy will require amending the 2006 Act, and amending legislation is rarely a quick and simple process.

2. Under the common law, negligence could only form the basis of a derivative action if the wrongdoer gained some form of benefit from the negligent act. This limitation has not been preserved in the 2006 Act and derivative claims can be brought for any negligent act. This reform has caused fears that derivative claims will increase sharply.

3. A common law derivative action could be based on an act/omission by a director or a member. A statutory derivative claim can only be based on the acts/omissions of a director (including former directors and shadow directors).

4. Permission from the court was required to continue a derivative action and this requirement is preserved for derivative claims. However, the 2006 Act provides guidance on what factors are relevant when determining whether or not to grant permission. Such guidance did not exist under the common law. To date, few cases have been granted permission to continue—be prepared to discuss these cases and their impact.

• One final point is worth noting. With the creation of the unfair prejudice remedy, derivative actions/claims are much less common and it could be argued that the shareholder remedy is of little significance in practice.

CHAPTER 9

Essay question

• Prior to the enactment of the **Insolvency Act 1985** UK company law did little to aid ailing companies, and companies that struggled with financial difficulties were 'left to die'. Highlight the severe consequences that can result from the liquidation of a company.

• Point out that the law needs to strike a delicate balance between aiding struggling companies and protecting the creditors of such companies. Should a rescue attempt fail and the assets of the company be depleted further, the creditors will receive even less than if the rescue attempt had not been made.

• The 1982 Cork Report favoured the UK adopting a 'rescue culture' whereby mechanisms are put in place to aid struggling companies. The result was the introduction of two notable rescue procedures, namely administration and company voluntary arrangements.

Administration

• Administration was introduced by the **Insolvency Act 1986** and is a clear example of the law's desire to foster a rescue culture and aid ailing companies. In recent years, the value of the administration procedure has been in evidence. Following the 2007–8 financial crisis and the lockdown following the COVID-19 pandemic, a number of prominent high-street companies experienced severe financial difficulties and went into administration in an effort to avoid liquidation. In adverse economic times, the value of the administration procedure is greater than ever.

• The pro-rescue nature of the administration process is evident from the hierarchy of objectives that an administrator is appointed to achieve. Discuss the three hierarchical objectives of administration, making sure to note that rescuing the company as a going concern is the first objective.

• The pro-rescue nature of the administration process is further evidenced by the statutory moratorium. Discuss the rationale behind the imposition of the moratorium.

• Discuss the advantages that a rescue procedure like administration can have over placing the company in liquidation, including:

1. It may allow a company to trade its way back into profitability.

2. Administration is likely to be less expensive than liquidation.

3. Upon liquidation, the company's assets are usually sold off for whatever price the liquidator can obtain, whereas assets sold by an administrator are likely to fetch a higher price.

4. The company's creditors may have better prospects of being paid than if the company were liquidated, and the employees (or some of them) may be able to retain their jobs.

Company voluntary arrangements

• Point out that the CVA is an important, but historically underused, rescue procedure. Explain the basic workings of a CVA.

• The pro-rescue nature of the CVA is evidenced in that, if the company is in the process of being wound up when the CVA is approved, then the court can stay the winding up and give such directions as it thinks appropriate for facilitating the implementation of the CVA.

• Initially, the effectiveness of CVAs was adversely affected by creditors who could derail the CVA by appointing a receiver or by petitioning the court for a winding-up order. Accordingly, a new form of CVA was introduced that provides the company with a moratorium similar to that which exists under the administration procedure. However, this moratorium was rarely used and, with the introduction of the freestanding moratorium, the moratorium accompanying the CVA has now been abolished.

• Remember to provide a balanced discussion of the CVA by setting out its advantages and disadvantages. Point out that whilst a CVA is a useful rescue procedure, there is little doubt that administration is usually a more effective one, largely due to the moratorium that comes with it (although a freestanding moratorium is now available that could be used alongside a CVA).

Discuss why administration is preferable to a CVA, but also state that, for directors who wish to retain office, a CVA might be a more appropriate procedure.

• Point out that, recently, the CVA has become more popular, especially amongst retail companies.

Restructuring plan

• The restructuring plan under **Pt 26A of the CA 2006** is a type of scheme of arrangement that is specifically aimed at companies in financial difficulty. Be aware of why the restructuring plan was introduced.

• Be aware of how the restructuring plan is designed to help struggling companies, namely:

(a) it is only available to companies in financial difficulty;

(b) obtaining approval of the plan in the stage 2 meetings is slightly easier than for a **Pt 26** scheme of arrangement; and

(c) the courts have been given the power to cram down dissenting creditors, meaning that the courts can sanction the plan even if there has been a meeting of creditors at sage 2 that did not approve the plan. Be aware of when the courts can exercise this cross-class cram down.

• To date, the restructuring plan has not been widely used, but there have been some notable plans approved (e.g. Virgin Atlantic, Virgin Active, Pizza Hut, DeepOcean).

Moratorium

• A moratorium has long been available to companies in administration, but placing a company into administration is a major step that may not be suitable in all cases. Accordingly, the **CIGA 2020** introduced a new freestanding moratorium by inserting a new **Pt A1 into the IA 1986**.

• Be aware of the procedures that need to be followed to obtain a moratorium.

• Be aware of the purpose of the moratorium, namely to provide financially struggling companies with breathing space to consider rescue or restructuring options. Be aware of how companies obtain this breathing space, namely by discussing the effects of the moratorium.

Glossary

agent A person engaged to act on behalf of another person (that other person being known as the principal).

allotted share capital The total nominal value of shares that a company has allotted.

articles of association The principal constitutional document of a company that usually provides for rules that regulate the internal affairs of the company.

authorized share capital The maximum total nominal value of shares that may be allotted by a company.

bonus shares Shares allotted to existing shareholders and paid for out of the company's distributable profits.

book debt A sum owed to a company by those who have purchased goods or services from the company.

called-up share capital Where a company calls for payment on shares that have not been fully paid for, the amount called for plus the paid-up share capital is known as the called-up share capital.

capacity The ability of a person to enter into certain transactions or make certain decisions. For example, a company's contractual capacity refers to its ability to enter into legally binding contracts.

capital maintenance regime A series of rules designed to protect creditors by maintaining a company's level of capital by preventing capital from being returned to the company's members.

charge Any form of security where possession of property is not transferred.

chargee A creditor who obtains a charge from another person.

charger A debtor who grants a charge to another person. Also known as the 'surety'.

class rights The rights that are attached to different classes of shares.

codification The process whereby law is collected and restated in statute.

Companies House An executive agency of the government responsible for incorporating and dissolving companies and for storing information relating to companies that can be inspected by the public.

company secretary An officer and agent of the company who is usually responsible for ensuring that the company complies with its legal and financial obligations.

corporate member A company member who is a body corporate (e.g. a company or LLP).

corporate personality The separate personality that belongs to legal persons (e.g. companies, LLPs). Also known as separate personality or legal personality.

crystallization The process whereby a floating charge fixes onto the charged assets.

debenture A document whereby a company creates or acknowledges a debt, whether unsecured or secured.

debt capital The capital that companies obtain through borrowing from others. Also known as 'loan capital'.

de facto 'In fact'.

default A general term used in many pieces of legislation that refers to a failure to perform a legally obligated act (e.g. to appear in court when required).

de jure 'In law'.

dividend The distribution, usually in cash, of profits to the members, usually at a fixed amount per share.

fiduciary The word 'fiduciary' can refer to:

(i) a relationship of trust and confidence (e.g. solicitor and client, doctor and patient, or trustee and beneficiary), or

(ii) a person who is in such a relationship and who is under an obligation to *act* in the other's interests (e.g. a doctor, solicitor, or trustee).

golden parachute An agreement between a company and an employee (usually an executive director) providing that the employee will receive certain benefits upon the termination of his employment.

identification theory A theory which states that the knowledge of certain persons is to be attributed to the company.

incorporation The process by which a company or LLP is created.

initial public offering (IPO) The first sale of shares by a company to the public at large.

insolvency A company is deemed to be insolvent if it is unable to pay its debts as they fall due.

issued share capital The total nominal value of shares that a company has issued.

joint and several liability Persons who are jointly and severally liable may be sued jointly for a loss, or any one person can be sued for the entire loss (although that one party can usually obtain a contribution from the other liable parties).

limited liability partnership (LLP) A business structure established by the Limited Liability Partnerships Act 2000.

listed company A public company whose shares are listed on a stock exchange.

memorandum of association Historically, the principal constitutional document which regulated the external affairs of a company. Its importance has diminished significantly following the passing of the CA 2006. It now merely provides basic information concerning a company at the time of its creation.

misfeasance The improper or unlawful performance of a lawful act. Can be contrasted with malfeasance, which is the performance of an unlawful act.

nominal value A fixed value attached to shares when they are allotted, which may bear no resemblance to the actual value of the shares.

novation The act of substituting one contract for another.

objects clause A clause in a company's constitution setting out the objects or purposes for which the company was set up.

ordinary resolution A resolution passed by a simple majority (i.e. over 50 per cent).

ordinary shares Where a company only has one class of share, its shares will be known as ordinary shares, which will entitle the holder to the normal rights of share ownership (e.g. to vote at general meetings).

paid-up share capital The combined nominal value of share capital that has actually been paid.

parent company A company is a parent company of another company if it:

(i) holds the majority of voting rights in the other company, or

(ii) is a member of the other company and has the right to remove or appoint the board of directors, or

(iii) is a member of the other company and controls alone, pursuant to an agreement with other members, a majority of the voting rights in it.

pari passu 'With equal step'.

partnership A business structure defined by s 1(1) of the Partnership Act 1890 as 'the relation which subsists between persons carrying on a business in common with a view to profit'.

pre-emption right The right of first refusal belonging to existing shareholders upon the allotment of a new batch of shares. The company must first offer the shares to the existing shareholders.

preference share Shares which entitle the holder to some sort of benefit or enhanced right, usually in relation to the entitlement to a dividend.

promoter A person who undertakes and enters into the process of setting up of a company.

proxy A person appointed to vote or act on behalf of another for another (e.g. at a general meeting of a company).

qua 'In the capacity of'.

quorum The minimum number of persons required in order to have a formal meeting. Meetings lacking a quorum are said to be 'inquorate'.

quoted company A company whose shares are listed on the UK official list, or in an EEA state, or on the New York Stock Exchange or Nasdaq.

redeemable shares Shares issued by a company which can be redeemed (bought back) by that company should the company or the member so require, or upon the passing of a stated period.

registered company A company created through incorporation by registration.

Registrar of Companies The Chief Executive of Companies House. The principal functions of the Registrar are to register the incorporation and dissolution of companies and to ensure that documents delivered to Companies House are accurate.

resolution A decision arrived at by a formal vote.

share A measure of a person's interest in a company. The owner of a share is called a shareholder.

share capital The capital that the company acquires through the selling of shares. Also known as equity capital.

share premium The sum paid for a share in excess of the share's nominal value, which usually represents the difference between the nominal value of the share and its market value.

sole practitioner A sole proprietor who is a professional (e.g. solicitor, accountant).

sole proprietorship A business structure consisting of an individual who conducts business on his own account and who bears the risk of business failure and is also entitled to the profits of the business.

sole trader A sole proprietor who is not a professional.

special resolution A resolution passed by a majority of not less than 75 per cent.

subsidiary A company is a subsidiary company of another company if that other company:

(i) holds the majority of voting rights in it, or

(ii) is a member of it and has the right to remove or appoint the board of directors, or

(iii) is a member of it and controls alone, pursuant to an agreement with other members, a majority of the voting rights in it.

substratum The purpose(s) for which a company is formed.

thing An item of property other than land.

thing in action An intangible thing (e.g. a share) which, being intangible, can only be claimed or enforced by legal action, as opposed to by taking possession of it.

ultra vires 'Beyond one's powers'. If a company acts outside the scope of its constitution, it will be acting *ultra vires*.

uncalled share capital The difference between the company's issued share capital and its called-up share capital.

unissued share capital The difference between a company's authorized share capital and its issued share capital.

unregistered company A company not incorporated by registration (i.e. one created through incorporation by Act of Parliament or through incorporation by Royal Charter).

Index